203

D0838062

THE COMPLETE BOOK OF CAT CARE

Revised

LEON F. WHITNEY, D.V.M.

Revised by George D. Whitney, D.V.M.

The Complete
Book of
Cat Care

REVISED EDITION

DOUBLEDAY & COMPANY, INC.

GARDEN CITY, NEW YORK, 1985

Library of Congress Cataloging in Publication Data

Whitney, Leon Fradley, 1894–
  The complete book of cat care.

  Includes index.
  1. Cats. 2. Cats—Diseases. I. Whitney, George D., 1918–   II. Title.
SF447.W5 1980   636.8'08'3
ISBN: 0-385-23296-9
Library of Congress Catalog Card Number 79-7216

For Dorothy

"A home without a cat and a well-fed, well-petted and properly revered cat—may be a perfect home, perhaps, but how can it prove title?"

—Mark Twain

Contents

Diagnostic Table

$\mathcal{T}$HE following table is designed to help you use this book easily and well. It will make it possible for you to identify many of the common diseases of cats and it will tell you where to look for information about them.

If your cat is sick it will exhibit certain symptoms—probably several. These symptoms are shown in the table in boldface, and under each of them there is a list of diseases or conditions with which they are most commonly associated. You will find in the book a detailed discussion of the symptoms, causes, prevention, and treatment of each of these diseases.

Here is an example of the way the table should be used: You notice that your cat is excessively thirsty, seems to be bloated about the abdomen, and shows signs of a soft swelling in its legs. Excessive thirst, abdominal enlargement, and swellings are all shown in the table as symptoms. The diseases listed under each of these symptoms vary greatly, but dropsy appears under all of them. By reading the discussion of dropsy, you will be able to determine whether your cat has the condition and, if it has, what you can do about it.

This table is *not* a cure-all chart. It will *not* make you a veterinarian. It *will* help you to recognize the signs of disease in your cat and show you where to get the information you need in order to decide whether you can treat the condition yourself or whether your pet needs veterinary attention.

ABDOMINAL ENLARGEMENT
Anemia (in young)
Bladder ailments
Bloat
Dropsy
Excessive thirst
Fat
Heart malfunction
Infectious peritonitis
Kidney disease
Liver disease
Metritis
Organ enlargement (spleen, liver)
Overfeeding
Parasites (in young)
Pregnancy
Tumors

ABDOMINAL TENDERNESS
Colon impaction
Enteritis
Foreign bodies
Peritonitis
Poisoning
Stomach inflammation
Tumors
Ulcers
Urine retention

ANEMIA (Pale gums)
Blood parasites
Hemorrhage
Infectious peritonitis
Intestinal parasites
Iron deficiency
Leukemia
Lice
Parasites
Piroplasmosis
Poisoning
Tumors

APPETITE (Difficulty in eating)
Foreign bodies in mouth or throat
Insect stings
Lead poisoning
Mouth ailments
Teeth loose
Tongue injuries
Tumors in mouth
Ulcers
Virus diseases

APPETITE (Loss of)
Any disease causing fever
Change of diet
Emotional problems
Malnutrition
Overfeeding
Pain
Parasites
Poisoning
Toxins
Tumors
Virus diseases

APPETITE (Ravenous)
Diabetes
Heat, onset of
Lactation
Pregnancy
Undernourishment

BLINDNESS
Cataracts
Cornea, opacity of
Eye ailments (various)
Glaucoma
Injury
Vitamin deficiency

BREATH (Bad)
Cancer
Constipation
Foreign bodies in or on teeth
Gum diseases
Kidney disease
Lip ailments
Poisoning, caustic or acid
Tartar
Tongue injuries
Ulcers in mouth

BREATHING (Abnormal; loss of breath from exertion)
Anemia
Collapsed lung
Emphysema
Heart ailments
Hernia of diaphragm
Hydrothorax
Infectious peritonitis
Pleurisy
Pneumonia
Pneumothorax
Pyothorax
Ruptured diaphragm

CONVULSIONS
Calcium-arsenate poisoning
Diabetes
Eclampsia
Encephalitis
Plant poisoning
Foreign bodies in stomach
Strychnine poisoning
Uremia
Worms

COUGHING
Bronchitis
Chronic infections
Drugs
Emphysema
Laryngitis
Pharyngitis
Pleurisy
Pneumonia
Viral diseases
Worms

DEAFNESS
Chronic infections
Drugs
Inherited

DIARRHEA
Enteritis
Exercise (excessive)
Fiber (excessive)
Horse meat, consumption of
Kidney disease
Liver disease
Parasites
Poisoning

Skim milk, consumption of

DIZZINESS
Accidents
Cerebral hemorrhage
Ear canker
Ear mites
Middle-ear infection

DROOLING
Gum disease
Insect stings
Lip ailments
Poisoning
Tartar on teeth
Teeth, loose
Tongue injuries
Tumors in mouth
Ulcers

EMACIATION
Chronic diseases (various)
Diabetes
Diarrhea
Kidney disease
Liver disease
Tuberculosis
Tumors
Undernourishment

GAGGING
Foreign body in throat
Postnasal drip
Tonsillitis
Tumors
Virus infections
Worms

HEAD SHAKING
Canker in ear
Ear ailments
Ear flap torn
Fleas
Foreign bodies
Hematoma in ear flap
Lice
Tumors

HOARSENESS
Asthma

Foreign body in throat
Infections
Injuries to throat
Laryngitis
Paralysis

LUMPS
Abscesses
Bone tumors
Cancer
Foreign bodies
Goiter
Hematoma
Hernia, inguinal
Leukemia
Salivary cysts
Tumors

MOANING OR CRYING
Abdominal ailments
Abscesses
Constipation
Ear ailments
Encephalitis
Fleas
Foreign bodies
Heart and lung diseases
Heat period
Pancreatitis
Poisoning
Skin disease
Urine retention

NOSE, RUNNING
Allergies
Infections
Nasal tumors
Pneumonia
Tearing, excessive
Virus infections

PARALYSIS
Back broken or injured
Chastek paralysis
Concussion
Meningitis
Rabies
Stroke
Thrombus
Toxins

SHEDDING (Abnormal)
Burns
Diabetes, incipient
Mange
Periodic shedding
Skin diseases

SHIVERING, TREMBLING
Cold
Eclampsia
Horner's Syndrome
Pain
Poisoning
  Caffeine
  Calcium arsenate
  Food
  Nicotine
  Strychnine
  Theobromine
Shock

SKIN AILMENTS
Acne
Allergy
Alopecia
Burns
Dandruff
Fleas
Mange
  Demodectic
  Notodectic
  Sarcoptic

SLOBBERING
Chemicals
Convulsions
Encephalitis
Foreign bodies in mouth
Gum diseases
Insect stings
Lip ailments
Oral ulcers
Poison
Teeth loose or broken
Tongue injuries
Tumors
Virus infections

SNEEZING, SNORTING
Allergies
Foreign bodies
Infections
Nose, ailments of
Pneumonia
Tumors
Virus infections

SWELLINGS THAT LEAVE PITS WHEN SQUEEZED
Dropsy
Edema
Heart ailments
Insect stings
Kidney diseases
Snake bites

THIRST, EXCESSIVE
Diabetes, incipient or sugar
Dropsy
Food too dry
Food too salty
Kidney disease

URINARY TROUBLES
Cloudy urine: bladder
Excessive urine: kidney disease, diabetes
Inability to urinate: bladder, urethra
Leaks (urinary incontinence): kidney disease, diabetes
Odor, foul: bladder, blood, kidney
Over-yellow: jaundice
Sand in urine: bladder

VOMITING
Diaphragmatic hernia
Gastrointestinal foreign bodies
Hair in stomach
Hernia, strangulated
Infections (various)
Kidney disease
Parasites in stomach
Peritonitis
Poisoning
Tapeworms
Tumors, brain or other
Urinary ailments
Virus infections

YELLOWING TISSUE
Gallbladder infections
Jaundice
Liver infections
Poisoning
Steatitis
Tumors

1. You, Your Cat, and Your Veterinarian

*Y*EARS AGO, when I began veterinary practice, I often wondered why some people seemed to get so much more pleasure than others out of owning and handling cats. As I talked with them, listened to their problems, and tried to answer their questions, it seemed to me that the difference lay largely in their general attitude toward animals, in their understanding of the nature of their cats, and their relationships with them. All of these things were important factors in the choice of their cats, in the way they handled them, and in the care they were able to give them. Having worked with thousands of cat owners, I am now more than ever convinced that a proper understanding of the nature of animals is the first and greatest prerequisite to being a good cat owner.

WHAT YOU SHOULD KNOW ABOUT YOUR CAT

The capacity to feel love for animals is a gift—to many people a gift as rewarding as any we have. There are those unfortunates—comparatively few, I think—who lack the ability to feel affection for animals just as surely as there are those who cannot distinguish red from green. They will never understand the pleasure and the gratification which every cat owner experiences, for the love of animals can never truly be taught. But most people do not have the sympathy and warmth and patience that it takes to get the most enjoyment from the care of a cat. What they lack more than anything else, I think, is a realistic conception of what they are to the cat and what their cat should be to them.

Just as so many humans feel the need of some higher power or individual and look to it or to him for support or guidance, so your cats look to you, their provider, for their support. To them you are a god, you are Providence.

If you are to get the most fun out of owning a cat, perhaps nothing is more important than learning to accept your cat for what it is, to cultivate the proper attitude of mind toward it. A dog is a dog; a cat, a cat; a pigeon, a pigeon; and a fish, a fish. Glorifying your cat in your own mind, thinking of it or treating it as a human being, is a basic source of many of the difficulties some people encounter in cat owning. You must learn to refrain from the natural tendency of projecting yourself into the cat. It is poor logic; it will make your cat unhappy and you dissatisfied.

Here is an example of what I mean. A woman I once knew had an outdoor frog pond. In it she had frogs and turtles. Every winter she spent a great deal of time feeling sorry for the frogs hibernating down in the cold. I have known others who think it cruel to leave pet raccoons in outdoor pens in the winter; instead they bring them into the cellars of their houses. Still others go out into the woods to feed animals and birds so that they will not have to prey on each other. They simply cannot accept the way of nature. They cannot believe what Charles Darwin said: "The war of nature is not incessant, no fear is felt, death is generally prompt, and the happy and the healthy survive and multiply."

Not all cat owners are as misguided as these people. Some recognize these natural processes and are not foolishly disturbed because nature seems to them needlessly cruel when judged by human standards. They realize that each species of animal has gradually adapted itself to its particular environment through a series of hereditary changes which have enabled it to live happily and without suffering. They do not feel sorry for the frog hibernating down in the mud. They understand that for a raccoon it is perfectly right to eat like a glutton because of some drive he cannot resist and then den up and become quiescent in a deep sleep for several months. He has been provided with wonderful equipment to protect him against intense cold and has stored so much food in the form of fat on his body that he semihibernates most happily indeed. The animal lover who is aware of this is more likely to be envious of the animal which has so perfectly adapted itself to its environment than to be unduly concerned about its welfare.

Though most people are willing to accept the laws of nature as they apply to wild animals, some of them are still reluctant to extend the same reasoning to the animals they keep as intimate pets. In principle, there is no difference. You should always try first to understand the nature of the species you are interested in, not just that of a particular animal. A pet's background in nature is still our most reliable guide to proper care. We learn our best lessons, particularly about food and feeding, from nature, and we would all be much better providers if we could bring ourselves to rely more on such guidance.

Take feeding, for example. Because we have learned to enjoy a great variety in food, we are inclined to project our tastes on pets. A horse will quite contentedly eat hay, oats, and a little salt for a whole lifetime. Wild dogs can live by eating what appears to be a single item, animal bodies. Even today, when cats become wild, they exist primarily on rodents.

From a study of the natural habits of animals we can and should learn a great deal about the kind of food that is best for them. It would, of course, be foolish to suggest that we slavishly follow the natural diet of animals. Cats will thrive on mixed diets all their lives—boiled kidneys, oatmeal and milk, fish—and on almost as great a variety of foods as dogs. No one with any sense at all would ever spend his time catching rodents for his cat, but he might well spend a little time considering that the rodent which the wild cat eats is full of vegetable matter which the cat devours. Do we always see to it that household cats have vegetable matter in their diets? Not the person who feeds them only boiled kidneys day after day. The principle applies equally to all species.

YOUR OBLIGATIONS AS A CAT OWNER

The obligations of cat owning are few, but you must fulfill them. All that the animal asks of you is food, water, comfort, exercise, health, affection, and protection. If you can't fulfill these simple requirements, it would be better for you not to have cats, for they will only be a burden.

One of the first requirements is that you know the kind of cat that is best for you. You should know enough about the species you select —and about your own needs—so that it will never become a liability. You should never obligate yourself to care for a pet that demands more attention than you can freely give it.

It is difficult to believe that thousands of human beings have been enslaved by pet ownership—by white mice, by goldfish, by parrots, by cats. These are the people who are convinced that it is impossible to keep a pet without being prepared to spend most of their time in looking after it. One man believes, quite wrongly, that he can't indulge his desire for tropical fish because they must be fed five times a day. Others believe that dogs and cats require elaborately prepared meals, which in 99 per cent of the cases are entirely unnecessary.

It is true, however, that some cats require more attention than others; that some breeds, in fact, are more difficult to care for than other members of the species. In choosing a cat you will be wise to get one of a breed which from long years of selection is best adapted to the purpose for which you want it. If you need a cat for a ratter, get a short-haired ordinary cat or a Maine Coon Cat, not a fancy, long-haired, ornamental variety. If you want a beautiful, ornamental creature to decorate your living room, and if you have time and patience to care for it as it deserves and demands, buy a lovely Persian or long-haired cat. But be sure to buy one from parents with dispositions which allow their owner to comb them. I see many long-haired cats that are such spitfires that no one can comb them properly. They must be anesthetized occasionally to be cared for. Their owners may even consider them "cute," but such cats should never be bred to perpetuate such temperaments. You should make inquiries in order to be as sure as you can that the long-haired litter comes from particularly docile parents.

Veterinarians often treat cats brought to them with their coats solidly matted and fleas having a regular Old Home Week beneath the mat's protection. No one could possibly comb them. The owners lament, "Oh, why didn't somebody tell me what he would be like when he grew up!" A cat allowed to get in such a condition is a medical problem and a nuisance to the owner as well. When the cat has been clipped all over, deflead, and the owner made to understand that from then on he must spend some time on the cat's grooming, he is likely to say, "But that's so expensive!" The owner should have known before he bought the cat that one with a shorter nap is cheaper to keep.

Beyond the few simple obligations which a cat owner assumes, there are a few things he learns to avoid. He soon finds that it doesn't pay to let his cats roam any more than he can help. It costs less to feed a cat on a neighbor's garbage—but the savings are deceptive. Sooner or later the animal gets some "tainted swill," sickens, and perhaps dies. Animals that roam free are in constant danger of being injured in accidents or hurt in fights.

Anyone who has known the history of many cats can attest to the fact that it is not uncommon for those kept in suburban homes to become feral (i.e., turn wild). They leave home for longer and longer periods and finally stay away, living mostly on rodents and occasionally birds, and keeping in top physical condition.

Trained cats, on the other hand, almost never become feral because they enjoy human companionship so much. City cats also tend to remain domesticated because there is no environment outside of their homes to entice them to become wild. One of our obligations to our cats is to spend some time training them. Later on in this book you will find some suggestions for training a cat that should help both it and you enjoy each other's companionship far more than if you let your cat go untrained.

HOW TO CHOOSE A CAT

When the first edition of this book was published, there were fewer breeds of cats than there are today. Persian, Domestic, Siamese, and Manx pretty much summed up the cat world, though a few breeds were then in the process of development. Now national cat associations and cat shows have become popular and, as a result, breeds classified under long-haired and short-haired standards have proliferated.

The currently recognized short-haired breeds are: Abyssinian, British Blue, Burmese, Domestic Shorthair, Havana Brown, Manx, Korat, Rex, Russian Blue, and Siamese.

The long-haired breeds include: Angora, Balinese, Birman, Himalayan, Maine Coon Cat, and Persian.

In addition to the above, there are a few newly imported breeds not yet recognized as such by one or more of the cat owners' associations. Chances are good that cats such as the Egyptian Mau and the Japanese Bobtail will eventually become popular enough to warrant recognition as separate breeds.

And finally, a number of cat breeders are combining certain characteristics with the aim of developing new breeds or colors, such as lilac and chocolate longhairs.

At one time cat shows offered classes in only two distinct breeds of long-haired cats—Persian and Angora. After many years styles changed and only one long-haired breed was recognized by the cat associations. This unique long-haired breed was divided into sixty-two classes, based on color and sex. Styles changed once more and six breeds are now considered sufficiently different to justify their separate classification.

It is worth keeping in mind, however, that despite the various classifications, some breeds bear striking similarities to others; for example, the Balinese is practically a long-haired Siamese, the Burmese is a brownish Siamese, the Himalayan is a Persian with color points, etc.

Every day hundreds, perhaps thousands, of people acquire a new cat. These figures might even be conservative if you consider that there are somewhere between thirty and fifty million cats in America, living anywhere from one day to twenty years. If you are contemplating the acquisition of a cat, I would like to help you make a choice that will be satisfactory after your kitten (if that is what you decide on) is grown. The following breed descriptions are of what the *mature* cat should look like. They do not apply to kittens, which, no matter how entrancing they may be as little balls of fluff, change, sometimes drastically, as they mature. For instance, Siamese and Himalayan kittens may appear white all over but will change in appearance as the points darken. Some Siamese kittens, and kittens of other breeds as well, develop darker colors when they are raised in a cold climate than they would otherwise. Eye color frequently changes as the kitten ages and because eye color is so important to certain breeds, you must take a chance that the kitten's eyes will turn out to be the right color or shade when it matures.

Allowance must also be made for rate of growth and maturing. The Abyssinian cat is notoriously slow in maturing, whereas some Domestic Shorthairs mature and come into heat early enough to surprise their owners.

Luck undoubtedly plays a role in the selection of a kitten that will mature into the cat of your dreams. It is my strong recommendation, however, that you regard the appearance of the kitten in the light of what that kitten will grow into. It pays to choose wisely, because once the choice has been made, your generous nature will make it next to impossible for you to dispose of an unfortunate selection.

One way of gauging the current popularity of a breed in the United States is to count the number of advertisements for that breed in a magazine for cat fanciers.* Some of these ads offer a variety of breeds, but most of them offer only one breed. The following list shows the number of advertisements for various breeds in a recent issue of *Cats* magazine:

Persian	140	Birmans	15
Himalayan	96	Balinese	13
Siamese	51	Somalis	8
Abyssinian	46	Korats	7
Burmese	37	Chartreux	5
Rex	21	Japanese Bobtail	5
Manx	20	Turkish Angoras	5
Russian Blue	19	British Shorthairs	4
Maine Coon Cat	19	Scottish Folds	4

The survey of cat breeds is by no means an inflexible list. Many other breeds are in the making, some of which will fall by the wayside while others will soar in popularity. It will be most interesting to see the configurations of the cat world ten years hence after fashion has once again decreed changes.

BREEDS AND THEIR TRAITS

The Abyssinian. This breed comes in two colors: ruddy (i.e., brown, ticked with black or darker brown) and red (a rich solid tan color). The body is strong, medium-sized, with slim legs and a rather small head. The tail is long, thick at the base, and tapering. The coat is dense and finely textured. The almond-shaped eyes are green, hazel, or gold and have a dark rim around the eyelids. Kittens of both varieties darken with age.

The ears help identify this breed: they are prominent, alert, and pointed, tipped with brown or black. The hair on the ears is very short while the inner ear is bare.

The British Blue. This cat, the most popular shorthair in England, is quite distinct from the Russian Blue. It is a blue, even-colored, medium-sized animal with a broad, massive head. Breed standards emphasize expressive large eyes set wide apart and usually orange, yellow, or copper with no green tinge. The body is well built and powerful, with a short, bull-like neck, and broad, flat shoulders. The coat is short, thick, and firm to the touch.

The Burmese. A compact, muscular, satin-coated cat of sable, blue, or champagne color and of surprising weight for its size. It has a cobby body with a bearlike walk. The facial expression is regarded among cat

---

* In reading cat magazines, remember that fanciers have special names for each of the colors, coat characteristics, sexes, and so forth.

fanciers as being "sweet" (i.e., pleasant or happy). Kittens often show faint stripings which fade as they age; most Burmese also darken as they mature.

The Domestic Shorthair. This is the common cat also known as the barn cat, alley cat, and even pussy cat. But let no one think it is an inferior animal. Among the millions of domestic shorthairs, there are those that conform to a standard established by professional cat fanciers, and are thus entitled to be shown in competition.

The ideal calls for a cat of medium-to-large size showing good depth, a full chest, and a powerful body. The head is broad in queens, but broader in toms. The face is medium in width and length. The ears are medium in size, rounded at the tips, and set forward. Eye openings are round, medium in size, and set wide apart. The muzzle is squarish. The medium-length tail, which is carried level with the back, is thick at the base and tapered. Legs are sturdy; the feet are round and not too large, with five toes on front legs and four on hind. Extra toes are undesirable. The coat is short, flat, lustrous, and of good texture, and may be of any color. (The eyes should match the coat.) There are twenty-six recognized color classes.

The Havana Brown. The body is medium in size, firm, and muscular; the coat, an even mahogany brown, is smooth and glossy with medium-length hair. The ears are large, round-tipped, with very little hair inside or out; the eyes are oval-shaped and dark chartreuse.

The Manx. The Manx body is medium-sized, short, with legs longer behind than in front, with an arched back, rounded rump, and deep flank. The head is large, longer than it is broad, with prominent cheeks— even in queens. The nose is longer and broader than in the Domestic Shorthair. Ears are medium in size, wide at the base and set slightly forward, almost naked inside but with ear tufts at the tips. The eyes should be round and full.

Manx coats, which come in all cat colors, are double, soft, and well padded, with a thick undercoat. Eye color should conform with coat color.

There are really three kinds of Manx, one of which should cause suspicion. The genuine Manx has a slight hollow at the tip of the spine. A second type has a tiny vertebra easily palpable. This is discriminated against by Manx breeders. A third exhibits a blunt vertebra at the end of the spine which usually tells us that the cat was "manxed" (i.e., had its tail amputated) when it was a kitten. If it was "manxed" when mature, the stump would be plainly palpable.

Many Manx cats move with a hopping motion due to a slight deformity in the lower part of the spine. One hears it said that such cats are part rabbit and some have been sold as "cabbits," which, of course, is absurd.

The Korat. This is a medium-sized blue cat characterized by a heart-shaped head, with the tom showing an indentation in the center of the forehead. The nose is short and has a downward curve; the ears are large, with rounded tips set high on the head with a large flair at the base, and almost bare inside. The Korat's back is short, but arched.

One of the distinctive features of the Korat is the silver tipping all over the blue-haired body. The blue is even throughout without shading or tabby markings. Paw pads and nose range from dark blue to lavender with a pinkish tinge.

The eyes seem unusually large, almost too large for the face; the aperture, when partially closed, shows an Asian slant. Eye color is amber or amber green, although a brilliant green is preferred. This is another breed whose eyes change color with age.

The Rex. A small- to medium-sized cat with a long slender body and neck giving the appearance of being delicate. The head is narrow, longer than wide; chin well developed, forming a straight line with the tip of the nose; whiskers and eyebrows curly. The ears are bare, wide at the base, and taller than wide. They are placed high on the head and stand erect.

The eyes are medium-sized, oval, with a slight upward slant. Legs are very long and slender, with dainty paws. The tail is long, tapering, and extremely flexible.

The chief differentiating characteristic of the Rex is its coat, which consists only of an undercoat with no coarse guard hairs. It may be of any color. The short coat is extremely soft and silky. Uniform "marcel" waves extend from the top of the head across the back, sides, hips, and continue to the tip of the tail.

This breed is known for its good disposition.

The Russian Blue. What distinguishes the Russian Blue from other breeds is its plush, soft, lustrous, bright-blue double coat with silver shading. The eyes are a vivid green. But one cannot select for eye color until the cat is two years old, because the kittens and adolescents have yellow eyes.

It is a medium-sized cat with a long graceful body which, because of its thick coat, appears heavier when the cat is in repose. The legs are fine-boned; the feet are small, neat, dainty, and well rounded. The head is narrow and the face quite long. The tail, which tapers from a thick base, is long.

The Siamese. This cat is a lovely, lithe, agile, pantherlike feline with a fawn-colored coat highlighted by darker points. Although you may have seen large, powerful Siamese cats, the show Siamese is a medium-sized, dainty, sleek, long-bodied creature. The head presents a pointed or wedge-shaped effect because of the rather large ears, which are pricked slightly forward as if the cat were listening, and because the face tapers to a point at the nose. The slant eyes are often slightly crossed, a characteristic now being discriminated against in shows. A good Siamese is intelligent, affectionate, aristocratic.

No breed has the unique voice changes of the Siamese, and few—if any—such loud voices. One tone, disliked by some people, is eerie. About the only criticism of the breed I have ever heard concerns this quality of voice.

Color is an important feature of the Siamese. Kittens are born nearly white with dark-shaded tails, ears, facial masks, and feet. The body color gradually darkens as they grow older. Their greatest beauty—the contrast of dark points and fawn body—comes about nine months of age. The mask, ears, legs, feet, and tail should be clearly defined in the darker shade, which may be chocolate, lilac, blue, red, or seal.

The Angora. Not many years ago all long-haired cats were referred to as Angoras. Then, for many years, one seldom heard of them; in cat exhibitions, all long-haired cats were called Persians. Around 1968, however, Angoras began to stage a comeback. A distinct difference between the Angora and the Persian is now recognized and some professional cat breeders are devoting themselves to restoring the Angora to its former status.

This cat is medium in size and of any color, with a soft, fine coat of abundant hair which stands out from the body. Its head size lies between that of the Domestic and the Persian. Ears are pricked slightly forward, with tufts. The tail is fully plumed, long, and carried more or less parallel to the ground. The legs are sturdy and covered with medium-length hair; feet are dainty and small with no extra toes.

The Balinese. Picture a Siamese but with a long flowing coat two or more inches in length, of a silky texture, and you have a Balinese. The eyes are clear blue, not crossed, and the tail has no kink. Eye colors are the same as those of the Siamese. The Balinese is also much like the Himalayan but with a thick coat colored like the Siamese.

The Birman or Burman (also called the Sacred Cat of Burma). This cat should not be confused with the Burmese.

The Birman was brought from Burma to France, whence its popularity spread to England and the United States. But cats with the characteristics of the Birman had appeared now and then in litters from pet cats and were kept because of their oddity.

The over-all appearance of the Birman is one of balance. The body is medium in size, back parallel with the ground, legs medium-long and stocky. Especially distinguishing features are the dark markings on the lower part of the legs, below which are white feet giving the appearance of gloves. The tail is carried high over the back.

The coat is unique, with guard hairs standing out above the shorter fine body coat. In many respects the Birman is much like a long-haired Siamese with white feet and points colored like those of the Siamese, but with less coat than the Himalayan. Its nose is straight; the ears, instead of standing sideways, are erect (they are also longer than the ears of the Domestic); the body structure is similar to that of the Domestic.

The Himalayan. It was only natural that long-haired cats should have crossed with Siamese. The offspring of the first cross are short-haired, but when two of the hybrids are crossed, 25 per cent of the kittens have long hair. Or when a hybrid is crossed with a pure longhair, 50 per cent of the kittens will be long-haired. This is probably the origin of the Himalayan, one of the new, beautiful breeds gaining in popularity. It is a long-haired cat with "points" colored in the same way as in the Siamese.

The medium-sized body is cobby with a short, level back. The neck is short and powerful; the legs short, thick, and heavy. The head is broad and massive, the nose almost as broad as it is long. The ears are small, set wide apart, rounded at the tip, and almost hidden in the long coat. The eyes are large and round. The tail is short in proportion to the body. The coat is long and fine in texture, soft and glossy, and stands out from the body all over. The ruff is immense, as is the tail plume. The ears should show long tufts.

The Maine Coon Cat. This is a long-haired cat with hair shorter on the neck and shoulders becoming gradually longer toward the tail, where it is like that of a Persian, with shaggy heavy coat and britches. The tail is long, well furnished, and carried straight up over the back, like a hound's tail.

The Coon Cat's body is large, long, and level, with the neck slightly longer in proportion. The eyes are large, slightly oval, with an alert expression. Eye color as well as coat color are the same as the Domestic Shorthair.

The Coon Cat got its name from the mistaken notion that it is half raccoon and half cat. Some Coon Cats have bars across the tail, reminiscent of a raccoon's markings. These rugged cats are usually excellent ratters and are especially well equipped to fend for themselves. Temperamentally they like to sleep in high places, in contrast to the Persian and Domestic breeds, which sleep closer to the floor.

Only recently have the cat associations decided to register this long-haired cat commonly found in the New England states.

The Persian. This is a medium- to large-sized cat, massive across the shoulders and rump, with a short back, deep chest, short neck, and a massive head with great width of skull. The jaws are broad and powerful; the forehead is rounded, the cheeks full and prominent; the nose is short and almost as broad as it is long.

Some Persians have been developed into a separate breed—the Peke-faced Persian, similar to the normal Persian but with a "pushed in" (retroussé) face like that of a Pekingese dog. Only red and red tabby Peke-faced Persians are recognized as a breed.

The ears of the Persian are small, round-tipped, pointed forward, and not unduly open at the base. Since the ears are set wide apart, the forehead seems broad and level. The eye openings are large and round, with eye color conforming to coat color.

Tails are short in proportion to the body. They are carried without a curve at an angle lower than the back, but do not trail when walking.

The coat is especially important. There are times of the year when the coat is sparse, but when shedding is over and the full coat is present, it is long, fine in texture, soft, glossy, and stands out from the body. The ruff should be immense with a deep frill between the front legs. The ear tufts are long and curved; the toe tufts are also long; and the tail plume is very full.

Persians come in all colors but only specific ones are eligible for showing. Each color must have a specific eye color to accompany it. Thus, a red tabby must have brilliant orange or deep copper eyes; silver tabbies must have green eyes. Some Persians have one blue eye, one copper.

As with all white cats, white Persians with blue eyes are occasionally deaf. Such deafness is not considered a fault by show fanciers, but a deaf cat is not as useful as a pet as one with normal hearing.

The Hairless. This cat is not hairless in the same way as the Mexican hairless dog, but it is hairless nonetheless. One strain that breeds true is a Siamese hairless. In some no hair ever develops; in others there in a downy fuzz which comes and goes with seasonal changes.

In Mexico a different hairless cat was bred which experts believe came from an Uruguayan ancestor. Some of the Mexican cats of this strain were partially hairless and others were entirely bald. Surely no one today would want such poorly protected felines as human companions, yet someone must have wanted them enough to have allowed them to continue propagation.

VETERINARIANS AND THEIR CLIENTS

History tells us that animal doctors practiced their profession in the Egypt of the Pharaohs as well as in ancient Greece and Rome. It appears that the more advanced a society is, the better care its animals receive. In the late 1700s animal care was a blacksmith's sideline in the United States, whereas Europe could boast of flourishing schools of veterinary medicine (ironically, this was at a time when human surgery was still a sideline of the barbers in many parts of the "civilized" world). The earliest U.S. veterinary schools date from 1849–60 and offered a one-year course dealing almost exclusively with farm animal problems. All failed until Iowa State University established its school in 1879.

Gradually, however, the veterinarian's scope began to expand, and until quite recently he was expected to be knowledgeable about all creatures (with one major exception, of course—man). To a great extent this is no longer the case. Given the ever-growing mass of information on all species revealed by research scientists, more and more veterinarians are concerning themselves with fewer and fewer species. Specialization is becoming the norm with both human and animal doctors, a situation which makes it all the more important for you, as a cat owner, to choose a veterinarian who enjoys and courts feline practice and who is up to date on the latest advances in feline health care. Of course, you can't ask a prospective veterinarian whether he takes regular courses in a continuing education program (actually you can ask, but it would be rather awkward), but there are other ways of finding out whether or not he is the right doctor for your cat.

If you are moving to a new area, ask your current veterinarian to suggest a colleague in that area. Tap your new neighbors or nearby cat owners for information on local veterinarians. Phone a breeder listed in the Yellow Pages and ask a few pharmacists. The latter in particular are in a good position to know who prescribes the most up-to-date medications. Usually a name will be mentioned several times but that doesn't solve the problem entirely, since there is still the matter of communications to consider. You should like the veterinarian and feel confidence in him or her.* You should also be assured that in an emergency help will be provided either by the veterinarian of your choice or someone he refers you to.

In selecting a veterinarian, don't overlook the newly established practitioners. Space has always been scarce in veterinary medical schools and for that reason it has traditionally been easier to gain admittance to human medical schools than to veterinary medical schools, with the result that those chosen have been excellent students. Over half of these students already have degrees when they begin veterinary studies and many have advanced degrees. All of which means that the new graduates are brighter and better grounded in theory than many of my vintage.

There are certain things you should look for immediately when choosing a veterinarian. You cannot fail to notice the cleanliness and efficiency of his office or of his hospital. You will probably see on his walls his credentials, which must include study at an accredited college of veterinary medicine and a state license to practice. What you cannot see is that he frequently takes continuing educational courses in his field and keeps up to date with all the latest advances by reading his professional journals.

A veterinarian must be completely honest. He will not give unnecessary injections at exorbitant prices, using five cents' worth of vitamin concentrates. He will not exaggerate the seriousness of an illness. He will try to effect a cure in a single visit. Not only does he do what he can for the patient in his office, but he respects the owner by instructing him in the care of the patient. If repeated visits to the office will give you added confidence, that is a matter for you to decide. The wise veterinarian, how-

---

* I will often refer to the veterinarian as he when we all know that a great many are she's. Since I don't think he/she reads well, even to a militant feminist, I'll stay with the traditional construction until someone comes up with an appropriate grammatical alternative.

ever, knows that the pet which costs the owner too much is a burden rather than a pleasure. On the other hand, the veterinarian who undercharges cannot afford the equipment necessary to do the diagnostic and surgical work of which the profession is capable.

The ethical veterinarian is democratic. He does not exclude from his attention the laborer in work clothes, or the man or woman of a minority group. Yet there are doctors who do discourage the poor and the laboring man. When a cat needs care, *it* is the patient, not the owner.

The ethical man thinks first of the service he may render. He does not ask to be paid before treating his patient. Money is not and cannot be the veterinarian's first consideration.

Some veterinarians have found, to their sorrow, that they have been too kind-hearted and generous in extending credit to pet owners. It is too easy to leave an animal to be treated, and then take it home with a "Thank you, Doctor. Send me the bill." Some excellent veterinarians have been put out of business by such practices. If a client can't give satisfactory references and establish credit, he should expect to pay when he picks up his pet.

The modern veterinarian shares his discoveries freely with the members of his profession. Through the presentation of studies at association meetings and in the proper veterinary journals, he makes his observations available to others so that they can be used to relieve suffering.

Finally, claims of unusual ability to effect cures by secret methods should instantly arouse suspicion. A veterinarian's picture should not be used to advertise products or to condone questionable procedures. He must not be a party to price fixing but may give a list of charges for standard procedures.

The man in whom you can place your confidence may not wear all his qualifications like shining armor. They represent an ideal, but more and more the conscientious veterinarian is approaching this ideal. The veterinary profession today is distinguished by many truly magnificent characters—men and women who have unselfish attitudes, who sacrifice themselves for their patients just as willingly and unstintingly as ever the family physician gave of his strength and knowledge. That should not be surprising to anyone. A veterinarian must of necessity love animals, and the man who truly loves animals must also love his fellow man.

There is another side of the veterinarian/client relationship and that is the doctor's reaction to you. At a first meeting, he will do some sizing up himself, trying to find out whether you will follow instructions or whether you will take it upon yourself to make some blunder rather than phone for advice. He also wonders if you will talk to him candidly or "fudge" in some way in order to make yourself look less inept.

I well remember diagnosing pregnancy in a queen presented by a gentleman with his eight-year-old daughter. "No way, Doc," he said. "She never leaves the house and we don't have another cat." The little girl pulled her father's sleeve and said, "But, remember when she stayed out that night a month ago, Daddy?" If looks could kill! The truth is that many people stand behind the Fifth Amendment when dealing with a veterinarian: they don't want to incriminate themselves.

Many of my colleagues rate their clients with an A, B, C, or D jotted down on the medical history form. A's are awarded to the best clients, while the D clients are the ones whose pets we pity.

The moral of all of this is simple: be honest with your veterinarian. You'll find that by working with him candidly, everyone, but especially your feline friend, will benefit.

2. The Cat's Body and How It Functions

$\mathcal{S}$O MANY high school and college graduates have managed to escape courses in human physiology and anatomy that I have long ceased to be surprised that few cat owners have any conception at all of animal physiology. If you are to get the most out of this book, it will be necessary to review briefly the structure and function of our pets' bodies. Even though the study of the mechanism of the living body is to me one of the most fascinating in the world, the general attitude toward the subject is such that I feel I must warn you that you are not in for an "organ recital." All that will be necessary here is to learn enough about your cats' bodies so that you may treat them sensibly.

The science which treats of the functions of living things or of their parts is called physiology. That which treats of the structure of the body and the relationships of its parts is called anatomy. Let us combine the two and see how the body is formed and how its parts function.

The body of every animal grew from a single cell. What is a cell? It is a unit of life smaller than our eyes can see. The whole body of some tiny animals is a single cell: the amoeba and paramecium, for example. Other animals consist of whole colonies of cells. All the visible animate creatures we see are immense colonies of cells, and each cell has some special function. Every one of these cells is composed of a covering within which is some protoplasm, a substance not unlike egg white, and a nucleus, which is its business part.

The first cell, which resulted from the uniting of a male cell (sperm) and a female cell (ovum), and thus started an animal, is complete in every detail. It is a favorite academic paradox to say that a cell multiplies by dividing, and quite true, of course. If one cell divides into two cells, it has divided, but because it is two, it has multiplied. The two become four; the four, eight. As they go on dividing and thus increasing in number, different cells become specialized at certain stages. Some may become skin, some liver, some heart, some germ plasm, some tonsils, and so forth. There are cells that may never renew themselves; brain cells, for example. Then there are other specialized cells, like those in the hair and nails, which constantly renew themselves. They all live together in a happy community or colony, doing their work unless hindered by improper nourishment or crowding (from overfatness), or disease. That's what our cats are—big colonies of cells.

THE BODY'S COVERING

The skin is composed of several layers, each made up of innumerable cells. Two main layers are recognized: the outer layer, epidermis; the lower layer or true skin, the dermis. Sometimes we hear the epidermis called the cuticle or the scarfskin and, colloquially, the scurfskin. The true skin, in turn, consists of two layers. The skin is constantly shedding and renewing itself, a fact that has an important bearing on the treatment of skin diseases.

Under the skin we find subcutaneous connective tissue, an interesting

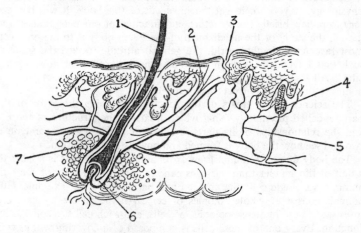

(1) Hair growing out of follicle. (2) Erector muscle. (3) Sweat duct. (4) Nerve end organ. (5) Blood vessels. (6) Bottom of hair follicle or papilla. (7) Subcutaneous fatty tissue.

part of the body made up of very elastic cells. Through it run nerves, lymph vessels, blood vessels; fat is often deposited in it.

Out of the skin grow the appendages we call hairs in mammals. Even the finest fuzz is composed of myriads of thin hairs each having the same general construction as coarser hair. Hair grows out of the skin from follicles. In the follicles (sacs or sheaths) are little muscles which, for example, cause a cat's hair to stand on end at times.

In some places on the bodies of pets sweat glands are found, and everywhere in some pets there are sebaceous glands which usually discharge their waxy secretion into the follicles. As the hair grows, it comes out coated with this sebum, a substance with an acrid smell, which, in dogs, partly accounts for the doggy odor. In cats the amount is so small that the coat is rarely gummy nor does it have an obnoxious odor. This helps to make cats the desirable pets they are. Other glands secrete oil, which helps the cat to shed water.

These protective coats, plus its natural resistance to water, make the skin waterproof. It is not, however, resistant to all oils, some of which can soak through it. In fact, the skin can absorb a good many drugs and substances which can be toxic (poisonous) to the pet.

In addition to its function as a protective covering, skin is also an organ of touch. Some parts are extremely sensitive. Through it, too, the pet responds to variations in heat and cold outside.

The skin heals by growing outward from the lower layers if it is not wholly destroyed by a gash, scald, or other injury. (Blisters usually are pockets of fluid between layers of skin.) When all the layers are destroyed, growth occurs from the sides. It is for this reason that your veterinarian, in case of injury to your cat, will want to bring the sides of the destroyed area as closely together as possible, so that the space to be covered over will be as narrow as he can make it. Moreover, if left open, the newly generated skin will be devoid of glands and hair. Great scalded areas become covered with skin, but not skin with the usual accessories.

THE BODY'S FRAMEWORK

The Skeleton.   The skeleton serves as the framework of the body and provides protection for the organs. The ribs cover the lungs, heart, liver, stomach, kidneys, and pancreas; the skull covers the brain and such delicate organs as the hearing mechanism and the organs of scent. These services that bones perform are not always fully appreciated, because we think of them primarily in their role of support.

Each species differs from the next in form; breeds within species differ from other breeds, and individuals vary in some respects. The skeleton on which the soft tissue of the body hangs is the basic cause of these structural differences. In some animals, for example, the mere absence of certain bones can cause a startling difference in appearance—compare the normal long-tailed cat with the Manx, whose lack of tail is one of its breed's characteristics.

Some bones are solid, others hollow or filled with marrow in which red blood cells may be generated. Some are mere beads and others long and strong. The way they are joined is an interesting study in itself. There are ball-and-socket joints (hips), hinge joints (knees), others made by one bone abutting another with a cushion between (vertebrae), and modifications of all three kinds. Some animals are more agile than others; some have difficulty turning around in a short radius, while others, because of their skeletal construction, can "turn on a dime."

The skeleton is a marvelous framework, replete with strength where strength is needed, rigidity where rigidity is needed, flexibility, swivels, and hinges where stretching, bending, and rotating are required.

Each long bone is made up of a shaft of hard, brittle material, a soft center of marrow, and ends of spongy material with a covering of dense, hard bone. Around the whole is a sort of skin called the periosteum. On top or on the bottom of the spongy end—if the bone terminates at a joint—is a springy, cartilaginous pad, called the epiphyseal cartilage, which takes the shocks. All through the bone small spaces form tunnels which carry blood and nerves; nourishment is also furnished by the periosteum.

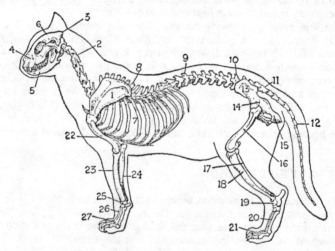

Skeleton of a cat. (1) Shoulder blade. (2) Neck vertebra. (3) Occiput. (4) Nasal bone. (5) Mandible. (6) Cranium. (7) Ribs. (8) Cervical vertebra. (9) Lumbar vertebra. (10) Lumbar vertebra. (11) Sacrum. (12) Tail vertebra. (13) Ilium. (14) Ischium. (15) Pubis. (16) Femur. (17) Fibula. (18) Tibia. (19) Tarsus. (20) Metatarsus. (21) Rear toes. (22) Humerus. (23) Radius. (24) Ulna. (25) Carpus. (26) Metacarpus. (27) Front toes.

Some bones are flat; ribs, head bones, and shoulder blades are examples. They are not so solid as they seem, but are well fortified with nourishment. The ribs join at the lower extremities with cartilages. These look like true ribs but are only extensions upward from a flat "bone"—the sternum or breastbone—to which all but one or two of the last ribs in some species are joined. The sternum is not actually a bone, but is composed of springy, tough cartilage, which is fortunate as the breastbone needs to be flexible, considering all the strains it undergoes.

At the points where the ribs and the cartilaginous extensions of the breastbone meet, one sometimes finds enlargements which may persist throughout life. These enlargements may be normal or an indication of disease, or evidence that the pet was inadequately fed or was sick for a considerable part of its growing period. Coupled with these one generally finds abnormal enlargements on the lower end of the radius, a large bone of the forearm, where it joins the wrist (carpal) joint. The spongy end may be so abnormal as to turn the leg, making it crooked (bandy leg), or weak, so that the leg from the wrist down bends out sideways. Some cats are born with hereditary "bench" legs, which are characterized by front feet that turn out sideways, a condition not due to rickets or other dietary deficiencies.

The process of bone healing is most interesting, and it is worthwhile to understand it in case you have to manage a pet with one or more fractured bones.

Let us suppose that a fairly simple break occurs in the bones of the foreleg of a cat. When our cat returns home after his accident the broken leg is obviously shorter than the others. He holds it up, cries with pain. Your veterinarian waits until the cat has recovered from shock, then he sets the leg. The ends of the bone are brought together; "in apposition," your doctor calls it.

Now the ends of the bone must "knit." Here is where it is worthwhile for the owner to know exactly what happens, so that he can give the pet all the attention and care required.

For several days the body decalcifies or withdraws calcium and other minerals from the ends of the fractured bone. Gradually they become soft, like cartilage. At this stage, it doesn't make much difference if the bones are not perfectly matched at the break. The second step, after the softening process, is the growth of connective fibers from each end. Once the bone ends are joined, the fibers shrink, pulling the ends closer. This process is completed in fourteen or fifteen days. During this period it doesn't matter how straight the bone is kept, so long as the ends are in apposition. At any time during this interval it is possible, but not desirable, to bend it at the break.

Next comes a stage when the junction, or *callus,* becomes impregnated with mineral salts of calcium and phosphorus—in other words, it hardens. At this point it is essential that the bone be kept straight, and meticulous care must be given to seeing that it is. If there is any change in the position of the bones your veterinarian will want to see the cat at once. Remember that a crooked leg he has set is a poor advertisement for him —to say nothing of its effect on the cat's future, with which both you and the veterinarian are concerned. You owe it both to your pet and to your doctor to pay careful attention at this point. Once the callus is strong enough so that the bone will not bend, the device holding the bone ends together can be removed (if an external device has been used).

The last period involves the shrinking of the callus. Some bones will set with what appears to be a disfiguring bulge about the break, but in time this largely disappears, leaving a bone that is even stronger at the breakage point than in the adjacent unbroken parts.

Many injured bones can't be set properly. Some are so badly shattered and infected that chips must be removed and nature trusted to do her best. The pelvis, that girdle of bones forming a framework for the rear part of the abdomen, is often broken into many pieces; it often, without any attention, heals itself without too much constriction of the pelvic passage.

There are breaks of such a nature that the bone breaks but stays in place; others where part of the bone breaks and part does not. These are called greenstick fractures. Compound fractures are those in which the broken bone protrudes through the skin.

Muscles. Skeletal muscles help hold the framework together and cooperate with it in locomotion. In addition to the skeletal muscles, there are other muscles not visible outside of the body. These are called the smooth muscles. Under a microscope, fibers of a skeletal muscle appear to have bands or striations, which do not exist on the smooth muscles. The duties of the smooth muscles are generally restricted to the functioning of organs and the digestive tract. The gastrointestinal tract, bladder, blood vessels, and sphincter muscles are all smooth and act more or less involuntarily (striated muscles, on the other hand, act under voluntary control). When nerves leading to muscles are injured those muscles shrink from lack of use. They can't function until the damage is repaired, at which time the shriveled muscles develop normally and become useful once again. If the nerve does not heal the muscles will not develop again.

THE CIRCULATORY SYSTEM

Heart and Vessels. The body is nourished by the blood, which delivers to the cells the substances they need, picks up the noxious and useless substances, and delivers waste to the organs of excretion. At the center of this marvelous system is a pump, the heart, an organ situated in the chest, as we know, and which for efficiency is not excelled by any man-made device.

The heart receives blood into two sides, then squeezes or contracts, so that the blood is driven into two large tubes (vessels). One leads to the lungs; the other divides and carries blood fore and aft into smaller vessels that, in turn, carry it about the body. In the lungs the blood liberates a gas, carbon dioxide, takes up another gas, oxygen, and is hustled back to the heart to be pumped around the body to distribute the oxygen and pick up cell wastes.

The great arteries, which carry the blood from the heart, start dividing into smaller arteries, these into other smaller and smaller ones, called arterioles, and thence into capillaries. From the capillaries the blood returns to the heart via venules, veins, and finally large veins. It also returns in lymph tubes or vessels. (The lymph may be thought of as concentrated blood without red blood cells.) So, blood leaves by arteries and returns by veins and lymph vessels.

The pump keeps up its contracting squeezes and relaxations rhythmically for the life of the animal. It sounds like a continuous lub, dub, lub, dub in the chest, and, in an eight-pound cat, pumps about a quart of blood every minute. Everything about it is wonderful: the delicate valves, the strength, its four chambers, the skin around it, called the pericardium, the nervous mechanism which causes it to beat.

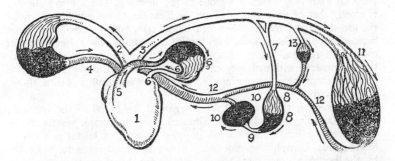

Heart and circulatory system. (1) Heart. (2) Anterior aorta, supplying front end of body. (3) Posterior aorta, supplying rear of body and organs. (4) Anterior vena cava, returning blood from front of body. (5) Pulmonary artery, carrying blood to lungs. (6) Pulmonary vein, carrying blood from lungs. (7) Celiac and mesenteric arteries carrying blood to (8), (9), and (10) stomach, spleen, intestines, liver, and other organs. (11) Blood supply to rear of body. (12) Posterior vena cava, returning blood from rear of body. (13) Kidney circulation.

The Blood. The blood is an organ. Even though it is fluid, it is a colony of specialized cells in a specialized fluid which, as we have seen, discharges carbon dioxide and picks up oxygen and nourishment, which it transports.

The liquid part (before it clots) is called plasma. In the plasma float red cells, disks concave on two sides. These contain a chemical called hemoglobin, whose job it is to handle the oxygen, as mentioned above. When arterial blood gushes from a cut it is bright red because of the presence of oxygen-rich hemoglobin. When blood runs from a vein it is darker and almost bluish, because the hemoglobin has given up its oxygen.

Plasma also carries white blood corpuscles of various sizes. Usually they appear spherical, but because of their softness and elasticity they can move through small openings, changing shape to do so. Moreover, they can engulf impurities and germs.

Platelets, oval or circular disks which help blood to coagulate or to clot, are another tiny component of blood.

Besides these microscopically visible entities there are chemicals, such as fibrin. Fibrin stays in solution until an injury allows blood to escape; then a ferment called thrombin causes the fibrin to clot. The blood slows as the clot develops and then stops.

Spleen and Lymph Nodes.   All along the path of the blood and lymph are filter organs, chief of which is the spleen. This varies in size with the size of the animal. A cat's spleen is small, three or four inches long, and three sixteenths of an inch thick. It is a flat, long, narrow organ, more purplish than red, which lies close to the stomach. The spleen's function is chiefly that of an organ of blood purification. Great numbers of bacteria are destroyed by it. When red blood cells become aged, the spleen breaks many of them down into liquid; in addition, the spleen manufactures both red and white cells. The blood spaces in the spleen are very large compared with ordinary capillaries; and when the organ is ruptured in an accident, hemorrhage into the abdomen may result in death, though not necessarily.

The spleen is the principal filter organ of the blood in the lymphatic system. Other smaller glands are situated along the lymph vessels and, by their construction, remove solid impurities, such as bacteria, from the blood fluids. Lymph does not move about by blood pressure, but rather by the body's movements. Muscle movement, breathing and the consequent expansion and contraction of the upper body, intestinal movements, and others, all force the lymph through the nodes and along its course. Valves in the vessels permit flow in but one direction (this is also true of veins).

THE RESPIRATORY SYSTEM

A pair of organs situated in the chest, one on each side, the lungs function in co-operation with the blood in the oxygen-carbon-dioxide transfer and, to a certain extent, in body temperature control as well.

In all mammals a partition—strong in some and almost gossamer in others—divides the chest cavity so that the lungs are separated. In the cat the membrane is extremely thin, and if the chest cavity is broken open on one side, so that air can enter, not only does the lung on that side collapse but the other as well. In humans, where the partition is stronger, if one lung collapses the other may not.

From the throat, a tube, called the trachea, made up of many rings of tough cartilage, runs down into the chest and branches into two bronchial tubes, one for each lung. (Bronchitis is inflammation in the linings of these tubes.) They, in turn, branch and subdivide into bronchioles, and finally into air sacs, each of which is surrounded by a network of blood capillaries so thin that gases can be absorbed or escape through them.

THE EXCRETORY SYSTEM

The Kidneys. Blood disposes of certain chemical substances, other than gases, through the kidneys. The blood travels through their intricate mechanism, disposing of waste and water. These wastes are principally urea, sugar, poisons, and substances such as carbonates, which can be eliminated in no other way.

Urea is the end product of the breakdown of the proteins in the body. Nitrogen, which is the principal constituent of protein, is also the principal component of urea. Everyone knows how urine gives off ammonia when hot. Ammonia also contains nitrogen.

In most animals the kidneys are located partially under the protection of the ribs and on either side of the body close to the backbone. They constitute one of the most delicate and ingenious filter plants imaginable. Everyone who has eaten kidneys or fed them to animals knows in general what they look like. But few have observed, microscopically, the minute inner workings, or wondered at their marvelous construction. If one slices a kidney lengthwise, one sees the so called pelvis, which constitutes a pocket for collecting urine, whence it is conducted via a tube—the ureter —to the bladder. That is about all one does see of the mechanism with the naked eye. The microscope reveals the most interesting features: the blood vessels, which divide to become capillaries, in tiny containers called glomeruli, and minute collecting tubules into which the urine filters and is conveyed to the pelvis. There are beautiful and ingenious arrangements to effect the transfer and reabsorption into the blood of certain useful substances and rejection of the useless—all of which is accomplished while the blood is passing through the kidney, entering under high pressure and coming out under much lower pressure.

Diseases can easily upset the normal function of the kidneys so that they cannot retain the useful nitrogenous substances like albumin or may lack absorptive capacity, so that too much water is secreted from the blood, causing great thirst. Albumin found in urine and excessive thirst are both indications of kidney disease or dysfunction.

Kidneys that function properly regulate the amounts of blood ingredients to a considerable degree. If too much sugar is present, some will be found in the urine. The same may be said of salt. Urine is composed mostly of water (95 per cent). Urea constitutes about 2.3 per cent, salt 1.1 per cent, and the balance, 1.6 per cent, is composed of other solids.

The bladder is a storage reservoir with elastic walls. It is amazing how it can stretch: to almost the size of a baseball in a large cat and the size of a tennis ball in almost any cat.

Other Excretory Means. Other impurities and surpluses from the blood—some mineral salts, for instance—are also excreted into the intestines; some gases are excreted by the lungs, and still other substances by the skin via sweat (although this is minimal in cats). Thus, the excretory system actually is composed of four parts.

THE DIGESTIVE SYSTEM

As we have seen, one of the functions of the blood is to transport nourishment to the body's cells. The nutrients are made ready for the blood by the digestive system.

The Mouth and Teeth. A cat's mouth is one of the most interesting parts of its anatomy and is most important to its health. The lips are the portal of the mouth. They are also remarkably sensitive organs of touch for some animals. The horse is an excellent example of this point. He can, with his coarse lips, feel among a lot of debris in a manger for a single oat grain! Monkeys use their lips with singular effectiveness. Watch one eat and you will see. Cats, on the other hand, instead of feeling dexterously with their lips, as monkeys do, seem to use their lips almost entirely for their primary purpose—to retain the food, as it is chewed, and the mouth juices or secretions.

The cat has two sets of teeth. The first, or milk teeth, fall out after their roots are partially resorbed by the body about halfway through the growing period. The eruption of the new teeth takes place so rapidly that it often causes loss of weight in growing animals and fever may sometimes accompany the teething.

Anatomists and students of natural history have a method of representing the number and arrangement of teeth of a species which tells the story, graphically, at a glance.

The front "biting-off" teeth are called the incisors. A cat has three on each side of the midline of the upper jaw and three on the lower. Observed from the front, there appear to be in the upper and lower jaws six nice teeth in a row. So the formula for these incisors is $I\frac{3-3}{3-3}$. Behind the incisors on each side is a long, strong canine tooth in both upper and lower jaw: $C\frac{1-1}{1-1}$.

Next we find premolars: $P\frac{3-3}{2-2}$. Finally there are the molars:

$M\frac{1-1}{1-1}$. We write the whole formula of the adult cat:

$$I\frac{3-3}{3-3} \quad C\frac{1-1}{1-1} \quad P\frac{3-3}{2-2} \quad M\frac{1-1}{1-1} = 30.$$

The deciduous teeth of kittens have a different formula:

$$I\frac{3-3}{3-3} \quad C\frac{1-1}{1-1} \quad P\frac{3-3}{2-2} = 26.$$

In my experience, I have noted some variation in the time of eruption of the permanent teeth, but here is an estimate:
The first incisors are full size at about four months;

the second at four and a half months;
the third at five months;
the canines at five to six months;
(the cat does not have a first premolar);
the second upper premolar at about five months;
(there is not a lower second premolar);
the third premolars at five to six months;
the four first molars at four and a half to five and a half months.

The part of the tooth that protrudes from the gums is called the crown; the part embedded in the socket is called the root; and the part between the crown and root is called the neck. Some teeth have one straight root, some several. Over half the length of each canine tooth is embedded inside the gums and bones; their roots are strong and exceedingly difficult to extract.

The tooth structure is interesting because of its toughness. When one sees a cat become angry and shear the end off a hardwood stick with its small, sharp teeth, as I have seen one do, our respect for animal teeth deepens.

Enamel, which covers a softer substance called dentine, adds to the hardness and strength of the tooth. The root has no enamel covering. Inside each tooth we find the pulp, a structure composed of nerves and blood vessels. These structures seldom give way, but cats can and do have tooth and gum troubles.

The teeth of no two species are exactly alike. It has been said that the natural diet of any species of animal can be told by examination of the teeth. This is probably true. With long, sharp tusks like those of cats or raccoons, it is logical to suppose that the animal's natural prey was some small animal easily killed and eaten.

Into the mouths of all animals is poured a fluid (saliva) from glands below or behind the mouth. Some animals have a starch-digesting substance in the saliva. Cats have very little. This explains in part why it is so important to cook such foods as potatoes before feeding them to these pets—to break up the starchy granules.

The roof of the mouth has a hard surface, the hard palate, going as far back as the last teeth and made up of ripples or bars extending across the mouth. Behind the teeth, the roof (soft palate) is flabby. By the time a pet's food is chewed and reaches the soft palate, it is practically in the throat.

The Tongue. The tongue, the principal organ for moving food into the mouth, is also the primary taste organ. Taste is experienced by the reaction to chemical stimuli of "buds," or sensitive areas, which stud this organ and produce the sensations of saltiness, sweetness, bitterness, and acidity. The taste buds are situated all over the tongue but are more abundant in the tip and at the back, in the throat proper.

The Throat. In the throat the delicate business of getting food properly started down the esophagus instead of down the windpipe is accomplished by the pharynx and larynx (pronounced larinks, not larnicks). The gullet is located above the windpipe, and an object called the epiglottis, which is part of the larynx, closes over the windpipe as food and fluid descend down the esophagus, then drops down to allow the passage of air.

Peristalsis. In order to understand how food moves along through the body, one must realize that those smooth muscles we mentioned earlier are at work carrying out this function. The only so-called voluntary muscles concerned are in the lips, the tongue, the throat, and the anus, and these are partly involuntary. Physiologists regard the inside of the digestive tract as continuous with the skin on the outside of the body. Actually the lining is of the same origin as the skin. The tract consists of a tube with valves and enlargements. Once food is swallowed, a constriction in the esophagus starts behind it and, as it progresses, forces the bolus (lump) of food into the stomach. The progress may be upward. A cat drinks with his head downward, and the water is moved upward for some distance before it goes downward into the stomach. The contraction which passes along the tube is called peristalsis.

In the stomach this wavelike movement continues. It mixes the stomach juices with the food. The exit valve of the stomach, the pylorus, opens and lets the food out into the intestine in sausagelike gobs into which constrictions have divided it. Soon other constrictions may start which cut the sausages in half, but all the while this marvelous process pushes the intestinal contents along through the whole length of the intestine as digestion continues.

The Stomach. Down the esophagus goes the swallowed food and into the stomach, which has walls sufficiently elastic to accommodate the varying amounts of food swallowed. Here in the stomach some digestion of food takes place, for it is a reservoir into which glands pour an acid liquid that helps digest proteins and fats. Starch digestion, begun by salivary enzymes, stops when the food in the stomach becomes acid, but few animals rely on such digestion.

The Intestines. The duodenum is a thickened area of small intestine starting at the stomach. It is important because into it two ducts or tubes discharge their contents. One is bile, which is made in the liver and stored in the gallbladder. Bile splits fat up into tiny globules so small they are invisible and at the same time has a laxative effect on the food. When an animal vomits a yellow substance, it is stomach contents together with bile which has been pumped backward into the stomach by regurgitation.

The second duct transmits more starch-digesting substance from the pancreas, which manufactures it. Starches are turned into dextrin, which, as the food is pushed along, is further broken down into glucose by another substance excreted by the small intestine. The glucose is then absorbed through the intestines and winds up in the bloodstream. Glucose is also the sugar of grapes and of corn syrup. And so in this way digestion transforms the carbohydrates in the food into a form transportable by the blood. Proteins and fats are also reduced to their component parts, amino acids and fatty acids—forms in which they, too, can pass through the intestinal walls and into the lymph and blood.

Absorption of materials from the intestine is increased by a unique arrangement. The inner surface feels—and indeed is—almost like velvet, being studded with microscopic, short, hairlike projections called villi. Each one, while minute in itself, increases the surface of the intestine by a little, and in the aggregate these tiny projections increase the area of the intestines immensely.

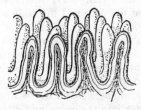

How the inside of a cat's intestine appears when magnified to show the villi. This arrangement enormously increases the absorbing surface of the intestine.

This efficient "factory" of the digestive system is like an automobile assembly line running backward, with the cars being taken to pieces bit by bit, instead of being built up. As it passes through the digestive system the whole mass of food which entered the mouth is reduced to its essential parts—fatty acids, glucose, and amino acids—and these disassembled products are absorbed into the blood.

The Liver. The liver is the largest solid organ of the body. It lies in front of the stomach and just behind the diaphragm, which is the partition separating the abdominal from the thoracic cavity, and is constantly massaged by the regular inhalations and exhalations caused by breathing. The healthy liver is a dark red with a glistening surface and several lobes, the number depending on the species.

All its activities are not concerned with digestion. Besides turning old red blood cells into bile pigment, it is a prime organ of regulation and manufacture. Bile, as we have said, comes from the liver. Besides the red blood cells bile contains bile salts, cholesterol, lecithin, fat, mucin, and pigments. Urea is made in the liver by converting ammonia left over from protein metabolism (chemical changes). Bacteria are destroyed in the liver to some extent, too, as they are in the lymphatic system and spleen.

As a sugar regulator for the body, the liver is essential. Suppose glucose is absorbed from the intestine in greater quantities than the body can use. The liver then changes it into glycogen (actually animal starch) and stores it. When the blood-sugar level gets too low, the liver obliges by releasing glucose from the conversion of the glycogen.

When the gall duct or gallbladder becomes obstructed or the bile cannot escape, the pigment gets into the blood, producing a yellow color known as jaundice. Jaundice is not a disease but a condition or a symptom.

Another function of the liver is the absorption of fat, which is then deposited in the tissues of the body to be used when needed.

The Pancreas.   We cannot leave the subject of digestion without mentioning another important function of the pancreas, besides that of furnishing enzymes (digestive ferments), which we discussed previously. That is the regulation of the power of the body to handle blood sugar. In this task it functions with the liver, which, as we have seen, stores up or liberates the sugar (glucose). In the pancreas are tiny islands that manufacture insulin, and it is insulin which in some unknown way regulates the percentage of glucose in the blood. If there is too much, it sees that the liver stores it; if too little, the pancreas sees that glucose is called out. A lack of insulin causes *diabetes mellitus*, or sugar (or honey) diabetes. The excess sugar escapes into the urine and may be measured. The disease also causes an increase in thirst and in the amount of urine excreted.

Final Steps in Digestion.   What is left of the food after it has traveled through the small intestine is deposited through a valve into the large intestine, where excess water is absorbed, and where a huge growth of bacteria takes place. In some species it has been estimated that over half of the feces is living and dead bacteria. The more unassimilated food ends up in the colon, the more there is for bacteria to work on and the more products of bacteria there are to be absorbed by the body along with the surplus water. This is another good reason for not overfeeding and underexercising pets.

THE GLANDULAR SYSTEM

Ductless Glands.   The blood acts also as a vehicle for transporting the products of the body regulators, only one of which has thus far been considered—the pancreas. (The spleen and lymph glands are also ductless glands but, as far as we know, do not secrete regulators.) A ductless gland is one which does not have an outlet except back into the blood.

Some glands, like the pancreas, are mixed ductless and ordinary glands. Salivary glands are good examples of ordinary glands because they have ducts which lead their products away from the glands, secreting saliva in the mouth. The important, strictly ductless glands are the pituitary, the adrenal, thyroid, and parathyroid. The important mixed ductless and ordinary glands are pancreas, ovaries, and testicles.

The Pituitary. Probably most important as a body regulator is the pituitary gland, located at the base of the brain, to which it is attached by a stalk. It has a front and a rear lobe. It seems incredible that such a tiny organ could be capable of performing the feats it does. Yet its direct and indirect chemical influence on other glands and organs coaxes them to extraordinary accomplishments. Here are a few of its capacities; it can:

Cause an animal to come in heat.
Make an unmaternal animal become maternal.
Affect the shedding of the coat.
Cause a pregnant female to commence labor.
Stimulate growth and cause giantism, if overactive.
Cause stunted growth if underactive.
Cause sexual development.
Help regulate metabolism of carbohydrates.
Cause overfatness if underactive.
Raise blood pressure.

Because the gland is so potent, the amount of chemicals required for these tasks is very small.

The Adrenal Glands. These glands, situated near the kidneys, are also known as the suprarenal glands. They produce epinephrine—also called adrenalin—a potent chemical that regulates blood pressure by its effect on the heart and vessels right down to the capillaries. These glands also determine in some manner the amount of salt in the urine and affect the use of fat and sugar. Their outer layers secrete a substance now being used in the treatment of arthritis.

The Thyroid. This gland lies in the neck on either side of the windpipe. It is attached to the larynx, so that with every swallowing movement the thyroid is moved too. An important chemical regulator, thyroxin, is secreted by it, and this is known to contain about 60 per cent iodine. Animals whose diets are low in iodine content become sick, and some young animals grow into cretins—peculiar abnormalities not often seen among pets. (A cretin is a dwarf, stupid, slow, dull, gross in appearance.)

Thyroxin regulates the speed of living in any animal. Slow, poky animals, overweight and phlegmatic, respond by quicker actions, more rapid pulse, restlessness, and sleeplessness when given the drug. When the gland secretes too much of its regulating substance, the animal becomes nervous, develops a ravenous appetite, wastes away, exhibits protruding eyeballs, and usually an increase in the size of the gland itself. Any such increase is called goiter in man or in animals.

Parathyroids. Located beside the two parts of the thyroid are two small glands whose function is the regulation of calcium metabolism. If they are removed, a condition known as tetany, involving violent trembling, is established and death ensues. It has been thought that they are also concerned with eclampsia, a condition characterized by trembling and rigidity in nursing mothers. Injections of parathyroid extract increase the percentage of calcium in the blood, even when none is fed, by forcing the body processes to draw it from the bones.

The Ovaries. Located behind the queen's kidneys are the ovaries. They have several functions. Their first and most important task, of course, is that of perpetuating the species, but we shall deal with that function later. Here we are interested in the secretions that regulate the animal's behavior.

The ovaries influence body development even before reproductive functions begin. Even such a thing as mental interest is controlled by them. If the ovaries are removed from a young kitten it grows somewhat ungainly and tends to put on fat more than a twin whose ovaries have not been removed. This propensity continues through life. The pet tends to become an intersex. A female kitten grows larger and lazier than her whole sisters; not a bad fault. In fact it may be considered an advantage when the owner has no thought of raising kittens.

Working in co-operation with the pituitary, the ovaries initiate the sex cycle. Once this occurs, the behavior of the female in heat is determined by an ovarian-secreted hormone in the blood known as the follicular hormone. This hormone produces the swelling of the vulva, and after several days, the desire for mating. (For more information on the function of the ovaries, see Chapter 5.)

The Testicles. Besides producing sperm, the testicles secrete the male hormone, testosterone, which functions in connection with the pituitary gland. Some grave errors were made in the use of testosterone in the mistaken notion that it stimulated the testicles to greater activity. It was administered in great quantities until it was learned that its use actually lessened testicle activity and caused the deterioration of the testicles. It is the pituitary gland whose secretions cause testicle activity and production of testosterone, which in turn affects the maleness of the animal. Some good stud animals have been temporarily sterilized by the indiscriminate use of testosterone, some possibly permanently. The natural secretion does affect the male animal profoundly, and without it he would be little good as a sire.

THE NERVOUS SYSTEM AND ORGANS OF PERCEPTION

The nerves may be thought of as the telegraph wires of the body. Thousands of miles of these fibers control the body's activities. They stimulate the muscles to contract, and each of even the tiniest muscles has its nerve supply. The brain is the central station from which the nerves radiate through several pathways, the principal one being the spinal cord. Most of the conscious body movements are regulated by the brain and cord. These two wonderful organs are exceedingly well protected by the skull and spine.

Nerves carry impulses to the brain from distant parts of the body. Organs of sense, such as the delicate nerves in the skin, telegraph messages to the brain. For example, feeling is a function of these nerves of the skin —sensitivity to temperature, to electrical stimuli, to wetness or dryness, to sharpness, as in the case of a pin prick. Some diseases—rabies, for example—may destroy the skin's sensitivity, so that a rabid animal may not even feel the bites of another animal.

Whereas telegraph wires carry messages both ways, nerves conduct impulses in only one direction, some *to* the brain and some *away from* it. Suppose a cat touches a hot electric-light bulb. Her sense organs alert the brain with the speed of electricity, and instantly the muscles are given an impulse which pulls them away from the hot object.

We used to talk about the five senses, but today, besides the ordinary five, psychologists recognize many more: the kinesthetic sense, or muscle sense, the sense of balance, which can be demonstrated even while animals are embryos, the sex sense, to mention only a few.

The Brain and Cord. The nerves are unlike other cells in that they are long, thin fibers. Many fibers may be grouped in bundles, and the largest bundle of all is the spinal cord, which gives out and takes in pairs of nerves between every vertebra of the back bone. The bundles of fibers branch here and there (the trunk divides into branches) until the final divisions are tiny individual fibers innervating some small area of the body.

Besides the cord there are other nerves that leave the brain, running to organs and other parts of the body. All of the body—organs, muscles, glands, intestines—is controlled by the cord and by "cranial" nerves.

For every sensitive area in the body there is a corresponding center in the brain. Sometimes when a cat has a paralyzed leg it is difficult to realize that the origin of the ailment is a part of the brain or spinal cord. Nor, when we see a pet scratch, do we think that a nerve somewhere in the skin telegraphed the brain, which set in motion the pet's hind leg. Nerves control the reflex actions of cats. Everyone knows about the human knee jerk—how tapping a definite area just under the kneecap produces an involuntary forward kick of the foot. Cats have many similar reflexes. Anyone who has grasped a big handful of skin at the cat's neck and shoulders knows how she tends to curl up like a kitten being carried by its mother. Some persons misinterpret this action as being due to early training; it's not—it's a reflex action. Everyone who has scratched a cat on the back close to the tail knows that the cat will stretch the hind legs as high as possible, hold the tail straight up, and move about. This is not only because the cat enjoys being scratched, but is also due to an involuntary reflex. (Do not become alarmed if your cat does not tolerate such affection. Many don't.)

When compared with our own, the brain itself is small in pets, chiefly because the forepart, called the cerebrum, is so much smaller in lower animals. The positive, willing, conscious actions are evolved in this portion of the brain. Ordinary living is a concern of the lower part, called the cerebellum. There are other parts, most of which, like the two mentioned, come in pairs.

Animals can function mechanically without the cerebrum, but have no memory, can't learn, and lack the will to do anything. Their existence is almost like that of a vegetable. They can breathe, eat if their faces are held over the pan, defecate, urinate, sleep, wander aimlessly around, bite or growl when hurt. But by the way some of our pets are trained (or not trained) one might conclude that all they had were cerebellums.

The cerebrum is the part of the brain which responds most to training. Let no one think a cat can have its brain "cluttered up" by training. Once a pet learns what is wanted of it and is properly rewarded, each succeeding act or trick taught it is easier to teach than previous acts. The most highly educated of all cats find learning easier and easier. Unfortunately our pets do not live long enough. Just as they become "almost human" mentally, they break down physically and die or must be destroyed.

The Eye.   Many misconceptions exist about the eye, which in fact is far less complex and much tougher than most people believe it to be. From the front of an animal one sees a big, round transparent part of a globe, the cornea. Surrounding it we see a ring of clear white, glistening tissue, the sclera. And under the eye, some animals, cats included, have a third eyelid, the nictitating membrane. This thin membrane acts as a protection to the eye. It is a minor detail which observant cat owners watch nonetheless because, in some unknown manner, a number of different problems can cause it to rise up across the inner side of the eye with the result that the eye seems to be rolling back in the head.

In the middle of the eye we see the pupil or the opening of the eye. In cats, it is a vertical elliptical slit, while dogs show a round pupil. The pupils get larger or smaller depending on the amount of light the eye needs for vision, and vary from drug action, or brain disease. An animal looking at a bright light shows a very small pupil; as the light dims, the pupil enlarges. The colored tissue we see around the pupil is called the iris. It ranges from pearl in some pets, yellow, green, blue in others, to blood color in albinos and dark brown in still others; cats often have eyes of a different color.

Behind the pupil lies the lens. It is tough, crystalline, and fibrous. Through it light rays are bent so that the image comes to rest on a sensitive, nerve-laden area behind the lens known as the retina. The retinal nerves in turn transmit visual images via the optic nerve to the brain.

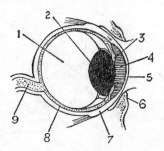

Cross section of the eye. (1) Vitreous humor. (2) Lens. (3) Iris. (4) Aqueous humor. (5) Cornea. (6) Lids. (7) Sclera. (8) Retina. (9) Optic nerve.

So many misconceptions surround the subject of cataracts that a definition is in order. A cataract is an opacity in the lens, not scratches on the cornea or anything else. When you look into the pupil and see an irregular white area, it may be a cataract.

Sometimes a cat's eye is pierced with a sharp object. If the hole is in the cornea and no deeper, the forepart of the eye will collapse as the fluid escapes. The opening will promptly heal and, if no infection has entered, the fluid will be renewed and the eye will regain its normal shape. The white cells, in healing, may produce a temporary milky effect in the cornea, and a scar may be formed that does not always show. If it is not in the line of vision, it does not interfere with sight.

Cats, as far as scientists have been able to discover, are color blind (i.e., they see colors as shades of gray).

The Ear. Though the eye is a marvelous organ, the ear excites just as much wonder. Here is a truly marvelous device for catching sounds and carrying the impressions to the brain through nerves. The natural four-legged animal has a cupped erect ear to enable it to pick up distant or faint sounds. By turning the head, the sounds can be captured as by a trumpet or radar antenna. The sounds are conducted downward through the external canal. Every cat owner has looked down into his pet's ear, probably cleaned it, and knows the projections to be found there. And that is all of the ear most people do know about. They often wonder about the possibility of piercing the drum when they are cleaning the canal. So long as they clean downward, they do no harm. The canal becomes smaller at the bottom, then turns upward slightly, and terminates in a very delicate membrane, the drum. All the rest of the ear is within the solid bone of the skull.

Behind the drum are three tiny delicate bones. This remarkable mechanism is activated by sound vibrations. The three bones transmit these vibrations, via the semicircular canal, to nerves which in turn carry them to the brain via the auditory nerve. From the small cavity (the middle ear)

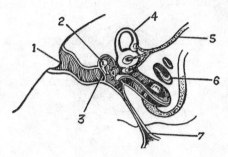

Cross section of the ear. (1) Auditory opening and canal. (2) Middle ear with mechanism for feeling vibrations. (3) Tympanum. (4) Semicircular canal. (5) Auditory nerve. (6) Cochlea (a spiral represented in sections). (7) Eustachian tube.

in which the three bones are found, a tube called the Eustachian tube, runs into the throat. By means of it, pressure on the drum is equalized. If we go up a high hill or mountain or under a river in a subway, we feel a sensation in our middle ear. If we swallow, the pressure is relieved or, in other words, equalized. If it were not for this provision, the delicate drum might be broken from the changes of atmospheric pressure.

Suppose some ear medicine is dropped into the ear canal of a cat. The canal is rubbed and squeezed by the fingers to mix the wax with the medicine. While that is being done, the pet sticks out his tongue as if he has experienced an unpleasant taste. Perhaps we open his mouth and smell his breath. There is the odor of the medicine. This is a certain indication that the eardrum is broken. Some of the worst cases of ear disease, and the hardest to cure, are due to infections in the middle ear. When the drum is broken, special medicines are required to effect a cure.

The Nose. That part of the animal's face which we call the nose is only a small part of his smelling apparatus; all the important parts are out of sight. These consist of a complicated pair of cavities with a partition or septum between. The front part is called the anterior nares; the back part, the posterior nares. The bones of the face cover the anterior nares. This part of the cavity is called the vestibule.

In warm-blooded pets the inspired air passes through the vestibule and thence through a remarkable shelf-like arrangement made up of turbinate bones covered with erectile tissue which can become engorged with blood. A mucous membrane overlies this tissue.

When the air is cold, the erectile tissue fills with extra blood, which helps to warm the air before it passes to the lungs. The arrangement of bones and erectile tissue also filters the air at all times, removing dust and bacteria from it.

Before animals can smell odors, the odors, which are gases, must be dissolved in the watery secretion that is present in the olfactory organs. A chemical stimulus received by large numbers of nerve fibers terminating in olfactory hairs in the mucous membrane goes to the brain via the olfactory nerve. At the first stimulus or acknowledgment of the new odor, most animals begin to sniff, which, of course, brings more of the odor into contact with the mucous membrane, where it dissolves. The stimulation is thereby increased. It is difficult for us to realize how minute an amount of odor is required to effect this remarkable recognition by cats and other pets.

THE REPRODUCTIVE SYSTEM

The sex organs exist as a means of producing the next generation. Eggs are produced by the female; sperm by the male. An egg and a sperm unite and the plans for a new individual are completed. The architectural scheme awaits unfolding. Mammals are arranged so that the egg or eggs develop within the female.

Female Organs. The female's ovaries contain her heritage—the germ plasm of which she is the custodian and which created her. At certain times the ovaries produce eggs in blisterlike follicles. The eggs are conducted to a resting place, but before they arrive they are generally fertilized by the sperm—a tiny tadpole-like cell containing the male's heredity. Yes, all the heredity from the male is in a "package" so small we would have to magnify it a hundred times to be able to see even its crudest details.

The female mammal has a uterus in which the fertilized eggs rest. This organ is of various shapes in the different species. In the queen it is like a letter Y, but the stem is short and the two horns are long and capable of growing much longer. At the lower end of the uterus is a muscular ring which constitutes its mouth and is known as the cervix. The cervix also constitutes the upper end of the vagina, that part of the reproductive tract into which the penis of the male is inserted during copulation. Close to the opening of the vagina (the vulva) is the clitoris, a small glandular organ known to be the equivalent of the penis of the male. If a female kitten is regularly injected with enough male sex hormone, this clitoris will grow to be almost as large as the penis of a male of the same species. The function of the clitoris in lower mammals is not known. Being of erectile tissue, it becomes somewhat enlarged at times. Probably it assists in making the sexual act pleasant for the animals and, if so, is helpful in stimulating procreation.

The vulva, which one sees below the anus, is the termination of the reproductive system of the female. Into it, urine is discharged, so that it serves two functions. During the mating cycle it enlarges considerably.

The breasts of the female mammal are glands of the skin. Richly supplied with blood, they make milk. Many people have an entirely er-

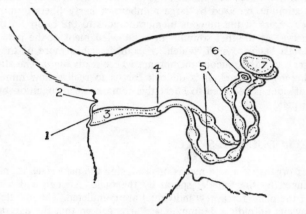

Reproductive system and related organs of a queen. (1) Vulva. (2) Anus. (3) Vagina. (4) Cervix. (5) Developing embryos in uterus. (6) Ovary. (7) Kidney.

roneous idea about the process of milk production (lactation). The young take hold of the teats and suck. Milk may not come at first, or if it does, not more than a few drops at best. Then it begins to come so fast in some animals that it may actually run out of teats to which no young are attached. This is because the mother exerts an involuntary pressure which

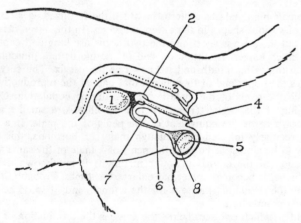

Reproductive system and related organs of a tomcat. (1) Bladder. (2) Prostate. (3) Rectum. (4) Penis. (5) Testicle. (6) Vas deferens. (7) Cross section of part of pelvic bone. (8) Epididymis.

forces the milk out easily. Milk is made by glands, from blood *while* the young are nursing. Except for a small amount held in a reservoir, it is not made up in advance and then drained out.

Male Organs. The male organs consist of two of each of the following: the testicle, in which the sperm are produced; the epididymis, which is attached to the testicle and in which the sperm are stored; the vas deferens, through which the sperm are transported to a common duct. Anyone with a knowledge of human organs may wonder why the seminal vesicle is not mentioned. Most male pet animals have none. The vas deferens from one testicle joins the one from the other side, and the resultant single canal joins the urethra through which the sperm are discharged during copulation. The penis runs out through the pelvis, under the anus, bends around between the hind legs, and emerges through its covering, the sheath. In mammals, the testicles must be located outside the body since internal body temperature is sufficiently high to prevent the production of sperm. A strong muscle draws the testicle up close to the body if the external temperature is too cold, and lets it down when the weather is hot. Notice in a cat how the testicles are low or high depending on the weather.

In addition to the vas deferens leading away from it, each testicle has a vein, an artery, and a muscle called the cremaster, which together compose the spermatic cord. This enters the body through the same opening in the abdomen through which the testicles descended.

3. What You Should Know about Food and Feeding

ANIMALS are usually divided into three classes—flesh-eating (carnivorous), plant- and seed-eating (herbivorous), and those which eat both plant and animal matter (omnivorous). These classifications are made not only on the basis of the food which the animal eats, but also on such characteristics as teeth and digestive apparatus as well.

The distinction between these three general types of animals is not so sharp and clear as most people think. There can be no doubt, of course, about the group to which some animals belong. Having observed large numbers of rabbits and cavies without finding a single instance in which they ate food of animal origin—even crickets—the scientist can be certain that they are as herbivorous as the cow or deer. But the classification of most household pets is not so simple. The layman is likely to think of dogs, cats, rats, and raccoons, for example, as carnivorous animals. The zoologist, however, very properly considers them omnivores, because he has observed that they eat *all* of the animals they catch—including the partially digested vegetable matter in the stomach and intestines. Despite the fact that their teeth are typical of carnivorous animals, well adapted to tearing the flesh and puncturing the skull and vital organs of the smaller animals on which they prey, studies have shown that most of the mammals we keep as pets are nearly as omnivorous as we are. With one notable exception, there is practically nothing that we eat which these animals cannot digest as well as humans. This one exception is, as we have seen in Chapter 2, that they must have certain starchy foods crushed for them. When wild cats consume the stomach and intestinal contents of their prey, they are getting the benefit of the chewing, mastication, and some digestion which has already been done.

Today we are beginning to doubt whether any of our pets, in fact, can live for very long on flesh alone without deficiency diseases developing sooner or later. It is fortunate that this is so—fortunate that our pets can assimilate foods of vegetable origin. It may well become increasingly so in the years to come, when the earth has more people and an insufficient food supply.

Nearly all the information we have about nutrition has been provided by the great laboratories of the world since 1900. And much of our knowledge of food values and human nutritional needs has come through feeding experiments with pets. Yet we have been extremely slow in applying this knowledge to the care of household animals. Recently, while reading a volume on dogs published in 1872, I found that the directions given in the section on feeding are just about what the average owner today thinks is the proper way to feed his dog! Cat feeding, too, is just as old-fashioned. We have put into daily practice innumerable scientific findings with regard to our own food requirements, but we still cling stubbornly to outdated ideas in feeding our pets.

No one should assume, of course, that because we are interested in adopting scientific methods in the feeding of animals that we intend to depart from their natural habits and tendencies. In Chapter 2 we stressed the point that if we want to keep pets healthy and happy, it is essential that we understand and consider their native inclinations. A cat is a cat, not a human being. In choosing or preparing our cats' food, we might well consider their natural propensities in choosing their own food. We, partly because of our training, enjoy our meat cooked, but Eskimos eat much of theirs raw. Even the raw intestinal contents of their food animals are eaten raw. How often do we provide our cats with well-chopped raw leafy vegetable matter? While it is true that we should interfere as little as possible with an animal's natural mode of life, it is also true that when we refuse to use what knowledge we have of their care we are being foolish and wasteful.

We know that cats differ from their remote ancestors because human selection of certain odd characteristics has made them most unnatural in many respects. Their mildness and ease of domestication are the most interesting illustrations of that fact. Few similar forms of animal have been domesticated to such a degree of dependability as the cat. Many of what we consider the finest characteristics of cats and many of those most useful to us are the very ones which would make them less able to survive if they were suddenly dropped back into a wild existence. And yet cats of all breeds have such marvelous qualities of adapting themselves to wide environmental changes that they rate among the most adaptable animals known to man.

Cats have been evolved to be useful to man, and while they were being developed they lived closely enough to man to share his food. They became accustomed to it as time went on, and those that could not manage it died off, while those that could lived and reproduced. Partially as a result of that selection, we find that cats today thrive on an almost unbelievable variety of diets. So the problem boils down to determining how to feed our cats *best* and most *completely* with the foods we have available, rather than to consider what they *must* be fed.

FELINE DIGESTION AND DIETARY NEEDS

Before examining the nutritional needs of cats, let us see first how their digestive apparatus differs from ours. Starting at the mouth, we find that the teeth are different. The teeth useful for ripping an animal apart and cutting the tissue off are longer and sharper than the equivalent teeth in our mouths. Our back teeth (molars) are flatter and more useful for grinding grain into powder. The cats' habits of eating consist of tearing their food apart, cutting off pieces with the back teeth, and gulping them with only sufficient chewing to make them small enough to swallow.

The next difference is in the saliva. We have a starch-digesting enzyme —called salivary amylase—which begins the process of turning starch into sugar. The cat has very little of that enzyme. It was this discovery that caused the early students of cats to say that they couldn't digest starch. Probably such students never saw a human eat a huge mouthful of doughnut and wash it down with a gulp of coffee—and stopped to think that that too is digested without the aid of the salivary enzyme.

Let's see how starch digestion works for man and for cats. Our pets' stomachs secrete somewhat stronger juices than do ours. Bones eaten by cats are acted upon by this juice, which is rich in hydrochloric acid and pepsin, and are actually dissolved in the stomach. A bone in a healthy cat's stomach becomes soft and pliable in less than an hour. Actually the same thing might happen in the human stomach, but it would take much longer.

Upon emerging from the stomach the food is mixed with the same kind of juices—pancreatic and bile—which affect our food. Here, then, is where most of the digestion of starch takes place. The boy who washes down the half-chewed doughnut and the cat who gulps his starchy meal both live and thrive because of the digestion that takes place in the small intestine. But here is the important difference to remember: we usually chew our foods, so that we crack starchy grains and nuts into a fine paste, but the cat doesn't. When the pancreatic enzyme (amylase) works on these starches, in our case, they are so fine that the enzyme has little trouble. In the cat, when the starchy foods are in too large lumps, the enzyme cannot do its work effectively. To some degree the same thing happens in the human digestive tract if a person fails to chew a nut or a kernel of sweet corn—neither is digested any more than it would be by a cat. A cat will usually regurgitate any such indigestible material, as he often does hair or mouse tails.

In feeding cats, it has been found that it pays well to feed either very finely ground raw starch or precooked starches. Corn meal fed raw is an inefficient food, but corn meal which has been boiled until the starch granules have been cracked open, so that they are vulnerable to the attack of the amylase, is an efficient, if incomplete, food. Another point of difference between the human and the cat is the length of the small intestine. Cats' food travels through more quickly and there is less time for absorption—another reason for feeding easily digested foods. Cooking facilitates the digestive process, especially for foods such as raw cereals, vegetables, and fruits, which pets do not chew. Meats are digested as easily raw as cooked. Fish, however, *should* be cooked, since if it is fed raw in large amounts, it may cause paralysis. Fatty meats, like pork, also may cause problems. When fat and protein are fed alone, the cat's system does not tolerate either nutrient as well as when they are fed in conjunction with carbohydrates. If very fatty beef is fed, the result is the same, i.e., the cat will regurgitate it. People who advise against feeding pork or fatty beef forget that if plenty of carbohydrate is fed along with either or both, the fat will be handled nicely and may safely be fed in reasonable amounts. They forget, too, that when a cat eats a mouse it may get as much as 30 per cent fat—but in that case there is sufficient carbohydrate to burn the fat up.

Although cats can and do tolerate a wide variety of foods, many people, including some so-called experts, apparently feel that great variety is essential in a cat's diet. They sometimes go to astonishing extremes to attain that variety, and if you were to follow their advice you would spend a good part of every day in obtaining, preparing, and storing the cat's daily rations. Fortunately most of their recommendations are based on personal opinion and preference and not on a scientific study of nutritional needs.

The fact that an elaborate diet is unnecessary to cats can be seen by studying the food of the feral cat, who thrives—and indeed stays in beautiful condition—by eating very few types of food. Several accurate studies have been made of the contents of the stomachs of wild cats trapped or shot by wardens. Some of the studies were made, incidentally, to determine the amount of damage done by cats to bird life, and the results seemed to indicate conclusively that cats destroyed far fewer birds than had been supposed.

One of the studies, which dealt with wild cats taken in Wisconsin, found that the contents of the stomachs were composed principally of the remains of rodents, birds, and insects. The fifty stomachs examined contained fifty-nine rodents, nine birds, and five insects. A few of the cats had eaten garbage, and in their stomachs were found potatoes, string beans, apple, boiled rice, and custard pudding. Two had eaten ensilage.

In Oklahoma a study of the stomachs of eighty-four wild cats taken from several groups showed that 55 per cent contained mammals, mostly rodents; 26.5 per cent contained garbage; 12.5 per cent contained insects; and 4 per cent contained the remains of birds. In a small group of cats caught in residential districts 6.5 per cent showed evidence of having eaten birds. Other studies have shown that as much as 25 per cent of the contents of cats' stomachs was insects. Lizards also were found in some.

Our principal interest in these lists is not so much in the small number of items in the diet. More important is the fact that these studies all showed that whatever animal the cat fed on was eaten in its entirety. Very seldom do cats open their prey and eat only a single part of the animal, such as the liver or kidneys. Even bobcats—living chiefly on rabbits, hares, squirrels, mink, muskrats, mice, grouse, pheasant, bluejays, grass, insects—eat most of the body of their prey. Red and gray fox fur and meat has been found in their stomachs, and occasionally deer and porcupine remains. But who ever heard of a wild house cat eating only the kidneys or liver of a mouse?

Wild cats do have variety in their diet, but that variety is largely the result of their eating the complete animal. Rodents eat great quantities of vegetable matter, and when the cats eat the rodents they get a certain amount of this type of material from the stomachs and intestines of these animals. In all probability a cat could live indefinitely in excellent health on a diet consisting exclusively of mice. That single item would provide ample variety—muscles, bones, liver, intestines, brain, glands, *and* vegetable material in its digestive tract.

While some owners err by overelaborating their cat's diet, others take the opposite, and equally unwarranted, route by unconsciously training their cat to demand one particular type of food. The number of cats that refuse all food but one kind of canned cat food, or kidneys, or liver, or halibut, or codfish, or horse meat, or lean beef is myriad. The problem should be handled as it is with any other animal. It is best to pay no attention to a pet cat's likes and dislikes. Get your cat hungry enough to eat what is good for it and provide a meal varied enough to satisfy all of a cat's nutritional needs. Make sure that the variety is of the sort that a cat obtains when it eats a mouse—variety in one meal. There is no harm, of course, in giving occasional tidbits as a *small* part of the diet.

In addition to striking the proper balance in a cat's diet, it is obvious that a cat must have *enough* food. This is another way of saying that there must be sufficient food to furnish energy for his day's living. We measure this energy in the food by burning it in calorimeters to see how many heat units, or calories, it holds. We know how many calories any resting animal of a given size requires. The more any animal exercises or works, the more calories it needs. Living, exercise, or work all require energy, and this energy is extracted from the food. If a cat eats too few calories, it will live on stored fat and get thin. If it consumes too many, the surplus will be discarded in the feces or stored as fat, an energy reserve, as it were, for a time when food is scarce. Laymen often forget that a pet doesn't have to consume food to obtain nourishment when it is carrying it around in the form of fat.

Besides having enough food, our pets need the following essentials: water, minerals, amino acids, fatty acids, vitamins. Some species can live without consuming certain essentials which other species must have. (Cavies, for instance, need vitamin C; dogs and probably cats make their own.) In the next several sections, we will examine closely these essential nutrients, beginning with milk, the so-called perfect food, about which there are a number of misconceptions. There is no one "best" diet that will supply all of these nutrients in the proper balance. Here are several, any of which is perfectly adequate. The decision should be made on the basis of convenience.

What you yourself eat, so well diced, mashed, or ground together that the cat can't pick out one part and leave the rest. Cats will eat all items of human diet when trained to do so. They have even been known to eat olives.

Good canned cat food.

Two thirds dehydrated cat food, plus one third canned fish or cooked diced meat. Some of the larger catteries feed dog meal and mackerel with sufficient water or milk to produce a moist consistency, thinner than crumbly.

Fish—always cooked—mixed with bread and table scraps.

Meat—beef, lamb, pork, horse—mixed with vegetable products.

Or variations and combinations of any of the foods listed above.

A well-fed cat is not a fat cat; a fat cat is a badly fed cat. Nor is the cat that is properly fed thin; a thin cat may be ravenous. A well-fed cat will eat what is set before it; it is hungry enough never to turn up its nose at wholesome food; it eats as though it enjoys it. Mealtimes are the big events in a cat's life—mealtimes and the return home of the favorite family member. Both of these events can be made more enjoyable by proper training. There are few things that give the owner more pleasure than to see his pet eat the food it is given with evident enjoyment.

MILK

For a number of reasons, some valid, some not, milk is the first food people think of giving to a cat. Some set a bowl of milk on the floor for the cat to drink instead of water—a great mistake. In many ways, milk is an unnatural food, albeit a good one. It is no more sensible to say that a cat *must* have milk than to say that an adult human being *must* have it. It is true that cow's milk is much like cat's milk in composition. It is also true that the composition of milk acts as a sort of guide for deciding what the relative proportions of protein, carbohydrate, and fat in a diet should be. Milk is 85 per cent water; the remaining 15 per cent consists of solid material divided up as follows: protein, 27.5 per cent; carbohydrates, 37.2 per cent; fat, 27.5 per cent; ash, 6 per cent—all of which refutes those who tell cat owners not to feed their pets fat. A pint (or pound) of liquid milk contains about 320 calories (a cat needs approximately 350 per day). Although 85 per cent of it is water, the remaining 15 per cent consists of almost totally digestible solids. This compares favorably with commercial canned cat food, which contains 450 calories per pound and is 70 to 75 per cent water. Less of the solid content in canned cat food is digestible in relation to milk.

It is very important to remember that milk is not water, even though it is fluid. If a cat always has milk before it and drinks a great deal, it needs very little other food. A cupful of milk contains half of a cat's nutritional requirements, and many cats drink at least that much a day.

When you forget that milk is food and give your cat all it wants to drink, you will find it very difficult to alter its diet. If you are trying to get your cat to eat anything and everything that is good for it, take away the milk. Don't coax it with specially tempting food and don't feel sorry for your pet. Just provide a little of whatever food you are trying to get it to eat, and if the cat doesn't eat it, don't worry. Next day, offer more. Eventually your cat will get hungry enough to eat all or part of it. There is no pain in starvation; the pain is in the owner's mind. It is not unusual for cats to fall in wells, be locked in vacant houses where only water is available, or even be locked out on a roof in a city, and live for thirty to sixty days without any food whatever. One hates to think of it, yet we must be sensible and honest. There is certainly no cruelty in letting a cat fast long enough to accustom it to eating wholesome food.

Cats, being cats, may leave home for greener pastures if they are deprived of the food they want, so confinement may be necessary while convincing them to eat a new diet.

There are some cats that refuse to drink milk. It has been estimated that about half of all domesticated cats will not touch it, but this is probably due to training.

WATER

That water is essential to living is obvious. Everybody who observes cats at all has seen what its absence produces in the way of dehydration, knows the sensation of thirst, the dry mouth, the way some sick, dehydrated cats develop a coat which stands in folds when it is squeezed together, the sunken eyes. And since blood, the very vehicle of transportation of nutrition to the cells, consists mostly of water, the need for water is patent. Besides its internal uses, its evaporation regulates temperature.

Water carries out waste products; it bathes the cells and totes off their excreta as it carries useful substances to them, to mention only a few of its uses. But supplying water is so easy that it is not a problem. A pan from which the pet can drink at will is all that is required. Then if there is enough water in his food so that he needs no more, he is satisfied, and if his food is of such a type that he must have additional water, he drinks.

Seventy per cent of our cats' bodies is water. Here are the percentages for the separate parts:

Teeth	10%	Brain	79%
Cartilages	55%	Blood	88%
Bones	60%	Urine	93%
Skin	72%	Lymph	96%
Muscles	75%	Gastric Juice	97%
Ligaments	77%	Saliva	99%

Nearly all the water drunk is absorbed. Normally about 20 per cent passes out with the breath, and in hot weather more is thrown off in this manner. Almost all the rest is passed in the urine. Very little water is used in combination with other substances. It acts as a solvent or vehicle. As water it enters the body; as water it leaves.

In foods, water content varies greatly. The juiciest meat contains about 75 per cent water. So do many brands of canned animal food. Dehydrated meals and baked biscuits contain about 7 per cent water. If they are dried below that, they often absorb enough water from the air to build up to 7 per cent. It is important that these facts be known because, when they are, the pet owner understands that some feeding schedules require that more water be fed. High water consumption need not be indicative of kidney disease or diabetes, as some pet owners surmise; perhaps the diet is too dry.

On the other hand, inferior canned foods contain so much water and so little actual nourishment that a growing kitten, to get enough calories, consumes so much food, and therefore so much water in the food, that it may seem to use its pan all too frequently. This predicament may be overcome by adding more dry food to the canned.

When water is taken into the stomach little of it remains when the stool is passed, and even in the case of enteritis-caused diarrhea, the water is absorbed in the upper small intestine and redeposited in the lower bowel. Only in unusual disease states does any significant amount of ingested water cause loose stools.

MINERALS

Some uncombined chemical elements are called minerals. A chemical element is a substance, made up of atoms, which cannot be decomposed by chemical means. Some of these elements are solid, some gases. Most of the pet's nutrition consists of very complicated combinations of elements.

Minerals compose about 6 per cent of the animal's body in the following proportions:

Calcium	40
Phosphorus	22
Potassium	5
Sulphur	4
Chlorine	3
Sodium	2
Magnesium	0.7

with many minerals in lesser amounts. Among these are: iron, manganese, copper, iodine, zinc, cobalt, fluorine, boron.

Ash. When you see, among the ingredients listed on the package or can of cat food, the item ash, don't conclude that the manufacturer included ash in the formula. What ash signifies is that a chemist, analyzing the food, finds a certain per cent of indigestible mineral matter. Part of the ash, calcium for example, is used by the animal to build bones, or blood. In a dry cat food, the percentage of ash is always higher than it is in a moist cat food, because the moisture content of the dry food may be 7 per cent while the moisture in the wet food is 74 per cent. If a dry food containing 10 per cent ash were canned (and moisturized) then the ash content would be about 2.5 per cent. So when you are considering a low ash diet to help control urinary problems add water to dry cat food for an even lower ash content than that of most canned foods.

Table I—Minerals: Their Functions and Sources

MINERALS	FUNCTIONS IN BODY	PRINCIPAL SOURCES
Calcium		
90% of body calcium is in the bones; 1% in circulation Stored in body	Bone building Blood component Reproduction Lactation Muscle function Nerve function Heart function Tooth component	Bones and bone meal Alfalfa-leaf meal Milk
Phosphorus		
Bones, blood, muscles, and teeth	Bone building Tooth component Carbohydrate metabolism Fat metabolism Blood component Rickets preventive Liquid content of tissues	Cereals Meat Fish Bones Milk So abundant in pet diets it is of little concern to owners
Iron		
Composes only 4/1000ths of the body weight Needed in minute quantities Is stored in body	Component of red blood cells Transports oxygen in blood 65% is found in blood 30% is found in liver, bone marrow, and spleen 5% is found in muscle tissue	Egg yolk Liver Kidney Gizzard Heart Bone marrow

MINERALS	FUNCTIONS IN BODY	PRINCIPAL SOURCES
Potassium		
	Body-fluid regulator	Blood
	Helps regulate blood	Potatoes
	Muscular function	Vegetables
Sodium		
Found in body in combination with phosphorus, chlorine, and sulphur	Regulates body fluids	Table salt
	Blood regulator	Blood
	Component of gastric juice	
	Component of urine	
Chlorine		
Found combined with sodium and hydrogen	Component of gastric juice	Table salt
	Blood regulator	Blood
	Regulates body fluids	
	Component of urine	
Iodine		
Most of iodine in body is found in thyroid gland	Thyroid health and normal growth	Foods grown in iodine-rich soils
	Regulates metabolism	Iodized salt
	Prevents goiter and cretinism	Fish meal made from salt-water fish
	In formation of thyroxine	Shellfish
Magnesium		
Needed only in minute amounts	Muscle activity	Bones
	Bone building	Vegetables
	Normal growth	Epsom salts
	Nerve function	
	Blood function	
Copper		
Needed only in minute amounts	Forms hemoglobin with iron	Blood
		Copper sulfate
Sulphur		
Minute amounts required but needed regularly	Body regulation	Meat
	Combination in salts as sulfates	Egg yolk
		Any food which, when decomposed, smells like bad eggs

PROTEINS AND AMINO ACIDS

A second general group of essentials for every diet is proteins. These complex chemicals always have the element nitrogen as a component. Every protein is composed of amino acids, which contain the NH_2 group as chemistry students know it. Proteins differ according to their amino acid content.

There are twenty-two amino acids, each of which has been studied both for its composition and its essentiality. There are ten without which life cannot go on and which must be part of the diet of all cats. These are: arginine, histidine, isoleucine, leucine, lysine, methionine, phenyl-alanine, threonine, tryptophane, valine. In Table II you will find some of the more common proteins listed, but no breakdowns into amino acids.

Two of the amino acids, cystine and methionine, are worth noting in that they contain sulphur. The most satisfactory way to feed sulphur is not as the element, because as such it is not absorbed, but as one of these two amino acids. Wheat, meat, fish, milk, yeast, egg are excellent sources of both cystine and methionine.

Unfortunately, there is too much sulphur sold to pet owners—in the form of additives for water or food, practically all of which is wasted. The way to feed sulphur—more than cats can use—is to feed foods containing amino acids that have sulphur in their composition. Chances are you are feeding these foods to your cat anyway.

The proteins found in various foods have unequal properties. Milk proteins possess all of the essential amino acids, and all are digestible. But corn, with its protein called zein, is not complete and is less valuable in feeding. Here, taking milk as a standard, are relative values of the proteins found in some common animal foods:

Beef	104	Yeast	71
Milk	100	Casein	70
Fish	95	Peas	56
Rice	88	Wheat flour	40
		Corn meal	30

Most proteins contain more than one amino acid. With their different assortments of amino acids, proteins can be mixed to produce complete rations of amino acids. Corn meal and horse meat, milk and cereals, alfalfa with wheat or oat flour—all are compatible mixtures. Even meat protein can be supplemented to advantage. It is the mixtures of proteins that produce the almost limitless variety in diets, varying flavors, aromas, and appearances.

Protein Requirements. If we could feed just the minimum of complete proteins, the average full-grown cat could, in all probability, get along on a diet that included 4 to 6 per cent of protein and for the growing animal, 15 per cent. Nearly all pet foods and rations contain over 20 per cent of protein mixtures, some complete, some incomplete, some supplementing others, so the results are excellent. Unfortunately, the amount of protein listed on cat food labels indicates the protein content but not all of it is digestible and therefore usable by the cat. For example, if blood meal is added to cat food, the protein content is increased but little of it can be absorbed by the cat. More properly cat food contents should read "available protein."

Protein is used primarily in building the body. Some is burned as energy, the nitrogen passing out in the urine, but protein foods, such as meat, are not primarily energy foods. And yet cat owners often make the grave mistake of feeding their cats only liver, kidneys, chicken, horse meat, etc., thus contributing to their ill health.

Table II lists the most important proteins together with their most common sources and some of their properties. It will be useful to those interested in checking the protein content of diets.

Table II—Some Common Proteins and Sources

PROTEIN	RICH SOURCES	PROPERTIES
Albumin	Egg white Milk Meat Blood	Soluble in water Does not precipitate by dilute acids or salts Coagulates when boiled
Casein	Milk Cheese Cottage cheese	Does not coagulate when boiled Coagulated by renin Coagulated by pepsin Coagulated by acids
Fibrinogen	Blood	Soluble in weak salt solutions Coagulated by heat Forms scabs Elastic Dissolved by weak acids
Myesin	Muscle meat	Dissolved by weak acids Flexible only while alive Semifluid consistency Coagulated by heat Shrinks Easily digested

Syntonin	Muscles and organs
	End product of digestion of
	  other proteins by gastric
	  juice
		Dissolved by weak acids
		Next step in digestion is to a
		  peptone

PROTEIN	RICH SOURCES	PROPERTIES
Peptone	An end product of protein digestion by gastric juice	Leaves stomach and enters intestines after protein digestion Can diffuse through intestinal walls Has more hydrogen and oxygen than proteins
Gelatine	Well distributed throughout animal body	Becomes solid on boiling Three per cent or more in a batch of food will solidify it Trick ingredient often used in cat food to give appearance of solid goodness Precipitated by tannic acid and alcohol
Chondrin	Ligaments, cartilage	Similar to gelatine in properties Requires longer boiling of the tissues which contain it to bring it out
Keratin	Horns, hair, nails, hoofs	Tough, fibrinous, indigestible, useless in pet feeding but sometimes found in foods Manufactured in hair follicles, etc. Contains much sulphur
Vegetable proteins	All vegetable matter Richest in seeds, especially legumes	Very similar to animal proteins In legumes one protein is found like albumin in milk Some are like fibrinogen, some like albumin with similar properties

CARBOHYDRATES

All carbohydrates are derived from plants. The chlorophyll of the plant leaf (much like the hemoglobin in the animal's body) is able to take six parts of carbon dioxide (CO_2) from the air, combine it with five parts of water (H_2O), and produce starch, $C_6H_{10}O_5$, and then have some oxygen left over which it passes out into the air. Starch granules are built up, layer on layer, and become the primary factor in nutrition. Plants add nitrogen to this starch to make proteins.

The starch granule has two substances in its composition: cellulose and granulose. The cellulose is fiber and gives plants their rigidity. When boiled it becomes soft but does not dissolve. Granulose will dissolve in boiling water. We find the starch diffused all through plants, some in seeds, some in tubers or roots, etc. Some starchy foods have large amounts of water (potatoes), some very small amounts (grains). When we buy starches we compare them on the basis of their dry components.

As a practical matter, it is important to remember this: raw starch is not soluble in cold water but it does dissolve in boiling water. However, about twenty times as much water must be added for the dissolving to take place. Mixed with an equal amount of water, it does not dissolve. Dissolving starch does not materially alter its composition, but when dissolved starch cools it becomes solid. This unimportant change explains why pet-food canners like to add to their products some starchy foods which are poured into the cans before processing and come out solid chunks. Many are excellent food but are not the solid goodness the buyer might think, since they contain 70 per cent or more of water.

Baking starch to 400°F. changes it to dextrin (not dextrose)—a gummy, sweetish substance, not unlike sugar, which dissolves easily. Biscuits taste good to animals because the heat has converted the starch to dextrin. Although it is sweeter, dextrin actually differs very little from starch; it has one more molecule of water (H_2O), $C_6H_{12}O_6$, whereas starch is $C_6H_{10}O_5$.

Starch is also found in animal liver and muscles as glycogen, or animal starch, soluble in hot or cold water. Animals quickly convert vegetable starch into animal starch, and they are also able to convert protein into glycogen.

Fasting uses up stored glycogen; eating replenishes it quickly. Within a few hours after a meal of starch there are abundant stores to be found in the liver. As it is circulated for the nourishment of the body, glycogen is converted into blood sugar, glucose. When the blood leaves the liver, it may contain as much as 3 per cent glucose. Sometimes animals are fed so much sugar they cannot store it. The excess is found in the urine; allowances for this must be made in tests for diabetes.

As we have seen, cats lack the salivary and other enzymes that break down starches in humans. Therefore, all starchy foods, such as potatoes or carrots, must be cooked and mashed in order to break down the starch to a form the cat can use.

Besides the starches, there are several carbohydrates common to most diets:

Milk sugar (lactose) is found in its only natural liquid form in milk. It is not, as a matter of fact, particularly sweet. Lactose is the food of acidophilus bacteria in the intestine and in such foods as yogurt cultures. Many very difficult cases of intestinal trouble have been greatly helped by the simple expedient of adding to the diet milk or some food like bread, which has considerable milk in its composition. Lactose is easily dissolved by the acid digestive juice. Its action on the bowel is laxative, which explains the effect of skim milk.

Cane sugar is good for animals but spoils their appetites as candy spoils those of children. It is, of course, usually fed in artificial forms. Honey is composed of the same sugar found in sugar cane and fruit.

FATS

The fatty acids are carbohydrates in a sense. They are composed of carbon, hydrogen, and oxygen, but have much less oxygen and more carbon than starches.

Unlike protein, fats contain no nitrogen. Like protein, they too are combinations of components, known as fatty acids. Only three of these are essential as far as we now know—linoleic, linolenic, and arachnidic acids, all believed to influence our pets' health in several ways. All are so very common in nature they may be almost neglected in our dietary considerations. Some other nonessential ones are butyric acid, caproic acid, lauric, oleic, palmitic, stearic acids.

Fats melt when heated, are smooth, lubricating when warm. Some fats like tallow are comparatively hard and crystalline; some, like vegetable oils, are extremely soft and fluid. All are made by the plant and the animal body.

When an animal consumes fat he stores it in his body largely in the same form in which he ate it. A cat eating lard mixed with his food in a sense first becomes part hog. Later his body slowly changes the lard to cat fat. Cats fed mutton tallow, which melts at 40°C., become part sheep until they change the sheep fat into cat fat, which melts at 20°C. The same applies to vegetable fats. Cats first starved and then fed corn fat become part corn for a while. All the fats in the body are fluid and pliable because they melt at body temperatures and harden after death when the fat chills.

Fats have a number of interesting properties which should be remembered by the pet owner:

Fats are able to emulsify; when acted on by bile salts produced by the liver, for instance, they can split into tiny invisible particles which stay in suspension in water or gastric juice.

Fat acts as a vehicle for carrying some of the vitamins—A, D, E, K. Because of this fact, mineral oil can absorb them from food in the intestines and prevent their absorption.

Fat slows digestion and renders it more complete. It enhances the availability of vitamin B in the diet, and affects fertility.

A balanced diet should contain not less than 20 per cent fat. An animal living on prey often eats 30 per cent or more of fat. The amount of fat animals can utilize depends on the amount of exercise they are getting. Cats that stay at home, show but little activity, and are in danger of becoming overweight need only a small percentage of fat in their diets; but farm cats, which hunt and prowl, can easily handle 25 per cent fat in the diet.

Cow's milk, with the water omitted, contains about 25 per cent fat, and milk is an excellent food for many pets—almost a criterion of what a food should be. But note that it contains a good amount of milk sugar. Feed milk sugar alone and the pet's stools become almost liquid. Feed fat alone and the same thing happens. Feed the two as whole milk and the

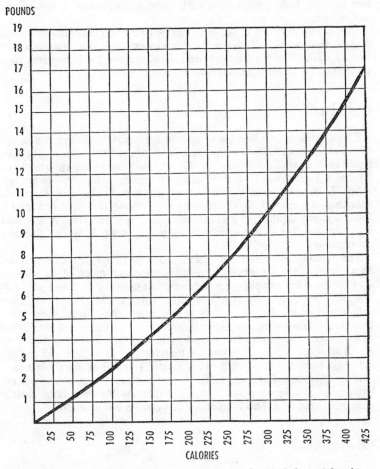

Approximate caloric requirements of cats by weight. Find the weight of your cat on the left-hand side and follow the line toward the right to its point of intersection with the heavy black line. Then drop downward to the bottom line, where you will find the daily calorie requirement (assuming your cat is not already overweight).

stool is perfect. Of course, the addition of a large amount of milk to the diet of a cat that has had no milk for a few weeks will cause the stools to loosen; but this should last only a few days.

Physiologists say: "Fat burns in the flame of carbohydrates." When you feed fat always see that there are sufficient carbohydrates present. On the other hand, if you fail to provide enough fat, the pet has to manufacture his own from proteins and carbohydrates in his diet—a less efficient and more costly process.

The economy of fat in pet food can be easily and conclusively demonstrated. One pound of rendered suet contains about four thousand calories; one pound of the best dehydrated commercial foods contains about 1,550; and the fat costs less than the cat food.

LAXATION

There often is considerable residue in the indigestible fiber and in part of the proteins and ash in many ingredients of pet foods. For a long while it was thought that the amount of this fiber was one of the criteria of how laxative a food would be and tables containing this information were published. It is now known that it is more a matter of the character of the fiber than the amount. If alfalfa meal is powdered like flour and used in food, it is not laxative; if it is ground coarse, like fine bran, it is exceedingly laxative; but if the same amount is fed as whole leaves, then it is constipating.

The question of residue in animal food is of considerable practical importance to the pet owner. Cats eating mice pass much of the hair and stomach contents and skin, but are not constipated by it. Some pets—rabbits and cavies—eat only vegetable food, which if fed alone to dogs and cats would cause diarrhea. With each species, the natural food habits have to be considered. In general, however, it is quite well established that animals whose stool has considerable bulk are healthier than those whose stool lacks bulk. It is unwise, therefore, to feed diets with as little indigestible residue as possible. Some residue is definitely an advantage.

It seems to me that hair, feathers, and perhaps bones of rodents and birds may contain elements that are important for cats since such is their diet in the wild. This is an area that warrants investigation.

VITAMINS

Another class of essential elements in food is vitamins. It may sound like heresy, but there is good evidence that far too much stress has been placed on this subject. Too many people drew rash conclusions from the scanty information available to them. We are now finding that a great many more facts are needed before we can speak with the confident tone many adopted some years ago. New vitamins are in the process of being tested daily, and there will be many others. Our knowledge will be incomplete and inconclusive for some time to come. Table III gives a brief review of the vitamins about which we do know something.

The definition: A vitamin is one of a class of substances, existing in minute quantities in natural foods and necessary to normal nutrition and growth, whose absence produces dietary diseases. Some are made synthetically.

Some vitamins are soluble in fat and are found only in foods containing appreciable amounts of fat. Some are water-soluble. Some are destroyed by heat, some by rancidity, some by age.

Vitamins are necessary only in minute quantities. With a few exceptions, all essential vitamins known at this time are present in the normal diet. When all our information is boiled down it seems certain that any animal among our pets, two- or four-legged, aquatic or terrestrial, can get all the vitamins it needs if its diet contains yeast, fresh alfalfa-leaf meal, and some form of vitamin D, irradiated yeast, etc. It is as simple as that. Is it an exaggeration to say that the talk about vitamins, essential as they positively are, has been too free, and often misleading?

Many vitamins have individual but very similar functions. In maintaining health some are useful only in conjunction with others. It is often difficult to break down the better sources into their individual components. For our purposes it is quite unnecessary to discuss each of the vitamins individually in order to understand the effects of the groups in which they occur and in which we handle them. The B complex is an excellent illustration. It embodies many essentials, all of which may be found together and are used together medicinally. A veterinarian seldom gives thiamin, rather the whole B complex. when he is using vitamin therapy.

Table III gives in outline form the major properties, functions, and sources of the principal vitamins and vitamin groups.

Table III—Vitamins: Their Properties, Functions, and Sources

VITAMINS	CONCERNED WITH	SOURCES
A (and carotene)		
Stable at boiling temperatures	General metabolism	Alfalfa-leaf meal
	Growth	Butter
Spoils with age if exposed to air	Skin health	Carrots
	Muscle co-ordination	Egg yolks
Body stores it	Fertility	Fish livers
Fat soluble	Calcium utilization	Glandular organs
	Digestion	Leaves of plants
	Hearing	Milk, whole
	Vision	Spinach
	Prevention of infection	Many dark green vegetables
	Nerve health	
	Prevention of one type of bladder-stone formation	

VITAMINS	CONCERNED WITH	SOURCES
	Pituitary gland function	
	Prevention of one form of diarrhea	
B Complex		
Biotin	Growth promotion	Yeast
Pantothenic acid	Nerve health	Cereals
Riboflavin, thiamin	Heart health	Milk
Folic acid	Liver function	Eggs
Niacin	Appetite	Liver
Pyridoxin	Gastrointestinal function	Alfalfa-leaf meal
Animal protein factor	Intestinal absorption	Rapidly growing plants
Water soluble	Lactation	Bacterial growth
Body storage—small	Fertility	Cattle paunch and intestinal contents
Some destroyed by high cooking temperatures, but not riboflavin	Muscle function	
	Prevention of anemia	
	Prevention of black tongue	
	Prevention of Vincent's disease	
	Kidney and bladder function	
	Blood health	
	Prevention of one type of paralysis	
C		
Ascorbic acid	Prevention of scurvy in some pets	Fruit juices and vegetables
Water soluble	*Not necessary in cats*	Alfalfa-leaf meal
Unstable at cooking temperatures		
D		
Irradiated ergosterol	Regulation of calcium and phosphorus in blood	Fish livers and oils extracted
Well stored by body	Calcium and phosphorus metabolism	Some animal fats
Stands considerable heat	Prevention of rickets	
Resists decomposition	Normal skeletal development	
Fat soluble	Muscular co-ordination	
	Lactation	
E		
Tocopherol	Muscular co-ordination	Seed germs
Fat soluble	Fertility in some species	
Body stores it	Muscular development in kittens	
Perishes when exposed to air	Sound hearts	
Stands ordinary cooking temperatures	Survival of young animals	
	Growth	
	Pituitary gland health	
	Prevention of steatitis	

VITAMINS	CONCERNED WITH	SOURCES
K		
Fat soluble	Blood clotting	Alfalfa-leaf meal
	Young kitten health	Cabbage
Unsaturated Fatty Acids		
(sometimes called vitamin F)		
Linoleic acid	Coat and skin health	Wheat germ
Linolenic acid		Wheat-germ oil
Arachnidic acid		Linseed oil
		Rapeseed oil
		Many seed oils

Scientists have made careful studies of what they often call "nutritional wisdom" in animals. In doing so they expose animals of one species or another—children, rabbits, dogs, cattle, poultry, and cats—to separate dishes of all kinds of foods. Each day they measure what is left and keep track of what the appetite dictates the animal needs. In making these studies the scientist tries to rule out "conditioning." He knows that once an animal is conditioned or habituated to eat only certain foods it is almost useless for experimental study of nutritional wisdom. In such studies the unconditioned animal will eat a reasonably balanced diet whereas the conditioned one may select a single inadequate food and suffer deficiency disease.

If cat owners had only a little realization of the effect of food habits on animals, those who judge the value of a food by how greedily a cat eats it would revise their opinions completely. Students have consistently found that the taste test is nothing but a test of previous conditioning. It is difficult to understand why pet owners should sometimes be so reluctant to accept this fact. Anyone working with humans knows that undesirable habits in food selection are amazingly difficult to eradicate. A man is asked, "Why don't you eat cabbage? It's good for you." "Because if I ate it I might like it, and I hate the stuff," is his reply.

How many people prefer bread made of white flour to whole-wheat bread! And yet it is distinctly inferior since most of the better proteins, iron, manganese, magnesium, copper, calcium, thiamin, riboflavin are removed. But white flour keeps better, so flour and bread manufacturers have conditioned the public to like it better. Fish is as valuable a food as meat and can cost less, yet many people refuse to eat it—and some have even trained their omnivorous pets to reject it.

A remarkable number of people have projected their own peculiar food habits to their pets. Animals can't reason, even as poorly as the man who wouldn't eat cabbage, but it is extremely easy to build up likes and dislikes by habit formations that are difficult to break. I have seen many cats, raised on dehydrated dog foods, which had to be starved several days to make them eat meat, and vice versa.

HOW MUCH TO FEED

Nobody should have any difficulty understanding a fundamental rule of cat care: *In feeding mature cats, the less they eat,* compatible with keeping them in sound condition, *the healthier they'll be and the longer they'll live.* It goes without saying, of course, that they should have a complete and balanced diet. They should not be allowed to get too fat or too thin. If you try to keep them too thin, they may get too little of some essential ingredient; if you permit them to get too fat, you will shorten their lives.

In growing pets, the faster they grow the cheaper it is to raise them. Yes, *but*—will they live longer, be healthier? Probably the best rule for sound health and longevity is to grow them moderately fast, but not to force them. This applies to all species.

Nearly everyone overfeeds. And almost every animal will eat 20 per cent more than it needs. There are some animals, like some people, that never get fat even though they are chronically overfed. The proper way to feed—the way people who are good feeders feed their cats—is to find just the amount which will maintain the pet's weight and feed no more. No rule in feeding is as important as this one. It applies, of course, only to cats whose weights are satisfactory.

If only Mrs. Jones and all others who allow cats to become obese knew a few truths about food storage in the body and something about fasting —which some people call starvation—how much better off their pets would be.

Starvation is the long-continued deprivation of food.

Fasting is total or partial abstinence from food.

Starvation is forced; fasting is voluntary. A sick animal fasts; an obese animal must be starved but not necessarily deprived of all food. When an animal is too fat he won't really starve, even though he takes no food until his fat is consumed. We say "he lives on his fat." In the winter the raccoon fasts. Not that he reasons what he is doing. He lazily lives on his fat. He has stored sufficient vitamins and minerals along with the fat and moves about very little except during the warm spells of winter. No one need be sorry for raccoons. Why, then, pity our fat cats when they have to forgo the habit of overeating for a while?

Most of this feeling sorry for pets that are reducing stems from the idea that starvation is painful. But it is not, so long as there is a reservoir of food in the stored fat of the body. If a little protein and a little carbohydrate are fed—say a slice of bread a day—to help burn the fat, there is no danger of acidosis developing. If a vitamin-mineral supplement is added, there is no danger of starvation at all.

Clients whom I have advised to feed a certain diet ask if a cat doesn't need variety. How can a certain canned, meal-type, or semimoist food which is fed day after day still be palatable? The reason is that our pets can smell each ingredient in a food. You and I smell hash. The cat smells separately each of the ingredients of which hash is composed. If you doubt this, watch a finicky cat trying to separate finely ground ingredients from each other in a mixture of foods. It isn't difficult to understand this ability if one thinks about it for a moment. Have you ever watched a cat raise its head and gently analyze air drifts for scents? They have uncommonly keen noses and are able to detect game, for which they are sometimes trained to hunt, at almost unbelievable distances. We so often overfeed house cats that few of them ever give us an opportunity to observe their actions when they are hungry.

In addition to reducing food intake, weight loss can be achieved through exercise, although with most pets a decrease in food consumption is the more practical and effective method. The close personal feeling between master and pet sometimes makes it difficult for the owner to reduce feeding sufficiently to achieve the objective (this is especially true in the case of cats), but no matter how you go about it, remember that it is far crueler to overfeed than to reduce. Not only is a fat cat a discredit to the owner, but overweight makes a cat sluggish and no longer fun to have around. It often brings great misery and suffering to pet and owner alike as the pet grows older. And although the problem of obesity is probably not so critical in cats as in other pets, it is almost definite that fat cats do not live as long as cats of normal weight.

GENERAL NOTES ON CAT FEEDING

The question of expense seldom is a consideration in feeding one cat; in feeding a colony of cats, it certainly can be. Approximately one third of all pet food sold in markets is bought by cat owners, and most of this is bought by families with one cat. The competition is enormous. Witness the many kinds of foods offered for sale; canned and semimoist foods of many flavors and package sizes, dry foods of all sorts and shapes and in a variety of attractive packages. Some foods are flat, some globe-shaped, some like miniature doughnuts, as if the shape made any difference to the cat. Most of the appeal is to the cat's owner.

The advertising to promote the foods is chiefly based on taste appeal—how avidly the cat will eat it. Considerable advertising is also based on the mistaken notion that cats must have variety. Thus we see one company advertising nine varieties of canned foods; another advertising four kinds of dry foods—all of which is unnecessary.

When a cat refuses food to which it is accustomed, the food may be bad or the cat is either overfed or sick. Your thermometer can help you to determine whether your cat has a fever (101°F. is normal). Its actions may tell you whether it was poisoned; its appetite may tell you by evening that it was overfed; a fecal examination can detect the presence of worms. The cat might have a mouth infection, a loose or broken tooth, but in those events it would probably act as if it were going to take a mouthful but stop just short of it. In this case, veterinary attention is called for. Here are some practical suggestions you may find useful in feeding your cat:

Warm all the food cats are fed. Cats dislike very cold food.

When you feed, place the food dish on an open newspaper on the floor or on a table. Cats like to drag food out of the bowl. The newspaper can be folded up with the crumbs and thrown away.

Remove any bones that might splinter—poultry and fish bones especially.

It pays to grind the cat's food. Enough for several days may be prepared ahead of time and kept frozen in the refrigerator. Grinding mixes the ingredients well too.

If meal-type foods are used, pour boiling water over them and then mix the additional ingredients.

Cats generally relish some green leafy vegetables well mixed in their food.

If a cat has a tendency to vomit but is otherwise well, feed it small amounts often.

Unlike dogs, cats do not like to eat crumbs. If you feed dry foods and find crumbs left in the bottom of the dish, pour some warm water on them and squeeze them into balls; the cat will usually eat them.

If a cat drinks little water add a splash of milk or even gravy to the water. This changes the surface tension and may be more appealing.

Fruit for Cats.   It is only rarely that a cat shows any desire for fruit. Some dogs love it, and cat owners, knowing this, offer succulent fruit to their cats and wonder why they refuse it. Probably because it is a most unnatural food. Surely, fruits are not a necessity, and they would certainly prove laxative if cats ate them.

Grass Eating.   Why does a cat eat grass? Is it harmful? Nobody has the answer to the first question. Cats on known complete diets will nibble grass. It is not digested and is clearly mechanical in its action.

As for the second question, the answer is probably not, if the grass is taken in moderation. Cats sometimes vomit after eating grass and occasionally it may become entwined with hair in the stomach, making accumulations too large to pass normally through the digestive system. In such cases, surgical removal is called for. Most of the time, however, grass passes uneventfully through the cat and is excreted normally, without causing any complications.

Catnip.   The leaves and tops of an herb, *Nepeta cataria,* constitute for a cat one of the most alluring playthings any animal can be given. Cataria was once used medicinally as a drug to reduce gas in the intestinal tract. It is also known as a mild nerve stimulant. In cats it is regarded as something of an aphrodisiac or a hallucinogen.

Cats do not digest catnip leaves nor do they regurgitate them as they do grass; in order for catnip to do any real damage, it is necessary to consume a large amount, which cats seldom do. In fact, it is the odor that produces the antics, not the actual ingestion of catnip.

The reaction to catnip is the result of a genetic factor. If your cat does not react, it means only that the factor is not present.

FEEDING THE NEWBORN

Before and after giving birth a mother needs a complete diet. The health of both the mother and young depends upon it. When the mother is carrying her young her food must not only keep her nourished, but must also build bones, blood, and bodies. She needs more fats, proteins, and minerals than usual. And a mother requires more water than usual while she is suckling her young, especially immediately following their birth.

The litter should be watched carefully to see that they are all getting enough milk. Very young kittens can starve in a very short time. They sometimes have to be helped so that they can find the teats or be fed artificially.

Sometimes a mother dies during parturition or when her litter is very young. Although it is not easy to save orphans, you can probably raise them successfully if you understand their needs. This means that you have to understand what their mother would supply if she were living.

Table IV shows the composition of natural milk in the cow and queen. If you want to raise an orphan kitten, you can use cow's milk, since the composition of cow's and cat's milk is similar, except for the protein, which is much higher in a queen's milk. Despite this difference, many kittens have been raised successfully on cow's milk.

People who are desperate to save an orphan often rush to buy goat's milk. Most people think there is something magical in it which will save the young of any species. Actually, goat's milk is very similar to cow's milk and much more expensive. It is richer in fat than most Holstein milk but not as rich as Jersey. About the only important difference is that in goat's milk the fat is broken up into much finer particles than in nonhomogenized cow's milk.

Table IV—Composition of Milk in Cows and Cats

	FAT	PROTEIN	CARBOHYDRATE	ASH	WATER	TOTAL SOLID
Cow	4.0	3.8	4.9	0.7	86.2	13.8
Cat	5.0	7.0	5.0	0.6	82.0	18.0

If no foster mother is available, the hardest thing in raising orphans is to arrange for a nipple of the right size. Kittens will seldom touch even the smallest baby nipple. Some people use medicine-dropper rubbers through which they punch holes. Others use children's doll nipples.

In the late 1920s a good deal of research went into the development of "artificial" puppy and kitten milk, in the course of which every conceivable method of administering formulas was tried. There were gang feeders, single tube feeders, and devices to keep the milk warm (important because milk cools off rapidly and kittens, especially in the first two weeks of life, are extremely temperature conscious). Two methods stood out as most satisfactory: the nipple and the tube feeder. And because it is difficult to find small enough nipples, and bottles to attach them to, the tube feeder wins out as the most efficacious method of artificially feeding a kitten.

The tube feeder is a syringe with a six-inch tube attached to it. Start with a 10-cc syringe and as the kittens grow graduate to a 25-cc syringe. The tube must be introduced into the esophagus and down into the stomach gently; care must be taken that it does not go into the windpipe. Once in, the plunger is pressed and the stomach is quickly filled. There appears to be no substance in the saliva needed for digestion, and kittens thrive on the tube method as well as on nipple feeding.

Today many veterinarians can supply you with specially made kitten-feeding tubes or nipples and show you how to use them. Needless to say, any device you use must be carefully washed between uses.

Many small orphans are killed through the careless use of medicine droppers. Unless you are very careful to put a drop at a time on the kitten's tongue and see that it is swallowing, its mouth may fill with the milk. It will then cry or wheeze and inhale some of the milk. This could lead to pneumonia and eventually death. Few of those using medicine droppers know how much milk to give. A day-old kitten needs two to three droppersful six times a day; day by day the dosage increases. The following table gives an approximation of the requirements for kittens by weight. As in humans, the amounts vary according to the individual.

Table V

WEIGHT OF ORPHAN	AMOUNT OF MILK REQUIRED	FREQUENCY OF FEEDING*
2 oz.	2 cc†	Every 3 hours
3 oz.	3 cc	Every 3 hours
5 oz.	5 cc	Every 3 hours
8 oz.	½ oz.	Every 4 hours
12 oz.	1 oz.	Every 5 hours
1 lb.	1¼ oz.	Every 5 hours
2 lbs.	2 oz.	Every 6 hours
3 lbs.	2¾ oz.	Every 6 hours

* All orphans under one week old do best on four-hour feedings or more often.
† A cc (cubic centimeter) is ⅕ teaspoonful.

At this point, we should mention the commonly available commercial formulas—proof that Madison Avenue can sell anything to the uninformed public. These so-called universal formulas are billed as being suitable for all manner of young animals—kittens, puppies, squirrels, etc. If you are tempted to buy such a product, remember that a formula should come as close as possible to the milk of the species involved. A formula ideal for puppies is not balanced for human infants any more than it is for kittens, who will thrive on a half and half mixture of evaporated milk and water. We can harm newborn creatures with poor diets and raise a percentage of them but this is no reason to use an inferior product. Such universal formulas are an expensive charade.

Although not part of the actual feeding, it should be mentioned that newborn kittens urinate and defecate as a result of the mother's licking. Lacking this stimulation, a kitten should be stroked with cotton or even a wad of tissue each time it is fed: rapid strokes over the genitals and anus will accomplish the results the mother obtains from licking. Many orphan kittens die because the owners are unaware of this simple, but necessary, ritual.

Nearly everyone has seen mother cats teaching kittens to play with a mouse she has caught and partially numbed. When she eats it, she shares it with them—their first solid food. Soon she may be bringing them dead or nearly dead rodents, and even at a month of age they know the taste of blood, vegetable contents of the intestines and stomachs, and meat of the muscles and organs. This also helps to supply iron, in which their first nourishment, milk, is so low. It should be a lesson to every cat owner that milk alone is not the only food for kittens. Their milk diet should be supplemented by more substantial foods as soon as they will eat, generally by their fourth week. Some cat owners use human baby foods; others use specially prepared foods for baby animals. Everyone to whom you sell or give a kitten will appreciate your having taught it to eat.

FOOD AND SKIN DISEASE

There was a time when food was considered the culprit behind a number of feline skin diseases. In retrospect that may have been the case when inadequate diets lacking certain vitamins were fed. We now have such a myriad of balanced diets for cats that that problem no longer exists. The term "eczema" means "boiling out" and at one time it seemed reasonable to assume that skin irritations were caused by blood overheated by improper food intake. But old ideas die all too slowly. In my experience the cases of food allergy are rare and those causing skin eruptions are close to nonexistent. I have never been able to diagnose a case.

There is ample evidence that the rare cat cannot tolerate a given food but the results are usually digestive upsets; so don't worry that what you feed, if it is a complete diet, is going to cause breaking out, itching, eczema, or mange.

Steatitis. There was a time when steatitis was a major problem in house cats. It was due to a lack of vitamin E, which is destroyed when the fats containing it become rancid. The rancidity was not sufficient to be obvious to man and was not obnoxious to cats. After eating canned fish food for a few months the cat became listless, had a fever, and was sensitive when touched. Many cats, and ranch mink too, died before researchers determined that vitamin-E-deficient diets were the cause. Now that manufacturers add vitamin E to canned food, the disease has vanished.

It should be noted that wheat germ is rich in vitamin E and retains it intact for long periods, whereas wheat germ *oil* soon becomes rancid and useless as a source of vitamin E.

4. Sanitation and Hygiene

*Y*OUR first concern as a cat owner must always be the maintenance of your pet's health and well-being. To be able to care for a pet in sickness is a necessary skill, but for many obvious economic and humanitarian reasons the prevention of disease is even more important.

The proper care of a cat requires that you have a fundamental knowledge of animal hygiene and sanitation, that you recognize the necessity of keeping the animal clean, that you provide quarters that are free not only of visible dirt and debris but also of disease-carrying agents. In short, it is essential that you have a thorough and realistic understanding of how to establish and maintain environmental and personal conditions which actively promote and preserve your pet's health.

Let us start first with the care of the animal itself and then consider its surroundings and how to manage them.

COAT CARE

When you think of an animal's coat condition, you must think both of his hair and of the skin under his hair.

The animal's skin, as we have seen, functions as an organ of the body, just as do the kidneys or liver. Its exposure subjects it to all kinds of abuse which better-protected organs never experience. In a healthy animal, glandular secretions of the skin keep the coat shiny. But a coat must be combed often. Dead hair must be removed and snarls untangled in all long-haired breeds. Only a brush or a comb and elbow grease will accomplish this. Burrs must be removed by hand. Hard mats have to be cut with scissors. To do this, push the scissors under the wad, pointing them away from the body, and cut the wad in half. Large wads may be cut into many sections which then comb out with little discomfort to the cat. It is almost never necessary to do the easy thing—snip across the hair. With patience, all the dead hair can be separated from the wad, leaving a lovely coat.

Combing of long-haired cats should be done as frequently as necessary to keep the coat in good condition. Animals should be taught from kittenhood to stand or lie on a table and expect and enjoy combing.

Short-haired animals need less attention, but a fine comb, even for them, is more efficient than a brush. Some people take a hacksaw blade and drag it, like a comb, over the coat. The teeth catch loose hairs and pull them out. The bare hand, moistened and rubbed over a short-haired cat's coat, will pull out many loose hairs and leave the coat looking glossier.

Brushes should not be the mainstay of grooming. Running brushes over the outside of a long-haired animal's coat accomplishes little in the way of loose hair removal, though it does sweep out some of the finest skin scales, accumulated dust, and a few loose hairs. There are many kinds of specialized brushes. Thousands of elaborate grooming brushes, with wire bristles on one side and fiber bristles on the other, are sold, but professionals do not use them. You can get along very well with: (1) a comb with very strong teeth, ten to fourteen to the inch, which can pull out snarls and do rough work; (2) a fine comb with twenty teeth to the inch; (3) a fine strong scrub brush; and (4) a pair of scissors.

If the animal to be groomed is a small, smooth-coated pet, a fine, strong comb plus a small scrub brush will suffice.

Have you wondered how the long-haired wild animals manage their coats in the wild? The raccoon and fox have their problems with matted hair particularly in the spring when their heavy winter coats are no longer needed. Raccoons examined in the spring have mats and snarls in their coats; then as the heavy coat is shed nature does what we do with our combs and brushes. As the animal forages for food, twigs and branches catch the loose hair and snarls and by fall the coat is luxurious and snarl-free. Perhaps if they foraged for food our cats would undergo the same natural grooming; but since we have developed coats so much longer than those found in nature, excepting the mane of the male lion, the job of grooming them is more than natural processes can accomplish.

The skin of many species of animals, including the human, has large numbers of sweat glands. Cats, however, have them in restricted areas—under the tail, for instance, and fewer about the rest of the body. But if cats do not sweat, how is the skin cleaned? Cleaning is accomplished by the renewal of the outside layer, which is constantly being sloughed off by growth in the layers beneath, and by the shedding of the hair itself. There is always a fine scaling of skin going on, more at some times than at others. Healing skin often sheds large, flaky, dandruff-like scales which must be combed or brushed out of the hair. Sometimes the shed-off scales will stick to hairs and one may find little disks of skin clinging to them, an eighth of an inch out from the body.

Cats are equipped with another small pair of skin glands, the anal glands, which are situated at either side just under the anus. They discharge their contents through the anus via two ducts. Pressure on them will cause the expulsion of the contents. These glands are found in a great many related species and their purpose has not been fully explained. We do know, however, that the anal glands discharge automatically when the animal becomes terrified. Dogs, skunks, minks, foxes, and weasels have them also, and each species is characterized by a distinctive odor. Everybody recognizes the penetrating odor of a skunk. Farmers are often able to detect the presence of a weasel by his odd musk. Many cat owners do not realize that their pets have these anal glands and that part of their body odor comes from them.

Because nerves are everywhere in the skin, it takes very little—only a fleabite, for example—for a pet to show its annoyance by scratching. With the other basic information necessary to care for an animal's coat properly, you should learn something about the nerve patterns in the skin. If you scratch your cat in certain places on the back, it will scratch, but not necessarily on the spot you are scratching. I mention this reaction only because cat owners frequently do not realize that when their pet scratches its shoulder, it is no indication of where the itch actually is. The cat may have a sore at the base of the tail. A better way to locate an itchy spot is to watch where the cat chews most, or else you can scratch the cat with your fingers and note his obvious enjoyment when you hit the right spot.

NAILS

The nails are appendages of the skin. Each nail has a hard outer crust protecting it, while inside there is a blood and nerve supply. Nails, being organs of defense as well as being useful in holding food while the teeth tear it apart, are strongly attached to the toes—much more so than our nails. Cats' nails are retractable.

Cats like to have wood to wear and sharpen their nails on and to exercise their toes. If the animal fails to keep the nails short enough, long claws are easily trimmed by cutting off the transparent tips.

SHEDDING

"Doctor," thousands of people ask of their veterinarians every year, "what makes my cat shed the year round?" The answer is—light. Nature intended animals to live without the benefit of electric lights. It has been found that as the days get noticeably longer the influence of longer periods of light on the cat's body (probably via the eyes) causes the hair to stop growing and fall out. New hair has slowly replaced the old. If the day is suddenly made much shorter, the new coat will grow faster and reach the acme of its beauty far sooner than if the days gradually shor-

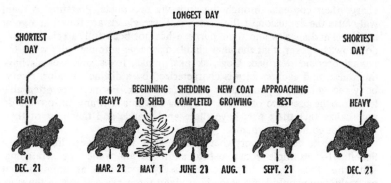

How the length of the day influences the shedding of the cat's coat when it is kept out of doors.

ten. Pets that are not subjected to the normal light cycle shed a little all the time and heavily in the late spring. Combing helps in removing the loose hair before it falls or is rubbed off on one's clothing, rugs, or furniture. Generalized shedding is a sign of good health whereas local shedding—in spots—is a sign of a problem.

BATHING

Dogs and cats are the only pets ordinarily bathed, and they are bathed simply to remove dirt and odors. The odors disappear with the dirt. There is no best way to bathe a pet, and no way has yet been found to eliminate the need for "elbow grease." The human fingers surpass any mechanical device for efficiency in bathing.

Bathing your cat may seem impossible when first tried, but persist and you will be the victor. The problem lies in that first application of water. The cat will try every trick of might and cunning to extricate itself from what must seem to be the brink of disaster. There are many methods used for the initial wetting, such as wrapping the animal in a towel and saturating the cat, towel and all, with warm water. I usually hold the cat by the nape of the neck and with a spray attachment thoroughly wet the body, excluding the head. After a few series of struggles, the wet pet lies seemingly vanquished and permits the remainder of the procedure to continue with an exasperated calm. Apply a detergent (the kitchen variety will do) and work it into a rich lather. Rinse, repeat the process if necessary, and towel dry.

Coconut oil liquid soap is effective and economical when purchased as 40 per cent soap, which you may dilute with an equal amount of water. Cake soap may be used but requires more "elbow grease."

By whatever means you apply the detergent or soap and water, the solution must be well worked into the coat and rubbed until the dirt is loosened or dissolved. After the lathering, the suds must be thoroughly rinsed from the coat. This is best accomplished by working the fingers through the hair, just as one does in applying the soap solution.

If a detergent containing vermin poison is used, no further medication is required. There are, however, vermicidal dips and rinses available that are well worth using for topping off a bath on any pet. The solution is prepared just before the bathing starts. After the pet has been rinsed, pour the dip or special rinse all over the coat, but do not rinse it off. Allow the rinse to saturate the coat for a few minutes, squeeze out the surplus with your hands, and then dry the patient.

A loosening of hair is generally a result of any bath. After the pet is dry, considerable combing is generally necessary to free the coat of the loosened hair and to give it a sheen and tone.

One of the questions about bathing most frequently asked is whether it is safe in winter. The answer is yes—provided the pet is well dried before being allowed outside in the cold air. For that reason many pet owners bathe their pets at night, knowing they are sure to be dry by morning.

Another common question is at what age is it safe to bathe a young animal. There is no rule about age. Small kittens that have become soiled and evil-smelling must be bathed if we are to keep them in a home. I have never seen a bath harm a pet provided it was properly dried. The fact is that kittens are frequently afflicted with parasites and various diseases. When one gets sick shortly after being bathed, the bath is all too often assumed to be the cause. Most of the harm attributed to bathing has its source elsewhere; in most cases, the pet was going to be sick anyway.

There are several dry shampoos available which are quite effective cleaning agents. These should be used according to directions, which vary with the type. Another alternative is a lather-free detergent, also readily available on the market.

Removal of Road Tar. Cats may run in newly tarred roads and return with a ball of tar and sand around each foot or worse, all over its body. Kerosene will dissolve the tar but it is too irritating to the skin. In most cases it will be necessary to massage lard, or any solid fat such as margarine, into the tar and then wash the area with a dish-washing detergent. Repeated applications of fat and detergent might be necessary to dissolve and wash away the tar completely. The discoloration caused by the tar is hard to eliminate completely but it does no physical harm.

Removal of Paint. Paint removal is a frequent problem. Though most paints are not as poisonous as many people think, some, like the lead-based pigments, are. If the cat comes home with fresh paint, still wet, on its coat, massage the paint with linseed oil and wash with a detergent. This procedure is of course for oil-based paints; water-soluble paints may be washed with water.

If the paint is dry, it will probably be necessary to clip the hair even if this results in a temporary disfigurement. There is usually no alternative, however, since cats will fuss over paint-matted coats and will often chew chunks of the paint out of their hair and eat it. Hair will grow back again on the affected area in a short time.

ANIMAL ODORS

The sources of animal odors, aside from excrements, are ear cankers, anal-gland secretions, and the sebum from thousands of body glands. All of these can be eliminated, as we have seen, by cleaning the ears, by expressing the anal glands, and by thorough bathing.

Skunk Scent.   Not infrequently the overcurious feline returns home smelling like a skunk. Chemists tell me that the odor is due to a chemical called mercaptan, which is neutralized by ascorbic acid (vitamin C). Fortunately we have inexpensive household sources of vitamin C in the form of canned tomato juice and concentrated citrus juice. Frozen orange juice mixed with half the water usually used makes a good nonirritating remedy. Since most of the scent is usually on the head and shoulders, these are the areas on which to concentrate.

Before beginning the treatment, add a few drops of baby or mineral oil to each eye to eliminate irritation. Soak the affected area well with the juice and wash with detergent as described in the section on bathing. Repeat the combination treatment until the odor is gone.

It may be comforting to know that skunk scent will not blind or otherwise injure the eyes. A few minutes of mild irritation may be experienced and self-inflicted injury is possible in an attempt to dislodge the odor.

Skunk scent is a volatile oil and as such evaporates in heat. So rather than burying or otherwise discarding your skunk-scented clothes, place them in a hot place until the odor evaporates.

THE MOUTH AND TEETH

A cat's unpleasant breath is often caused by dirty, broken, or tartar-covered teeth. Tartar, an accumulation of minerals and bacteria on the teeth, has been known to reach a depth of one eighth of an inch. Your veterinarian can snap it off and clean the teeth, which will do much to sweeten the breath. You can also do the job yourself with a tartar scraper available at most pet-supply houses.

Animals fed on soft foods have more tartar than those fed on hard foods. To help keep teeth clean and prevent tartar from building up, let your pet chew occasionally on soft rib bones or hard biscuits. Examine your pet's teeth at least once a month for the presence of tartar and loose or broken teeth. Animal teeth do not need brushing to keep them clean.

In the case of a difficult-to-handle cat or one with too much tartar, it is preferable to leave tooth care to your veterinarian, who can administer an anesthetic prior to cleaning and, if necessary, extract diseased teeth. Cats, by the way, do not develop cavities. Excess tartar appears to be influenced by genetic factors since unrelated animals eating identical diets in the same home often have different amounts of tartar. One cat might need frequent attention whereas another might not.

THE EYES

Our cats' eyes require very little attention. The only hygiene necessary is the removal of surplus hair that may curl inward and irritate the eyes, and the removal of exudate on the nasal side where the tears overflow in some breeds.

Foreign material such as a grain of sand or a piece of bark may become imbedded under the lids and cause excess tearing. Such a problem usually corrects itself; if you detect the problem shortly after it occurs, two drops of mineral or vegetable oil may lubricate the affected area and ease the object toward the inner corner of the eye where it works out. If excess "sleepers," or matter, are persistent, an infection may ensue for which your veterinarian will prescribe a medication.

THE EARS

Ears are often troublesome in cats and should be examined occasionally under a good light. Dirty ears have a nasty odor which pervades the animal and may cause him to shake his head and dig constantly at the ear with his hind paw. If you see a pet moving his front paw over an ear as if it itched badly, he probably has canker or ear mites.

A mixture of ether and alcohol has commonly been used to dissolve wax in cats' ears but ether is not easy to come by. Propylene glycol, obtainable from a drugstore, is quite effective as an ear cleaner. But remember that it is just that—a cleaner. If the condition causing the excess wax persists, by all means consult your veterinarian.

If you use cotton-tipped applicators use them with care since a cat will shake its head so quickly that damage to the ear is possible.

COLLARS AND HARNESSES

An animal's health should be considered when collars and harnesses are bought. Salesmen do not always have this in mind in making recommendations. Round collars for long-haired cats, strap collars for short-haired cats, are usually most satisfactory while harnesses are used for all cats. A cat's collar is useful principally to hold an identification tag. Some owners hang bells on them to track the cat's whereabouts or to frighten birds. For the latter purpose the bell is less protection to a bird than is commonly believed; a prominent ribbon which birds can see moving is more effective. Some persons take their cats walking on leashes; some tie them out part of the day, while others tie them up in the house. A harness is more comfortable for walking, but it must be quite tight or the cat can hold its front legs straight in front and back out of the harness. Some cats learn to reach down and chew the leather breast strap in two. There is no cruelty in a harness and often greater security.

Every collar or harness should be examined to see that no sharp points or rivets protrude to scratch the animal's skin or wear off the hair. It is most important not to get a lot of hardware on these accessories that can injure a cat's ears. When a cat shakes its head and the ears flap against a heavy buckle and license tags, the ears can be damaged. A cat that has worn a heavy combination of hardware sometimes has the hair entirely worn off its neck.

BEDS AND BEDDING

Bedding for cats can also be a problem especially since the alternatives are many. You can buy several different kinds of mattresses, canvas stretched across metal or wooden frames, and all sorts of beds. You can make beds out of pieces of thick carpet or castoff mattresses cut down, or you can allow pets to sleep in old chairs.

Some people like the smell of cedar padding stuffed into cat mattresses or pillows, but stale cedar has an unpleasant aroma. After a while the smell pervades a whole house—even the clothing hanging in closets. If wood shavings or other wood products are desired for bedding, ordinary pine can be bought for a fraction of the cost of cedar. With some flea powder sprinkled in it, pine makes a very much better flea and louse destroyer and repellent than cedar, and without the smell.

Even though you may know cat owners who go to great lengths to provide shredded bedding and soft springy materials, don't try to follow their examples. Cats actually need no such soft cushions; many prefer bare boards to anything else—your mantelpiece, perhaps. Years ago when I was a farmer, I had four Maine Coon Cats that chose to climb the posts at the end of the horse stalls, curling up on top of the harness where it bent hanging over the big hook. The space was not much larger than a peron's hand and yet those cats slept there every night without falling. A more uncomfortable place could scarcely have been found in the barn with its supply of soft hay.

SANITARY PROVISIONS FOR CATS

The type of pan, if any, that is furnished to a cat and the cleanliness with which the pan is kept are both highly important to its health.

In deciding on the proportions of the pan or box and the material to be used in it, you must consider both the natural habits of all cats and any unusual habits your particular pet may have. A cat generally digs a hole, voids, then covers the excrement. When you place a flat piece of newspaper on the floor you should expect your cat to scratch it to shreds, deposit her feces on the floor, and then cover it with the bits of paper. Instead of getting angry, you should remember that the cat is merely following one of its hereditary behavior patterns.

If the pan furnished a house cat is shallow and small, you may expect the litter to be scattered all over the floor near the pan. If it is too large, you, being human, are likely to neglect changing it, realizing there is room for other deposits. You must realize, however, that if you allow the pan to sit in the warm cellar or kitchen too long, the worm eggs in the stools will have time to incubate or pupate. Hookworms may have risen to the top of the litter to contaminate the cat's feet when it returns to the pan. Roundworms and whipworms will be in their infective stage. The litter in even a large pan should be changed every five days as a maximum.

Pans twelve inches wide and eighteen inches long with sides four or five inches high make excellent cat pans. Large dishpans are ideal. Many people prefer long, narrow pans. One cat fancier uses metal pans, six inches deep, seven inches wide, and eighteen inches long, and places two inches of litter in the bottom. She keeps many cats and finds that the narrow pans take less room in the cages. Pet stores sell various types, of which the stainless-steel models are best. Whatever type of pan is used, it must be scrubbed regularly unless you use plastic disposable liners, which are excellent. Filthy pans repel cats and people alike, and certainly they breed parasites—worms and fleas.

The location of the pan is often an important factor in sanitation. If a tomcat stands in the pan and sprays the wall, the odor will last for weeks, and wallpaper can't always be washed. Frequently, moving the pan away from the wall will correct the cat's habit.

Opinions as to the best materials to use in pans vary. Sand, peat moss, ordinary garden soil, and paper, whole, shredded, or cut in strips, are the usual alternatives. Sand has a number of advantages: cats like it; it is inexpensive, and it acts as an odor absorbent. It has disadvantages too: it is not too easily obtained by city folks, it is sometimes difficult to dispose of, and it is likely to be tracked out onto the floor. For catteries, though, it is excellent. Some people fill a barrel with new sand and keep an empty barrel outside into which they throw the used sand. Kittens broken to sand have some difficulty in learning to use newspaper in the homes of their new owners. A wise owner can first ascertain what the kitten is used to and use it. If the cat has been habituated to sand, then sand should be put in the new box, and if it is desirable to change to paper, strips of newspaper can be placed on top of the sand. By daily increasing the amount of paper, the sand may soon be dispensed with.

Paper is commonly used because it is cheap, it can be cut or torn quickly through many folds into inch-wide strips, it absorbs urine, and it can be gathered up and burned or wrapped in a whole sheet and disposed of. (When possible it should be added to a compost pile to be used as vegetation nutrient in a year or so.) Cats learn to use it quickly. Shredded paper can be purchased in bales, and some cat owners prefer it. If too finely shredded, however, it may catch in the claws or long hair and be dragged out of the box.

Several pan litters are sold by mail and at pet stores and supermarkets. They are excellent, quite deodorizing, and do not track about the house to any extent. If you buy one, you will still need to change the litter often enough to prevent worm infestation, if not odors. Of the commercial cat litters, dried clay (Fuller's earth) and alfalfa pellets are the most common (both are available from most supermarkets and pet shops). In my opinion, Fuller's earth is the most absorbent litter available commercially at a reasonable price. It may be purchased, usually in fifty-pound bags, at automobile parts supply houses, which stock it as an absorbent of oil or grease from garage floors.

Cat Pan Odors. Pet-supply stores now sell a number of devices, sprays, evaporators, and specialized cat pans to eliminate cat odor, at least partially. One such cat pan comes equipped with a rake and a bottle of deodorant. Feces can be removed every day with the rake and disposed of in the toilet. The chemical is then sprayed on the litter and the urine odor is dissipated.

For owners who want to discourage a tomcat from urinating in a particular place (on a wall or a piece of furniture), a number of spray repellents have been developed to discourage this habit. One of them is an extract of the rue plant. If you have let the habit go unchecked for too long a time, carbonated water is useful in removing urine stains.

OUTDOOR ACCOMMODATIONS

Scientific studies on acclimatizing animals show that they should not be exposed to sudden changes in temperature. An animal that might die of exposure when taken suddenly from warm to cold can stand much lower temperatures if it is introduced to them gradually. One reason for this is that cold stimulates the growth of the coat, which in time becomes much thicker and so provides better protection. When southern cats are sent north, their coats are so much heavier in their second winter in the north that they look like different animals. An animal that has become accustomed to cold can stand a great deal of it, far more so than many people realize. I have treated cats that have been caught in traps during sub-zero nights and lived, without even frostbitten feet. Some cat owners have learned that cats, given snug shelters, can become hardy and beautiful without artificial heat.

There are many cat breeders who believe their cats do much better in outdoor pens. Some of the loveliest cats I treat are kept out of doors the year round. Of course, weathertight, well-bedded hutches, free from drafts, are provided.

We cannot consider the problem honestly without mentioning the feral cats and how they live. Many take up abodes in woodchuck burrows, deserted houses, under hen coops, and even in hollow trees. Their marvelous adaptability enables them to eke out a satisfactory existence and to cope with the cold as well as our pampered, overstuffed pet cats cope with the other extreme of steam-heated apartment houses.

So adaptable is the cat to unusual environmental conditions that it would probably be one of the last species to die out in an environmental cataclysm.

Although the cat can adapt very well to life in the outdoors, there is very little scientific evidence indicating that a cat requires outdoor exercise. Most cats in the home will lounge around all day; a little playing several times a day seems to be sufficient exercise to keep them in good health.

DISINFECTANTS

Disinfectants must be chosen with care. Cats and foxes cannot stand phenol derivatives. Their nest boxes, beds, and their coats should not be disinfected with these products. Some time ago, when an owner used a phenol disinfectant in fox nest boxes, many of the fox kits were killed from the fumes long after the product had dried out or soaked into the wood of the boxes.

Odorless deodorizers are excellent and can be purchased reasonably. "Phenol coefficient" on a label may not mean a phenol product. It simply compares a product with phenol in germ-killing ability. Some of the odorless deodorizers do have high phenol ratings.

Some pet owners like the odor of pine oil; some prefer others, which often simply outsmell the odor to be removed. Good soap-and-water cleansing is usually adequate around pets, and if there is an odor left after scrubbing, it is a safe assumption that the spot or place is not clean. Disinfectants that give off chlorine are perhaps the best but are also bleaches and must be used judiciously on that account.

PERIODIC HEALTH EXAMINATION

One of the best bits of advice a veterinarian can give to his clients is that they keep careful track of the health of their cats, especially those that have passed middle age, through periodic physical checkups. A competent veterinarian to whom you entrust your animals' health can perform tests that may be instrumental in prolonging their lives by many years.

When you telephone your veterinarian for an appointment, ask if he would like a sample of the stool and urine. To obtain a urine specimen put new paper in your cat's pan and, as soon as it has urinated, before the urine has had time to soak into the paper, pour it into a container. If the cat has been trained to use only sand or sawdust, however, you will be unable to obtain a sample of urine. Occasionally wax paper shredded in a pan that has previously been scoured clean can be substituted for the usual litter and the cat in desperation will use it, thus enabling you to obtain a urine sample.

Let us consider how a periodic health examination can prolong the life of an animal. Suppose you know of nothing wrong. All you notice is that your cat hasn't the pep it used to have. You take urine and feces samples and ask your veterinarian to examine your pet. But don't expect him to make an examination worth the name unless you have the urine and stool, because so many facts may be learned from them. In addition to examining the excrements, your veterinarian may also remove some blood for a whole battery of laboratory tests.

The veterinarian asks you whether the cat drinks more water than it used to. You have noticed that this is the case. A urinalysis may very well point to urinary tract disease; in which case the doctor may also examine the blood for more clues. Occasionally he may want to hospitalize the animal and inject a dye in a vein that will show up on X ray indicating kidney malfunction. The veterinarian may give you medicine to administer at home and tell you not to feed much meat, fish, liver, and just about everything your cat loves. He explains that the pet will learn to love its new diet when it gets accustomed to it.

He may see that your cat, who weighs twenty-five pounds, is thirteen pounds overweight, and show you how to reduce him. The number of diseases that can be uncovered in cats whose owners had no idea they were even sick is legion. Fortunately the majority of them can either be eliminated or relieved by proper care and medication. A proper examination, which reveals many diseases in their early stages, when treatment is most effective, is one of the surest ways to ensure the health and longevity of your pet.

HOME PHYSICAL EXAMINATION

1. Place cat on table under a bright light.
2. Observe the coat. Is it lustrous and normal for the time of the year? Is there excess shedding in need of combing? Part the coat and look for fleas, lice, and ticks. Is there dark pepperlike material (usually flea dirt)?
3. Are the eyes clear, with no discharge?
4. Is the nose too dry or excessively moist?
5. Examine the outer ears for hair loss—blemishes.
6. Examine the ear canals and if necessary use a flashlight. Are they

clean and glistening or do they have excess wax or moisture? Do they smell clean?

7. Examine the lips. Raise the lips, first one side then the other. Are the tongue and gums a healthy pink? Are the teeth clean or stained?

8. Examine the anal area for sores or tapeworm segments.

9. With your fingertips feel the cat's skin and body—start with the head and neck—each leg, and finally the tail.

10. Put your ear to the chest behind the left elbow. Does the heart sound regular, with no sounds except the rapid lub dub? No wheezing?

11. Examine feet, toes, and nails. Should the nails be cut? Any broken nails?

12. Check your records. Are the inoculations up to date? (The preventive inoculations available will be suggested by your veterinarian.)

I recommend that you, as a responsible owner, perform your own home physical examination once a month. It takes about five minutes to accomplish everything on the above list and it's the best preventive medicine available. If you find a problem you can't solve, telephone your veterinarian for his advice.

5. Breeding and Reproduction

*T*HOUSANDS OF people breed and raise cats. Some enjoy breeding to improve the species, to originate a new strain, or even to originate an entirely new breed. But for the thousands more, pleasure in their cats is contingent on their pets' reproducing. On the other hand, in crowded city areas, in small homes, among busy people, litters of kittens are usually out of the question. Whether you want to breed your queen or prevent her from breeding, you will want and need to know how her reproductive organs function.

Cats give their owners less trouble in raising young than almost any other species. Show standards have not demanded abnormalities, as is the case for some dog breeds, and Cesarean operations are infrequent. But unspayed females and unaltered males can cause ample trouble for an owner if he is unequipped to handle them during mating, pregnancy, and delivery.

General preparations for breeding include deworming the female, if necessary, and making sure that she cannot pick up infestations while pregnant. Remove all external parasites and feed her well.

Biologically speaking, the basic reason for the existence of any animal or plant is to pass along the germ plasm of which it is the custodian for the next generation. Everything about it that helps it to live in harmonious relationship with its environment is working toward that end. The creature is a bundle of tricks of nature to ensure its perpetuation. One of the most interesting tricks or arrangements is the female mating cycle.

At maturity the female is said to come in heat or come in season. Most animals come in season in what are called mating cycles. The primary influence that causes different species to start their mating cycles is the length of the day. We do not understand how light accomplishes these changes, which vary from one species to another. Dogs have mating cycles that usually occur in spring and fall. Cats have several mating cycles in succession in the summer and fall unless they mate—in which case the cycles stop. If the female is not mated she may repeat the cycle three or four times. An understanding of the mating cycle of the cat will help you handle reproduction in your pet intelligently—and may save you embarrassment if you own an unspayed queen.

Outwardly, the first signs of the season are a slight swelling of the vulva and increased appetite. The queen often becomes more affectionate. The first preacceptance period lasts several days.

The second stage is initiated by a willingness on the part of the queen to copulate. This is the period that is called "calling." The queen rolls on the floor, becomes more affectionate, sometimes even becomes a nuisance. This is considered the first day of the second, or acceptance, period. Often the cat will hump its back and hold its tail straight up like a "Halloween cat." To the uninitiated this is thought to be some kind of painful condition.

Inside the queen in heat, the follicles are enlarging on the ovaries, and the uterus and blood vessels are greatly increased in size. The queen's follicles, each with its ovum (egg), do not rupture spontaneously as they do in the case of many other mammals. Copulation, with its stimulation and irritation to the vagina, is necessary for this to happen. If copulation does occur, the sperm from the male (thousands of them) will wait around the ovaries for the discharge of the eggs (ovulation), which takes place shortly after copulation. Each egg is fertilized by a single sperm cell. The fertilized eggs move down the fallopian tubes and eventually come to rest at fairly even spaces from each other in the uterus.

As soon as ovulation has occurred, a blood clot forms in each follicle. This changes into luteal bodies, solid yellow areas that secrete the hormone whose presence in the blood effectively stops the mating cycle and mating behavior. Luteal bodies remain throughout pregnancy. If they are dislodged, the queen aborts. After birth, the luteal bodies last for several months, thus preventing another mating cycle.

If the queen does not mate, no ovulation occurs and no luteal body forms. No luteal body means no chemical influence to prevent recurrence of another heat period. Therefore, the pet may have two, three, or even four periods one after the other before she stops. Just what causes her to stop after the last one is not yet known.

During the copulatory, or acceptance, period the queen mates repeatedly, if allowed, but toward the end she "goes out" of heat rather suddenly. As the luteal hormones take effect, her behavior changes. She may fight off willing males, and then just when the owner is sure the period is over she may play and be teased by a male until she accepts him. These late matings often result in large litters. Gestation, the period in which the eggs develop prior to birth, ranges from sixty-one to sixty-three days in cats.

MATING CHARACTERISTICS

Cats mate in such a haphazard manner that they must be considered genuinely polygamous. A female free to roam is often surrounded by a large ring of males, any one of which may leap, catch hold of the back of her neck with his teeth, and impregnate her. A queen may mate many, many times with male after male in the barn or back yard. How a queen would act in the choice of mates if she were wild we are not sure. Some of the wild cats closely allied to the Egyptian cat are monogamous.

Under natural conditions, there is usually a fight when more than one male is courting a female. But it isn't always the winner that the female chooses. A pair of males may have a frightful contest of tooth and claw, and while this is going on a small male on the sidelines may copulate with the female. There is some evidence that certain queens are selective in the males they choose and will not mate with just any male. Breeders usually let a queen call for two or three days before allowing her to mate.

Queens have been known to come in heat for the first time well before they are anatomically mature enough to bear kittens. A number of cases of cats breeding at four and a half months have been recorded. Five months is not an uncommon age, but most cats are seven months old before they copulate for the first time.

COPULATION

The tom's penis is unusual in that it is covered with small horns or barbs. When the female elevates her pelvis, the male thrusts the penis in, and while it stays, the female appears to feel no pain. Emission occurs, and then the male withdraws the distended penis quickly, with the result that the barbs on the penis tear the tissue lining of the vagina. The female then squalls characteristically, which often causes a person who is unaware of what is happening to think the cats are fighting. It is this irritation which causes ovulation in the female. Considering the apparent pain to the female, it seems incredible that any animal goes through this ordeal as many times in one mating cycle as some queens do.

Males are usually fertile at seven months, but they often seem emotionally incapable of copulating that early. As they gain in age and experience, they become more reliable breeders.

How often may a vigorous stud animal be bred? Cat fanciers allow three or four matings within two days. One copulation at the right time is enough, but queens, whose ovulation depends on copulation, should be allowed to copulate several times.

Among common misconceptions concerning breeding is the belief that if a female is bred to several males she will conceive from only one mating. This is not true. An animal can produce young in one litter that have been fathered by different males. Since the female produces a varying number of eggs (ova), it is possible for a sperm of one male with whom she has mated to fertilize one egg and for a sperm of another male with whom she later mates in the same heat period to fertilize another. If a purebred female is bred to two males that vary greatly in type, it is easy to distinguish the young sired by each father. When mongrel cats mate with other mongrels, or when animals of like appearance mate, it is impossible to tell which male sired which offspring.

STERILITY

Sometimes successful matings do not result in offspring. Why? The queen's breasts may develop, her abdomen may increase in size, she has a much larger appetite, makes a nest, but produces no litter. This condition is called a false or pseudopregnancy—a perfectly natural phenomenon in all fertile queens.

Anyone who has bred an animal unsuccessfully wants to know why the female failed to conceive. There are several possible explanations.

The male may have been infertile at the time of the mating even though he was known to be fertile at other times. Overbreeding, infection in the genital tract, improper diet, sickness of a general nature—one or more of these and other less obvious conditions may cause his temporary sterility. In addition, if a male is too young he will produce sperm that are not virile enough to fertilize the ova.

It has been found that a good "sperm swarm" is necessary to ensure proper fertilization. At one service several million sperm are discharged to fertilize only half a dozen eggs. Thousands of sperm surround an egg, yet only one enters to combine its germ plasm with that of the egg and start the new individual. If a male cat is overbred, the sperm swarm is depleted and fertilization is less likely to occur.

Lack of vitamins, such as vitamin A and the B complex, lack of proper amino acids, minerals, and possibly certain fatty acids in the diet of a tom, may produce sterility.

Undescended testicles are yet another cause of sterility. It is not advisable to breed to a male unless both testicles are in the scrotum because this defect often runs in families.

Sickness of a general nature will debilitate a cat so that he will lose his vigor. Even though he can copulate, he will often be unable to produce virile sperm. Convalescing males are generally sterile. Severe worm infestations also decrease virility, as does anemia.

Cysts on ovaries are a common cause of female sterility, though they can be removed surgically. Improperly developed reproductive tract, infection in the tract, tumors, or general debility due to disease all cause female sterility.

In rare instances fully grown females fail to come in heat because their reproductive organs fail to mature. Nothing practical can be done with such animals. Though medications (such as hormone injections) can bring the animal in heat, she will not conceive.

Great quantities of vitamin E have been fed in the form of wheat-germ oil to produce fertility. Its value is questionable. Many wild animals of other species eat nothing for three months before they copulate and still produce young successfully, even though their fat may be almost exhausted.

Wheat-germ oil loses a great deal of its vitamin E content within three weeks of the time it is produced due to a rancidity which is not obvious to our sense of smell.

It is common for very old animals, which will still come in heat, to breed normally, conceive, and then to resorb their fetuses. One may feel the little lumps along the reproductive tract as they grow large, day by day, and then feel them grow smaller and softer until they disappear. One remedy for this is female sex hormones in small doses. Your veterinarian can supply it in proper dosage for your female provided you are interested in breeding valuable old animals whose strain you want to perpetuate.

A single queen in a home usually has no problem in producing two litters of three to six young a year, but in a breeding colony, some problems do arise. In the first place we have suggested that the photo period, or the exposure to light, affects heat in cats, as it does in most other animals. Since the house cat experiences the change of seasons more directly than cats in a breeding colony, its mating cycle tends to run a more normal course.

Frequently a new queen added to a colony will have a normal litter or two and then, without much exposure to the lengthening of the day with the changing of the seasons, she has fewer and smaller kittens. If the colony is maintained in quarters with a lot of window exposure they cycle normally and have larger litters. This is comparable to leaving the lights on in the hen coup to produce more eggs.

There is no doubt in my mind that disease conditions that do not appear to affect the adults themselves are responsible for smaller litters with a high mortality during the first three weeks and particularly during the first week of life. Blood tests may reflect a viral infection by a low white blood cell count; a low red cell count may indicate a borderline anemia. Either condition could affect the health and size of a litter. If a virus is the culprit I believe the queen eventually builds an immunity after which she has normal litters once again. But this may take years. This is an area of feline practice in dire need of research.

PREGNANCY

After the queen's ova have been fertilized—that is, after each has become united with a sperm—they nest against the uterine wall. As they grow, each fetus is surrounded by amniotic fluid, which is enclosed in an amniotic sac. There is evidence that this fluid is produced by the lungs of the developing fetus. Each fetus has a placenta attached to the lining of the uterus from which nourishment is carried to it through its umbilical cord.

To be sure that the queen is definitely bred after mating, feel through her abdominal wall for the lumps which constitute the developing fetuses and "envelopes." The diagram below indicates their size at various stages. In palpating, use great care and gentleness. After thirty-three or thirty-five days of pregnancy, there is no longer any firmness. Do not again attempt palpation until the seventh or eighth week, at which time the nearly formed kittens can be felt. When more than one kitten is developing within the queen, the abdomen will be obviously enlarged after six weeks. Also the queen's breasts become fuller than in the case of a pseudopregnancy.

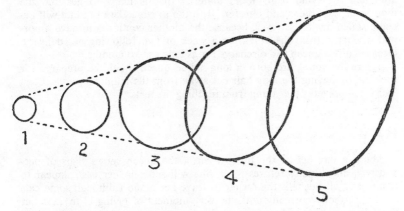

The size of the uterine lumps in a female cat at various stages of pregnancy: (1) 22 days. (2) 25 days. (3) 28 days. (4) 31 days. (5) 34 days.

It is difficult to predict the size of a litter from the appearance of a pregnant animal. If she is very large, it may mean that she is carrying a small litter of large young or that she is carrying a large litter of small young. X ray is the only dependable means of determining the number as term approaches, and it is easily employed if necessary.

As the time of birth approaches (sixty-one to sixty-three days after conception), the queen will make a nest. If she is a house pet, she may fix a nest in a closet, on a bed, or out in the garden. Many queens will start seeking a nest a week or more before the kittens are born. Some owners let them find a nest, learn where the nest has been chosen, and place a nest box of proper dimensions in that spot. It may be in the spare-room closet, in the attic, in the barn, in the woodshed, or under the porch. Others, the professional breeders especially, put the queen in a cage with the proper nest. She can have her kittens there as well as in a place of her own choosing. The difficulty lies in letting her out. If she is made to have her kittens in a spot selected by the owner, the first time she gets the opportunity she will almost certainly take them one at a time right to the place of her own selection. For that reason experienced cat breeders try to learn the location of the chosen nesting spot well in advance so that, if the kittens do disappear, they will know where to find them.

The bed can be a box eighteen inches square with sides about eight inches high. Since the kittens will have to stay in such a box until they are fairly large, the sides should be too high for them to climb over.

The bedding can be of absorbent cloth, which should be changed after the birth of the kittens. Loose threads, particularly nylon, may be a hazard as they have been known to wrap around a kitten's leg and practically amputate it. Avoid using loose material that is likely to get into the mouths of the kittens and interfere with the nursing. The bedding will become soiled again, however, because the mother continues to have a normal discharge from the vulva for a week or two following her delivery. Occasionally a queen will discharge for as long as two months.

Before the young are born, a long-haired queen should be prepared for suckling by having the long hair cut away from the mammary area. Long hair often prevents the young from reaching the teats.

BIRTH

About a day before the time of birth, the queen shows signs of nervousness and usually refuses food. She will settle in her nest, appear to strain, and all but tells the owner to leave her alone (although some cats behave perfectly normally until the very moment of giving birth). As her time draws near, the frequency and intensity of her uterine contractions increase.

The length of time for the delivery varies, according to the queen's condition and the size and number of her young. Large kittens take longer than small ones; and the same holds true for large litters. A queen kittens in an average time of about two hours but may take as long as twelve hours. If her whelping lasts beyond twelve hours, she may need hormone injections to stimulate uterine contractions, or she may need a Cesarean operation.

As a rule of thumb if a queen strains in full labor for two hours without producing a kitten telephone your veterinarian—even in the middle of the night.

The contractions of the uterus push the young animal out through the vagina. The kitten appears in one of several ways. It may still be in the amniotic sac. If so, the sac must be broken or the young will suffocate. If the mother doesn't do this, an attendant should do it for her. The kitten may still be in its sac, but the sac may have ruptured. Or the young may be born with the sac remaining inside the mother. In this case the umbilical cord is still connecting it to the sac. The mother may chew this cord to break it, and the sac and placenta will be discharged later. But an attendant can wrap a cloth or tissue about the slippery umbilical cord and pull gently until the sac comes out with the placenta.

If a placenta is not discharged from a queen she may develop metritis and even peritonitis, a serious infection. It is desirable for her health that every placenta be discharged shortly after the birth of a litter.

Normally a female will chew off the umbilical cord at varying distances from the kitten's abdomen, then eat the placenta and lick her young dry. This is unpleasant for most people to accept, but it is part of a natural function and there is no indication that interference is called for. However, it may be necessary to cut and crush the umbilical cords with blunt scissors at least two inches from the body if the mother is unable to do it. Rarely is it necessary to tie an umbilical cord.

If you attend a queen during birth you will find that your assistance and affection are reassuring and that she will trust you with her young.

Two postparturition infections are commun—uterine infections and infections of the breasts. Infection of the uterus is unlikely if no placentae remain in the uterus. Normally a female discharges from her uterus the lining to which the placentae were attached during pregnancy and through which the young were nourished. This takes the form of a dark red discharge and may last for ten or twelve days.

Breasts often cake because a mother produces more milk than her young need. This is inevitable when her litter is small. Caked breasts are normal and usually disappear without medication. Infected breasts, however, are extremely dangerous to both a mother and her young. They require immediate veterinary attention.

For information on feeding newborn and orphan kittens consult Chapter 3.

PROBLEM BIRTHS

When it is time for the kittens to arrive careful palpation may reveal if a kitten is unable to pass out of the pelvis and if the mother must be saved by an operation. If the kitten has been in the birth canal for an hour or two and its face can be felt through deep palpation of the vulva, get the cat to your veterinarian. He may be able to deliver the kitten with a pair of special forceps, or he may have to resort to a Cesarean operation.

If the tail and hind legs of the kitten protrude, take hold of them with a piece of cloth and pull gently but firmly; the first kitten—usually an oversize one—can thus be delivered, and the rest may be born easily. Give all help possible.

I am constantly amazed by clients who bring queens to our hospital and say that "they have something the matter." A glance shows the dried front or hind end of a kitten which may have been stuck in the vagina for half a day or longer. There is *indeed* something the matter! A veterinarian's services are not needed—only common sense. If you find your pet in such a predicament, wrap a cloth about the half-born kitten and pull. If the mother strains and helps, so much the better. Out comes the kitten, and behind it comes a great deal of dark brown evil-smelling fluid and perhaps the placenta and membranes which enveloped the kitten in the uterus.

In queens that have labored long trying to pass large kittens, the last one may stick because the mother suffers from sheer exhaustion. The longer the kitten stays in, the harder it is to expel, because of a dryness that develops. Help the mother in such a case. Nothing is likely to be hurt, especially since the kitten will probably be dead anyway.

An ideal birth takes under two hours from first to last kitten. Occasionally a queen will produce four kittens in a leisurely manner over a six-hour period. Sometimes four will be born in less than thirty minutes. Forewarned is forearmed.

Many delivery problems are caused by a malformation of the queen's pelvis. If you suspect that this is the case, don a sterile glove, examine the pelvis through the vaginal opening, and note its shape. It is not uncommon for a small kitten to have its pelvis broken and to grow up without anyone noticing its condition. Or a mature queen's pelvis is occasionally broken in an accident. In such cases, the pelvis almost always sets in a partially collapsed shape. (It feels like a V rather than an O.) If the pelvis is abnormal, a Cesarean operation will almost certainly be necessary. Have the queen spayed after the kittens are weaned. If she is spayed at the time of the Cesarean, her milk will probably "dry up," although there have been queens spayed at such a time who continued to give milk long enough to raise their kittens. Hormones may help keep adequate milk flowing.

Palpation is again invaluable in telling when the queen has finished giving birth. It is very easy to feel all about the abdomen with thumb on one side and fingers on the other. If there is an unborn kitten still within the uterus, it will be felt. If your sense of touch is untrained, shut your eyes, feel a kitten that has already been born, and then feel through the abdominal wall of the queen from the last ribs to the pelvis. An unborn kitten feels quite large inside the mother.

After the last kitten has been born, the uterus shrinks rapidly. Palpation may reveal a retained placenta. Let your veterinarian remove it. He may use an instrument or high douches or injections. This is not a job for a layman. Don't delay having it removed as decomposition occurs rapidly.

Queens are extraordinarily clever with their kittens. A mother cat is almost never clumsy enough to lie on a kitten, nor is she likely to lie down among her kittens with some behind her. She sees that they are all together and curls about them. If she is awkward with her first litter, however, she usually will be so with every litter.

Saving Chilled Kittens. It is not unusual for a queen to have her kittens somewhere outside in winter where the cold stiffens them until they appear to be frozen. In trying to save the kittens most persons will apply dry heat, which sometimes revives them. But there is a better way. Remember that baby kittens have developed floating in amniotic fluid within their mother's body. Therefore, to save the chilled kittens, use hot water, as warm as you can comfortably stand it with your bare hand.

Hold the kittens with their heads between your fingers. Immerse them so that only their mouths and noses are out of the water. There will be a rapid transfer of heat and the water will need heating frequently. Be patient. Kittens that seem dead often slowly revive and once they are back to normal may not show any harmful effects from the experience.

If kittens are lost and it becomes necessary to "dry up" the mother, just let her alone. Her breasts will cake, and in a short time the inflammation and discomfort will disappear. It is a common misconception that massage, camphorated oil, or more drastic treatment is necessary.

Queens will often nurse their kittens for many months. It is not uncommon for a new litter to arrive before the mother has weaned the last. Pets brought to our hospital to be spayed frequently have several sections of breast functional, and the owners are amazed to learn that a new lot of partly developed fetuses has been found inside.

ORPHANS

Every year we see newspaper pictures of unusual foster parents—adopted pet combinations—a cat nursing a young rat or tending a chicken, a mare pony caring for a puppy or a goat, a bitch nursing a kitten. Behavior of this sort stems from an extreme case of "mother complex." In the case of a queen that has not had kittens and has no milk, a hormone (prolactin) can be injected that will make her into such a good mother that she will steal other queen's kittens in order to have something to love and protect. She'll curl up with them and accept them as her own.

Almost any female with enough prolactin in her blood will try to mother some animate thing. Perhaps it is a bitch mothering a duckling, or a rat mothering a young mouse. The trouble with getting a foster mother to adopt young not her her own is generally that she already has become accustomed to her own and substitutions become difficult. Most people have heard what pains a shepherd must take to get a ewe that has lost her lamb to accept an orphan.

The best way to encourage an adoption is to smear the orphan all over with vaginal fluids and milk from the foster mother. This makes the orphan smell like one of her own. The queen will lick the fluids off and this licking tends to make her want the kitten. There is no quicker way. Persistence will win over a foster mother even if she at first refuses an orphan. It may be necessary to hold it to her breast, remove it so she can't bury it or kill it, and bring it back at the next nursing. If you are there, she won't harm it, but if you are not, she may kill it. However, once a foster mother starts licking an orphan it is usually safe to leave them alone.

Raising orphan kittens or supplementing the milk of those whose mothers produce insufficient milk is easy but takes time and patience. If possible, leave the kittens with the mother, because she will keep them clean and warm. If the mother is lost, killed, sick, or refuses to care for her kittens, gently rub the external genitals and anus with a piece of cotton and the kittens will be stimulated to urinate and evacuate. If they are not cared for, they will keep each other and their nests in a nasty condition. Tending to them each time they nurse will usually be sufficient.

If kittens are not getting enough milk from either their mother or from supplementary feedings, they cry, become thin and woodeny to touch, and may suck on each other. Contented well-nourished kittens are hungry at the proper times but are generally quiet. Their thriftiness is shown by their plump little bellies.

And one final word about a too often neglected precaution. By the fourth week the sharp nails of little kittens need cutting. If this is not done, one of the kittens may in play scratch another's eye and seriously injure or blind it.

PARASITES

Many litters of kittens which have not been dewormed will be found to harbor intestinal parasites. If they have hookworms, they will be anemic. Roundworms are the most common internal parasite found in kittens; and, while they are not so lethal to the hosts, they do produce toxins sufficient to cause fits, distended abdomens, and general unthriftiness. It pays to have stools tested for parasite eggs beginning at four weeks of age and to deworm the kittens when and if eggs show up. Occasionally there will be an invasion of roundworm larvae so heavy that the kitten has verminous pneumonia. In post-mortems on some kittens enough roundworms have been found in the stomach and intestines to have caused death and yet not one worm old enough to lay eggs. Although such an infestation is not common, the fact that it can happen should make one alert to the possibility of parasites in a sickly young kitten even if a fecal examination is negative. Another examination the following week may reveal great numbers of eggs, because by then the worms will be old enough to lay.

No deworming of a kitten is complete unless done twice at two-week intervals. The first eliminates the worms in the bowels but will not kill the larvae in the blood. The second kills this lot when they have become intestinal inhabitants.

HOW TO TELL THE SEX OF A CAT

To the cat lover who has had considerable experience with animals it may seem strange that in a book of this sort it is necessary to discuss the ways of distinguishing sex. Actually the determination of sex is not always easy even for an old hand. When you realize that a certain few experts with exceptional powers of observation are paid large sums of money for their services in "sexing" baby chicks, that a few scientists in any university are often called upon to "sex" young laboratory rats and mice for others, you will realize that distinguishing the sex of many species is not as simple as you might have assumed.

Sexing the newborn is even more difficult than sexing an adult, for obvious reasons. The simplest way of determining the sex of your kitten (or of a mature cat) is to compare the distance between its sexual opening and its anus with that of a littermate (or a comparably sized cat) you think to be of the opposite sex. The two openings will be closer together in the female since the rectum, which terminates at the anus, and the vagina, which terminates at the vulva, emerge through the pelvis together.

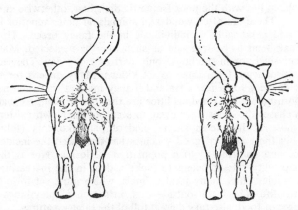

External sexual differences in male and female cats. Left, male; right, female.

In an adult male you can of course feel the testicles, too, and even if your powers of observation are not sufficiently keen to tell the sex by looking, you can surely tell by feeling. Rarely is a cat a cryptorchid, but if it is, you will be able to feel only one testicle or none at all.

Many cat owners do not realize that all male animals have rudimentary teats. Finding them on a tomcat, they often become confused and may sometimes wonder if their pet is an intersex—a hermaphrodite. Or they may find one or two and conclude that they are pimples caused by a skin disease. As a wit once remarked, these rudimentary nipples are there "just in case a male animal ever should have babies."

It is amazing how often cat owners make mistakes concerning the sex of their cats. For a time I kept track of the cats brought to our clinic to be "spayed." I found that one out of every ten cats brought to us for spay-

ing was a tomcat—which can only mean that at least 10 per cent of the
cat owners can't tell the sex of such a commonplace animal as the cat.
This fact is corroborated by the number of clients who bring their cats to
the clinic to find out their sex. Some people are uncertain even about the
sex of dogs. But what's so strange about that? Ask your physician some
time to tell you some of the strange conceptions that people harbor about
human sex, anatomy, and childbirth.

POPULATION EXPLOSION

There is no population explosion in the pedigreed felines. These animals represent an investment, although usually a modest one, and people
tend to protect their investments. Such cats are usually given prophylactic
(disease-preventing) injections and their owners tend to keep them inside and out of the many dangers that confront the roaming animal.

The problem lies with the poor Domestic Shorthair, otherwise known as
the alley cat. These are often wonderful animals, at times superior in tem-
perament and personality to individuals in the fancy breeds. However,
these animals tend to be free and as such may be neglected. Many live
outside exclusively or in the house only part of every day. They mate at
each heat, producing from three to six kittens. Many queens recycle ten
days after delivery for a few days and if they mate at that time new kittens are born before the previous litter are through nursing. At that point
the queen chases the older litter away to seek out their own existence. In
the past most of the excess kittens died of panleukopenia (feline distemper), but the advent of good vaccines has decreased the incidence of
the disease and contributed to a population explosion. Nor is the high
highway mortality rate sufficient to make a dent in the increasing numbers. The result is that many feral animals, which must eat to live, prey
on local wildlife. The inside-outside cats, in search of playthings rather
than a source of food, also take a great toll of the same creatures.

The answer to the problem is of course confinement and neutering.
Confinement is unfortunately inconvenient for most feline owners, which
is a sad commentary on many of our citizens. An excuse I have often
heard is that such cat owners believe in freedom for their animals. "If I
had to keep my cats cooped up I would rather get rid of them," they say
and as far as I'm concerned they should get rid of them.

Some well-meaning parents tell me they are keeping an unaltered
queen for the educational experience of procreation for their children. To
them I suggest that part of the educational experience would be to take
the children to the veterinarian to observe euthanasia of unwanted kittens.

Never—and I repeat *never*—permit a queen to breed unless you know
you will have homes for the kittens.

6. Heredity in Cats

*J*UDGING by the few breeds of cats to be found in the world today, the average cat fancier in the past has known and cared little about heredity. It has, of course, been difficult to know much about their heredity because of the elusive habits of cats during the mating period. Today, however, cat breeders are clamoring to know how to improve their strains. They want to be able to tell in advance the outcome of proposed matings. No doubt cat shows should be credited with stimulating some of this desire for information. Pride in ownership also has a lot to do with it, as does the financial aspect of cat breeding. Cat breeders know that certain colors are more popular than others in certain sections of the country and they want to be sure to produce the most popular colors. Many persons, too, prefer to breed for specific forms of cats such as Manx cats and cats with extra toes.

A number of highly unfactual ideas about heredity have been bequeathed to us by our fathers, and some of them are still widely revered as scientific facts. To understand the essentials of the science of genetics, we must first rid our minds of these ideas and, secondly, we must adopt the scientific method of thinking.

The scientist is a doubter. The fact that a self-constituted "authority" said or wrote in the past that a given statement was true means nothing to him. He knows that having written it doesn't make it true unless facts substantiate what has been written. *Truth is opinion which has been verified by test to conform to nature.*

Another difficult but necessary step for the layman is to rid his mind of the false idea that, because one event follows another, the first was necessarily the cause of the second. Simple minds are nourished on that kind of reasoning. Someone sits in a draft and a day or two later develops a cold; therefore, the draft caused the cold. We forget that millions of people sit in drafts every day without developing colds.

The scientist keeps accurate, usually mathematical, records, and that helps him with his work. Keeping records is particularly important in uncovering the facts of heredity. The scientist formulates a hypothesis and then assembles all the facts *on both sides*—those which show it to be true and those which show it to be wrong. When he has all his facts, he says, "My data seem to show such and such to be the case." The scientist never rationalizes—that is, tries to show that what he wants to believe is true.

Remembering this, let us consider the wrong ideas about heredity which were bequeathed to us. These are the discarded, erstwhile "facts" on which no reliance should be placed; each of them illustrates fallacious reasoning; they failed, when tested, to correspond with nature.

1. Birthmarking. If a cat who has been raised in a room with a colony of rabbits gives birth to a litter of kittens that hop like rabbits, it does not mean that constantly seeing the rabbits caused her to mark her embryonic kittens. Nor was she mated with a buck rabbit, as some theorists have insisted. Her kittens are not "cabbits," a name coined by those who mistakenly believe that a cat and a rabbit can mate. The frights or other experiences of the mother during pregnancy are not transmitted to the offspring.

2. Prenatal influence. The belief is still widespread that if a pregnant cat is taught many tricks or is starved so that she will become an excellent ratter or mouser, she will tend to impress her kittens through the exercise of these learned abilities, and they will be more easily taught tricks or will be better ratters. Books have been written on this subject to prove the idea, but when scientists, by scientific methods, began to test it, they soon learned that all the effort spent by animal owners who believed in this false principle was completely wasted. All it did was to help in the selection of more vigorous animals.

3. Telegony. The fact that queens produce great variation among kittens has often been said to be the result of earlier matings to a male of a different breed or to a mongrel whose influence was said to carry over to the later litters. Literally millions of worthwhile brood females have been unnecessarily destroyed because of such accidental matings. Perhaps this antiquated idea has made owners more careful in the choice of mates for their queen, but it has also done tremendous damage. There isn't a word of truth in it, as far as science can demonstrate.

4. Blooded inheritance. Nearly all breeders still talk about pure-blooded cats, blue-blooded cats, cats with the blood of some famous cat ancestor coursing through their veins. We have come to use the word *blood* to mean heredity, and, because it gives us such a completely erroneous picture, it would seem best to discontinue its use in this respect. We know today that blood has nothing to do with heredity; its only function is to nourish and protect the embryo. Even the blood with which a kitten is born is lost in a few months and a new supply manufactured, a process that continues throughout life. A pure-blooded cat is one with

clean blood. When we want to talk about heredity, we should say the cat is purebred, not pure-blooded, and certainly not a thoroughbred, which is a breed of race horse.

GERM PLASM

The complete heritage of the offspring is contained within the sperm cell of the male and the egg or ovum of the female; from here on let us consider some of the essentials modern science has uncovered to help you understand better the complicated process of hereditary transmission of characteristics.

As long as man has been able to observe, he has noted that certain characteristics seem to skip a generation, but he couldn't explain how or why. He invented strange theories, some of which seem logical but which, we have seen, were not borne out by facts. What we know today makes us realize that the germ plasm contained in the male's testicles and the female's ovaries is the basic reason for the animal's existence. It lives in order to perpetuate its heredity. The germ plasm is an endless stream of life that goes on from generation to generation, regardless of the appearance of the individuals that carry it.

The germ plasm usually goes on for generations without changing at all or only in the very slightest degree. The sudden changes such as taillessness or extra toes are called mutations. When such a change proves to be hereditary (a change in the germ plasm), fits the environment, and helps the animal or, at least, does not hinder it, the change in the germ plasm will be perpetuated. However, mankind has seized upon these mutations, often curiosities that are detrimental to the cat under natural conditions, and by selective breeding has incorporated them into the strain. A good illustration is the Pekingese face that one finds in some Persian strains, or the blue-eyed white cat—both of which mankind perpetuates as a fancy, not for any particular value to himself or the cat.

GENES AND CHROMOSOMES

Every hereditary characteristic is determined by a pair of genes—certain little packets of chemicals in the germ plasm. If you will keep this fact in mind, it will help you to understand heredity. At certain times during division of the cells, the genes congregate into strings called chromosomes; these, too, are in pairs. When the sperm are formed in the male testicle, each sperm has half the number of chromosomes required for the new offspring. That is the male's part in heredity. The female egg also contributes half the necessary number of chromosomes. When the two join, therefore, the new embryo has the total number—getting half its characteristics from each parent.

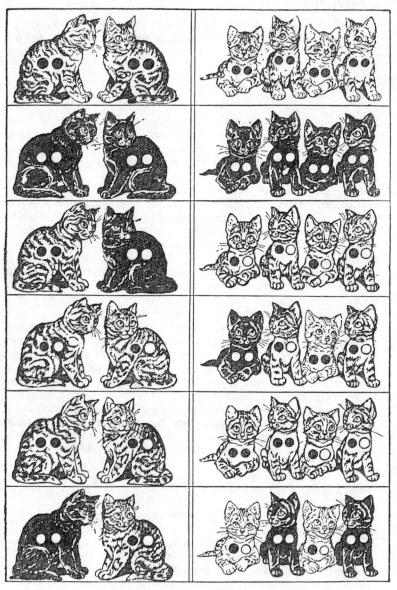

The six possible ways in which individual characteristics may be inherited. Black dots (genes) represent dominant characteristics (in this case tabby color); white dots represent recessive genes. Cats with either one or both black dots appear as tabby. The recessive (black) must have a pair of white dots. A cat having one white and one black is a hybrid and capable of transmitting the recessive character if it mates with another carrying the recessive.

Why then, you may ask, does the offspring seem to favor one parent more than the other? This is because certain of the genes are dominant over others. Suppose we mate a pure black cat, that is, one with two genes for black, with a pure tiger cat, that is, one with two genes for tiger. The kittens will have one gene for tiger and one for black and will be tiger cats because the banded hair is dominant over black. Now suppose two of these tigers, each of which carries a black gene in its germ plasm, are mated. What the kittens will look like is just a matter of chance.

You can conduct a little experiment to see the results for yourself. Place in a container twelve black marbles, representing the tiger pattern, and twelve white marbles, representing the black pattern. Without looking, reach in and pick out two marbles. Keep picking, two at a time, until there are none left. Keep a record of what you got each time. The expectancy is three pairs of blacks, three pairs of whites, and six pairs of white and black.

You may not get these results in one experiment, but if you will try it ten or twelve times you will have large enough numbers to find that you have definitely realized this expectancy.

The results of the marbles test are what you can expect in breeding the cats we have been discussing—three purebred black kittens, three purebred tiger kittens, and six tiger kittens carrying a recessive gene for black. Obviously you can't tell what you will get unless you have a record of which characters are dominant and which recessive.

The subject of genetics becomes a little more complicated when we consider two characteristics instead of one. We know that short hair is dominant over long hair. Suppose we mate a pure black, long-haired cat with a pure tiger-striped, short-haired cat. Tiger, being dominant, is represented by T; black, being recessive, by t. We represent short hair by L and long hair by l for the same reason. To predict the results of the mating, we have to compute, on the basis of chance, all the combinations of these two traits in the germ plasm.

One cat is LT, that is, short-haired and tiger-striped; the other is lt—long-haired and black. The progeny will have one of each of these genes, so they will be LlTt.

Now, let's theoretically mate two of these kittens when they grow up. What can we expect? Again, this is a matter of mathematical chance. What will the sperm and eggs carry in the way of genes for these four characteristics that we are considering? Each will carry the following assortment of genes: LT-Lt-lT-lt. The simplest way to see what will happen is to make a checkerboard like that shown below, putting the genes of the sperm along the top and the genes of the egg along the side, and then filling in the squares where the two cross. Altogether, we have sixteen possibilities. These represent the chances for each kitten carrying the four genes.

We find that we have nine possibilities which are represented by the two dominants LT, three by Lt, three by lT, and one by lt. Our two hybrid kittens, therefore, can produce kittens in the following expectancy

—nine short-haired tiger-striped, three short-haired black, three long-haired tiger-striped, and one long-haired black. Because we know which traits are dominant and which recessive we know what we can expect.

In the same way you can determine the expectancy where three characteristics are considered simultaneously, but this makes a table of sixty-four squares, and the ratio on the basis of appearance works out twenty-seven, nine, nine, nine, three, three, three, one. If you are interested in mathematics, you will enjoy such computation.

Sperm Genes

		LT	Lt	lT	lt
Egg Genes	LT	LT LT	Lt LT	lT LT	lt LT
	Lt	LT Lt	Lt Lt	lT Lt	lt Lt
	lT	LT lT	Lt lT	lT lT	lt lT
	lt	LT lt	Lt lt	lT lt	lt lt

This method also shows how traits appear to skip a generation. The dominant traits always mask the recessive. When in the next generation the individual has two recessive genes, he shows the recessive trait and thus takes after one of his grandparents. The trait, therefore, seems to skip a generation.

WHAT DETERMINES SEX—SEX LINKAGE

The chromosomes determine sex as well as other characteristics but in quite a different way. Among the many pairs of chromosomes in the individual there is one pair that contains the sex-determining chromosomes. In the male these two chromosomes are unlike. Geneticists call one chromosome X; the other Y. In the female they are always alike—the queen always has a pair of Y chromosomes. Therefore, the sex chromosomes of the male are XY, of the female YY.

Remember that each sperm has only one chromosome of a pair. Half the sperms will have an X chromosome and the other half will have a Y chromosome. Since the female has two Y chromosomes, all the female eggs will have Y. There is a 50–50 chance that an egg will unite with an X-bearing sperm. If the X-bearing sperm unites with an egg, the kitten will be male; if a Y-bearing sperm unites with the egg it will be a female. The sex chromosomes also contain genes that determine other characteristics. One of these, borne on the Y chromosome, is for orange color.

A convincing theory has been developed to explain the phenomenon of tortoiseshell coloration: When a tom has a gene for orange, the black-producing gene is masked. When a queen has two genes for orange, the black is also masked. But when a queen has one gene for orange on a Y chromosome, the black is not masked entirely and the result is a tortoiseshell.

For those who want to go a little more deeply into the genetics of cats, the following information should prove helpful. First keep in mind what a wild-type cat looks like. It is a tiger-striped animal (tabby) with yellow as well as gray in the banded hairs. But it is not the banding alone which makes the stripes, for if you will inspect a tabby, you will find some black-tipped hairs in the light stripes.

COLOR CLASSIFICATION

We will need to know what the colors are and how they are classified before we can see how they are inherited.

The Tabby Cat.   Tabbies are found to be of three basic types:
1. Stripes narrow, close, clear. Hairs are banded with gray and black. This pattern is often called the Abyssinian, although Abyssinian is also the name of a breed. The genetic symbol is T^1.
2. Medium wide striped with fairly clear, black stripes. The genetic symbol is T^2.
3. Blotched, stripes few, broken up. The genetic symbol is T^3. Tabbies may be black, blue, orange, or cream.

The Black Cat.   As mutations of the germ plasm occurred and bred true, cats showed different coloration. Black, for instance, is simply a loss of the hair banding. Genetic symbol is t.

The Orange and the Tortoiseshell Cats.   A good show-type tortoiseshell has clear, distinct spots of red and black. A tortoise-and-white is black and red, with white spots—the famous "three-color cat." If the cat carries the tabby gene, it will be tabby striped (one without the tabby gene would be black). If it carries the dilution gene, it can be blue tabby and cream and still be a tortoiseshell.

The orange cat is one which came from another mutation. Orange cats are black cats with the black masked or repressed by orange-producing genes. They are often called yellow cats and may be tabby or nontabby.

The Blue and the Cream Cats.   In the germ plasm there is a pair of genes which determine whether the color shall be full expression or

Major coat colors of short-haired cats. Except for the white spotting, these same colors are found in longhairs.
Left to right, top row: blotched tabby; wide-striped tabby; narrow-striped tabby. Second row: black; blue. Third row: black with small white spot; black with white collar; mostly white tabby. Bottom row: chinchilla; smoke.

Left to right, top row: blotched red tabby; wide-striped red tabby; narrow-striped red tabby. Second row: solid red; solid cream. Third row: tortoise with small white spot; tortoise with white collar; mostly white tortoise. Bottom row: seal-point Siamese; blue-point Siamese; Burmese.

diluted. The black and orange cats show the full expression of their color (D). But if they carry a pair of dilution genes (dd), these cats will be respectively blue (Maltese) or cream. These dilution genes apply equally to cats with or without tabby stripes. A tabby with the dilution genes will be blue striped instead of black; and the orange will become cream striped. This must not be confused with silver, which is produced by an altogether different pair of genes.

The "Siamese"-Colored Cat. We are not going to consider the breed —just a color (c^h)—because that color can be, by breeding, transferred to any breed. Long-haired cats with typical Siamese markings are already in existence.

Students of heredity consider the Siamese to be part of an albino series —imperfect albinos. The cat with albino genes has no color. The Siamese has weakened, but not totally absent, color-producing genes. The Burmese (c^H) has more color. The silver is a light tabby.

The Siamese and Burmese have light bodies and modified black ears, nose, feet, and tail. When a pair of dilution genes are also present, the points of the Siamese become blue. This explains the seal-point and the blue-point patterns. How can we explain the orange-point Siamese? The very fact that such cats have been deliberately created shows that the Siamese is a color pattern. If, by selective breeding, the orange color has been substituted for the imperfect black (seal), then the cat is an orange Siamese. Those so far produced do not yet all look like pure Siamese in body shape or hair texture, but it will not be long before such cats can be typical Siamese, if breeders want them.

A Siamese crossed with a black cat appears black but the undercoat is grayish. This is an important fact to know because it can help to determine the paternity of a cat.

The Smoke Cat. This is a silver (C^{ch}) lacking the tabby gene. The smoke color in a short-haired cat lacks the typical appearance of the long hair. The blending effect of long hairs which become intertwined produce the true smoky effect.

The White Cat. We have three kinds of white cats:
1. The pink-eyed albino (c) (very rare). This is a cat with a total absence of color.
2. The white cat with pigmented eyes. The genetic symbol is W. In this group we find blue- and green-eyed cats and, not infrequently, cats with one green and one blue eye. I personally have known of dozens of such cats. Blue-eyed whites are frequently deaf. Some students consider them partial albinos. True albino cats, however, are not deaf.
3. The white-spotted cat. White spotting is produced by a distinct gene or group of genes whose genetic symbol is S. We recognize three types of spotting (actually I have never seen a cat without at least one white hair): The cat with a white spot on the chest (S^1). The general white

collar pattern, consisting of a band of white over the neck, white on the chest and about halfway up each leg, a white tip on the tail, and a white blaze on the face has the genetic symbol of S^2. Lastly, we have the pattern of large areas of white which produce the effect of pigmented areas appearing as color spots on a white background (S^3).

GENETIC SYMBOLS

Some geneticists use the symbol A for the tabby strain, and the lack of it is designated by a. The a then stands for black. Others use T for tabby hair banding and t for the lack of hair banding. We shall use T for tabby because there are orange tabbies with lines as distinct as those on black and gray tabbies. Then too, there are orange cats with no tabby markings. You will see how easy it is to use symbols in predicting the outcome of any mating. The dominant character or gene is always represented by a capital; the recessive by a small letter.

> T—tabby banded hairs
> t—lack of tabby (black, blue, red, and cream)
>
> Dominant in this order:
> T^1—blotched
> T^2—wide striped
> T^3—narrow striped
>
> W—white (dominant)
> w—pigmented
>
> Y—orange (or yellow)
> y—not orange
>
> D—natural expression of color
> d—dilute
>
> C—full color
> C^{ch}—silver
> c—albino
> c^h—Siamese
> c^H—Burmese
>
> White spotting series—dominant in this order:
> S^1—small amount
> S^2—moderate amount
> S^3—large amount
>
> H—normal hair
> h—hairlessness
>
> L—short hair
> l—long hair

P—polydactyl (extra toes)
p—normal

R—normal eye
r—ruby eye

The table of symbols tells us what to expect from any mating. The explanation of what the symbols represent will be found in the description of coat characteristics on pages 97–101. Now let us make practical application of this seemingly theoretical material.

COLOR INHERITANCE

The tabby and the black constitute a series. The banded hairs and striped effect, as we saw, constitute the natural color (TT), but when the cat inherits a pair of genes for the loss of banding (tt), he or she is a black. The chart on page 94 clearly shows the six possible ways in which this pair of characteristics can be inherited.

When a pair of dilution genes (dd) are put with the tabby or black, the kittens will be blues (Maltese).

When the queen has a pair of genes for orange, this color will mask the black; when she has one orange gene, she will be a tortoiseshell. If the tom has even one gene for orange it will produce orange kittens or, in rare instances, tortoiseshell.

The tortoiseshell toms, when fertile, seem to produce kittens of orange color rather than tortoise. One such tom sired fifty-six kittens. Of the progeny from his matings with a black queen, thirteen were black toms, fourteen tortoiseshell queens, and one black queen. Matings to a yellow queen produced nine yellow toms, eight yellow queens, and one yellow with black spots. Matings with another tortoiseshell produced one black tom, two yellow toms, five yellow queens, and two tortoiseshell queens.

A Siamese mated to a black produces black kittens with grayish undercoats showing the black to be almost dominant over the Siamese. Two of these kittens, when mated, can produce the Siamese color in 25 per cent of their kittens.

Black is dominant over every color but tabby, red, or the dominant white.

Dominant white is dominant over all other colors.

The lesser amount of white on white-spotted cats is dominant over the greater amount. S^1 is dominant over S^2 or S^3. S^2 is dominant over S^3. A pair of S^3 cats have kittens which are mostly white. A pair of S^1 cats, if not pure S^1 parents (if they carry S^2 or S^3 genes), may have part white or nearly all white kittens.

Normal color intensity is dominant over silver, Burmese, or Siamese. Silver is dominant over Burmese and Siamese, and Burmese is dominant over Siamese. All are dominant over albinism (white with pink eyes).

Two new colors have been introduced in England: the lilac and the chocolate. These appear either as points or covering the whole cat.

The chocolate is a rich chocolate brown with no shading or stripes. The gene that produces chocolate is recessive to most other colors, according to the expert who has fixed the type. The lilac color is produced by mating a cat with the recessive chocolate gene with another carrying a gene for blue dilution.

In England the long-haired Siamese is called the Colourpoint. In America it is called the Himalayan. There is enough difference between the Siamese and the Colourpoint/Himalayan to distinguish them as two breeds. How did they come about? Given a knowledge of basic genetics, anyone could have predicted what would happen if enough Siamese and Persians were kept in contact. Short hair is dominant over long hair. So, if a Siamese crossed with a Persian, the offspring would be short-haired, each carrying the long hair recessively. When two of these half-breeds mated, the kittens would carry a reassortment of the characteristics. Long hair would combine with the Siamese points in some cases. And they did, both here and in England. They did not necessarily come from the Himalayan Mountains, but they are exquisite animals.

Compared to the Domestic Shorthair, Colourpoints have longer coats (sometimes as long as five inches). In addition they have shorter noses, and smaller ears (the latter tend to stand sideways) than the Siamese or their American counterpart, the Himalayan.

HAIR LENGTH

Short hair (L) is dominant over long hair (l). That is why a pair of shorthairs carrying the long-hair factor recessively so often have long-haired kittens but two longhairs never produce short-haired kittens.

When considering the length of a cat's hair, remember that a castrated male tends to grow longer hair. At the clinic I have noticed that when clients show me a castrated male, they will often mention that he must be half long-haired cat. Later I sometimes see cats from the same litter with definitely short hair. It is quite obvious that, while there are intermediate hair lengths in cats, allowances must be made for the effects of castration.

TAILLESSNESS

Although the tailless condition of the Manx is due to a dominant gene, it is only imperfectly dominant. When we study the same condition in other species as well as in cats, we are forced to admit that it is actually a deformity. When two pure Manx cats are mated, the kittens sometimes are cripples. This condition is also found in the offspring of other tailless species—rabbits or dogs, for instance.

When we study the mode of inheritance of the short tail we find that it is practically impossible to predict the outcome. Parents with natural bob-tails about two inches long may have kittens with no tail vertebrae, with little short stubs which do not show through the skin, or with tails three quarters of normal length. Sometimes a pure Manx mated with a cat with a normal tail produces all tailless kittens.

EYE COLOR

Unfortunately, the mode of inheritance of eye color has been studied very little. The students who have reported on coat color inheritance have not mentioned the eye colors in enough instances to give us the needed information which would enable us to breed the eye colors to order, or predict eye colors in kittens when we know the eye color of the parents.

However, the rarest eye characteristic—the capacity which some cats have to reflect red rather than the golden-yellow color—has been studied. If, when driving, you have seen red cats' eyes reflected in the glare of your headlights, you have seen one of these cats. The ruby eye color has been found in combination with nine different coat colors, proving there is no linkage as there is with blue eyes and white color. The characteristic may appear in any breed. I have seen it in longhairs and Maine Coon Cats, and several cases in Siamese have been reported.

HAIRLESSNESS

This is decidedly an undesirable characteristic in cats. Some specimens are completely hairless and others have a transitory fuzz. Strains have been established that breed true with either condition being recessive to the normal hair length. This accounts for the fact that hairless cats are sometimes born to normal parents. They are not necessarily mutations but the result of the recessive trait having been carried, masked, often for generations, waiting only for another gene in another cat with which it can combine to produce a hairless kitten.

DEAFNESS

So far as can be learned, deafness is usually associated with blue eyes, although it does not follow that all blue-eyed cats are deaf. One report lists a blue-eyed cat with normal hearing, a cat with one green and one blue eye, completely deaf, and an albino with the usual pink eyes with normal hearing.

POLYDACTYLISM (Extra Toes)

This is a characteristic determined by a dominant gene. A cat with a pair of these genes will produce only kittens with extra toes. A cat with one such gene mated to a normal-toed cat will put extra toes on half the kittens. A pair of cats with extra toes, each having only one gene for the trait, may produce 25 per cent of their kittens with normal feet.

Suppose that you wanted to write out the genetic composition of, let us say, a long-haired tabby, half of whose body was white, and whose feet had extra toes. You would first look at the table and set down the symbols. Tabby (T), white (S^3), long hair (l), extra toes (P). You would need a pair of each of the symbols. Since you could not tell whether or not the cat carried genes for recessive traits, you could only determine the secondary genes by breeding. She could be TT, $S^3 S^3$, ll, PP, or Tt, $S^3 S^3$, ll, Pp.

Suppose you decide that, from your newly acquired knowledge, you were going to breed a blue-pointed, Siamese-colored, long-haired cat. How could you accomplish it? There are several ways. One would be to breed a blue longhair with a blue-point Siamese. The kittens would be blue short-haired cats. You would then mate a pair of these and you could expect one out of sixteen kittens to be just what you want.

BEHAVIOR PATTERNS

As yet we know but little about inherited behavior patterns of cats. Every farmer who has had much experience with cats will tell you that certain strains will be good ratters, while some refuse ever to catch a rat, even when hungry. The tendency for viciousness to run in cat families is very marked. Some of the best show toms have produced large percentages of kittens that turned out to be completely untrustworthy unless they were spayed or castrated early in their lives.

The tendency of some cat families to sleep on high places has also been noted. I have already mentioned this characteristic in certain Maine Coon Cats. One cat family I know could not be kept in the house because they insisted on climbing the window curtains. The mode of inheritance of the characteristic has not been determined.

INBREEDING AND LINE BREEDING

Some mental characteristics, like viciousness, are often attributed to inbreeding. We are told that such and such a family produces such cats because they are too closely inbred. This means virtually nothing and is only an excuse for sloppy breeding. Inbreeding, of course, does tend to purify the strain. If a certain stud cat is known to be vicious and his progeny are mated together, the greater part of the offspring will eventually also come to be vicious, if the viciousness is hereditary. Inbreeding simply tends to make a strain pure for characteristics, good and bad.

The closest form of inbreeding is brother-to-sister mating. If brother-to-sister mating continues, bringing together only the finest characteristics and eliminating all inferior characteristics by refusal to breed their possessors, inbreeding can definitely improve a strain just as fast as it can impair it. It is true that close inbreeding tends to make the offspring somewhat smaller than the original. A certain amount of outbreeding is necessary for size and vigor. However, laboratory animals are bred brother to sister for many generations with no harm. In short, it is not the inbreeding that is bad; it is the lack of proper selection on the part of the breeders.

Line breeding is usually considered to be the mating of animals farther removed by heredity than first cousinship. Mating first cousins is generally considered inbreeding, but mating second cousins is considered line breeding.

SELECTIVE BREEDING

In the final analysis, it is most important for the average cat breeder to know the dominant and recessive traits and what to avoid. Beyond that, breed improvement consists of mating to the best possible animal. All too many cat fanciers do the easiest thing and mate their queens to the most accessible toms, usually one of their own. The careful breeder, however, looks around and obtains the use of studs that are noted for producing high-quality offspring.

If you have a choice between two studs, one of which is excellent and one of which is fair, look into their hereditary background. It will tell what you can expect much more than you can tell from their individual appearance because you must always keep in mind their recessive characteristics.

There is a Norwegian proverb at least 2,500 years old which says, "If you would have good children, marry not the maid who is the only good maid in the clan." Applying the proverb to the problem we have just been discussing, suppose that the excellent cat is one which just appeared in an otherwise poor family of cats, and the fairly good cat is the poorest one of the best family of cats that you know about. The latter would be the one to use as a stud because all the kittens will tend to be better than he is, whereas the progeny from the former will tend to be poorer than he is. This is not theory; it actually works out in practice. If you have already had experience in breeding cats, no doubt you yourself can testify to this.

7. How to Train Your Cat

CATS HAVE the reputation of being too independent to be trained. But isn't that simply an excuse given so often by cat owners too lazy or lacking in the necessary knowledge to succeed in cat training? It is true that many persons have tried to use the force system of training and found their cats to be quite unmanageable. Those owners, however, who have tried training by modern psychological methods have found that they can teach their cats as easily as they can teach their dogs.

It isn't necessary to understand the psychological terms scientists use, but it is necessary to know the principles in layman's language. The basic principle involves coupling a sound with the action you desire of the cat. At the same time, you must make the action pleasant to the cat. The simplest way to make the action pleasant is to provide food (either a regular meal or a prized tidbit) as soon as the action has been performed. For instance, feed your cat a dry, complete, wholesome food as a regular diet, and when you train use morsels of some food infinitely preferred over the regular diet. That's one way.

Another is to fast the cat for thirty-six hours. Suppose you feed once a day. Simply withhold the meal for twelve hours more, and the cat will be hungry and eager to respond to your signals. To reinforce the cat's proper responses, a tiny tidbit is all that is necessary; a piece of roast beef one inch square and one eighth of an inch thick.

The food is not really a reward but a reinforcement of the act—something given a little at a time. It is used to establish a habit and is given thirty or forty times in two sessions. For good results the cat should hear the signal you decide on and should receive the reinforcement the instant it responds. If there is a delay, it will take much longer to establish the habit.

A good, if slow, illustration of this technique is provided in the way your cat trains you. Imagine that your cat wants to go out. It has a need.

It will stand before the door and meow. The meow is the signal to you. You have a need—to "shush" the cat—so you open the door, let the cat out, and close the door. As another example, think of your cat standing in front of the refrigerator and meowing. Again in order to silence it, you obediently open the door, take out the milk, and pour some into a saucer. In both instances, you responded to your cat's signals; in other words, you were trained, although slowly because the response and reinforcement were too far apart. Consider, in contrast, the following more efficient method of teaching a cat to jump up on a chair:

When the cat is hungry we present it with a tidbit, held above the seat of a chair. As it jumps up we say "chair" and pop the tidbit into its mouth as it lands on the chair seat. The cat has probably jumped up from hunger and hasn't yet connected the word "chair" with the action. If we put the cat on the floor, say "chair," and simultaneously give the tidbit, the cat jumps up. If we continue this at least twenty-five times, the lesson will be learned. We allow thirty-six hours to elapse and go through the exercise twenty-five more times; our cat will be trained and we can expect it to jump on the chair when it hears the word "chair."

A word to the cat is a signal. A snap of our fingers, the sound of a bell, the sound of a whistle are all signals. Having taught our cat to respond to the word "chair," we can then have it respond to "table" (a great asset when you want to groom your pet). Next we can teach it to lie down, to roll over, to sit up. How? Put a collar on the cat and attach a string from the collar to a hook in the wall behind a table on which we will train the cat. As the cat comes to the edge of the table, hold a tidbit below the table top and as the cat lies down to try to reach it, we offer the tidbit while moving it downward. As the cat lies down we say "down," and give it the reward. Repeat this at least twenty-five times and the cat will be what the psychologists call conditioned, or as the layman says, trained. The cat will need another session of twenty-five repetitions to establish the habit and occasionally single commands will be necessary so that the habit will not become extinguished.

When the cat is on the table attached to the hook, you can teach it several responses: Sit up, roll over, stand on hind legs, and so forth. None of these responses is a useful one, but there are useful responses any cat can learn. Cats can be taught to retrieve or to respond to ringing bells.

Suppose an elderly person is deaf and owns a cat. She wants the cat to notify her when a bell rings. How can she do it? The owner of the pet will need the co-operation of someone after she has conditioned the cat to respond to the ringing of a bell. She has the pieces of tidbit, a hungry cat, and a bell. When the cat is wandering about the room she watches her pet and when she is looking at it she rings the bell and drops the tidbit into a dish. It will require a few minutes, a few repetitions, before the cat associates the sound of the bell with walking toward the dish and getting the tidbit. Twenty-five repetitions is not too many. Thirty is better. Two days later the cat is again put through the performance another twenty-five or thirty times.

Now comes the assistant. He or she rings the doorbell. The cat may go to the door or to the deaf owner. If it goes to the door, it gets nothing to eat, but if it goes to the owner, it gets a tidbit. The cat soon learns to respond to any ringing bell.

If the owner can't hear the telephone bell ringing, when the cat responds by coming to the owner the owner knows some bell is ringing. With some patience a cat can be taught to jump into the owner's lap when one bell rings, to rub against the owner's leg when another bell rings.

When we speak about training a pet most people think of housebreaking, while others think training means responding to the word "come."

To teach a kitten to use a pan, it is usually necessary only to keep it enclosed in a cage with a pan filled with some loose material such as sawdust, dried clay (Fuller's earth), fine pellets, shredded newspaper, or sand. A kitten likes to dig a hole, deposit its excrement, and cover it. This is instinctive, one of those actions no cat needs to be taught.

To condition a cat to come at some signal, make sure it is hungry when you put it outside. Call to the cat, saying, "Kitty, kitty, kitty," or ring a bell or blow a whistle. As soon as it comes, give the tidbit, pick it up, show affection, and put the cat back out. If you live in a one-story house, or the first floor of a house, you can put the cat out of the back door and go to the front door and call. It will respond. Give the tidbit and pet it. Put it out and go to the back door. Keep alternating this procedure twenty-five times. The cat may catch on to two responses: (1) to respond to the signal, and (2) to alternate. So at the next session two days later, break up the alternating by putting her down and when she runs to the other door, stay where you are; when she has alternated, signal from the same door. Do this several times and the alternating will become extinguished.

Scratching. Most cats love to extend their claws, hook them onto some resistant substance such as carpet, wood, or cloth, and pull. If no unwanted material is provided, the cat may use the legs of valuable pieces of furniture, causing considerable damage.

Training a cat not to scratch furniture simply involves providing a proper scratching place and discouraging it from scratching elsewhere. Pet shops sell scratching posts, or you can use strips of carpet hung on the wall or split logs placed on the floor.

Some cats stop scratching if their nails are clipped closely. When this does not avail, then the cat is due for a visit to her doctor. The veterinarian will anesthetize the cat and remove the nails from the front feet. No more need to scratch and no need for negative training! This is a last resort. Declawed cats are handicapped and their ability to escape danger by climbing trees is somewhat hampered.

To Gentle a Wild Cat. Occasionally, one finds a wild cat with certain characteristics one would want in a cat: perhaps special beauty or a specific trait needed for scientific research. Suppose the wild cat is caught in a box trap. In the author's cat colony there were two such cats. Both loved to be fondled and no one could guess that either was ever wild. How were they gentled?

First, they were made hungry. Some food was offered on the end of a stick. After three days of hunger both ate. Each day the stick was shortened until finally the food was fed from the hand. Next, my fingers were folded about the food so the cat had to poke her nose between my fingers. While she was doing this, my fingers gently scratched her neck. In a short time both cats permitted my scratching anywhere on the body. A few days later neither objected to being lifted by hand under the abdomen. Today both are satisfactory cats.

Negative Conditioning.   How does one condition a cat against doing undesirable things in the home? The chief problem is to keep your cat from practically living on the furniture. Some of the long-haired varieties leave hair four or five inches long when they lie down on furniture or curl up on your lap. Many cats jump on the bureau or on the dining-room table.

To stop this behavior, a rubber fly swatter comes to the rescue. Every time the cat jumps up, swat the furniture next to the cat and frighten it away. If this fails, swat the cat. Never permit it to enjoy being up on something. Or else provide a chair on which your cat may lie and enjoy itself.

(By the way, some vacuum cleaners do not remove cat hair satisfactorily. There is nothing better for this purpose than a rubber sponge.)

Occasionally a cat, disregarding the pan provided for it, may decide to defecate under the bed or in a closet. In such cases, the material provided in the pan is not what the cat likes. Or the pan is too small. Try a different sort of material: sand, pellets, Fuller's earth (sold under various trade names). Put the pan where the cat defecates and when it gets the habit of using it in that position move the pan by stages to where you want it to stay.

If you can catch the cat in the act of defecating in the wrong place it is permissible to swat it and put it in a small enclosure, containing a pan. The enclosure can be a wire cage, the front of which opens. The pan is left in it until the cat uses it constantly, after which the cage is removed and cat goes to the location of the pan.

Two responses are especially useful in managing cats and both are simple to establish. These are jumping in and jumping out of a carrier. Some carriers have openings in the end but most of them open at the top. The top openers are most satisfactory because the paper in the bottom can be changed more easily.

For these responses you can train your cat on the floor but it is more comfortable on a table. Set the carrier with the hungry cat in it on a table. Open the lid and let the cat smell the tidbit you are holding between your thumb and first finger. As it follows the movement of your hand the cat will jump out onto the table. Immediately say "out" and the cat's effort will be reinforced. Pop the reinforcement (tidbit) into its mouth without delay.

Return the cat to the carrier, close the lid. Wait a few minutes. Open the lid and repeat the performance. After half a dozen repetitions you can open the lid and say "out" and the cat will jump out and receive the reinforcement. Return it to the carrier and repeat the response twenty-five or thirty times.

Two days later, go through it all again to ensure that your cat is conditioned to jump out of the carrier whenever you say "out."

To condition your pet to jump into the carrier, open the top, let it smell the tidbit, and it will follow your hand as you move it to the bottom of the carrier. As the cat jumps in, say "in," and offer the tidbit immediately. It knows what "out" means, so give the signal "out."

Let the cat stay out a minute or so and then lead it again into the carrier by enticing it with the tidbit. As the cat jumps in, say "in" and give it the tidbit.

Do this twenty-five times. Wait a day and repeat it again. Once a week or so exercise your pet in its new knowledge. You'll be surprised how long the conditioning will last!

Toilet Training. A clever owner can circumvent the messiness of the litter box by training the pet to use a toilet. It was many years ago that this phenomenon first came to my attention through a photograph of a Siamese perching on the toilet seat. That was a case of choice on the part of the cat; but there is a system of training that works well.

It is necessary that the cat be trained to a litter box first. Next, place the box in the bathroom near the toilet. After a week in its new location, discard the box and replace it with another fashioned to fit under the seat of the john. Place the cat in this box a few times, and, with no alternative available to it, the cat soon learns to accept the new accommodation. Incidentally, this new litter box should be removable for obvious reasons. After a week of use the box should be replaced with a one-inch mesh wire to prevent the cat from falling in during the training period. After another week, discard the screen, as our friend should now be able to perch safely on the rim of the seat. I have heard of no cats trained to flush the john; but no doubt an enterprising inventor will solve that problem before long.

8. What You Should Know about Restraint, First Aid, and Emergencies

*A*DEQUATE CARE and intelligent handling are usually sufficient to keep a cat in good health. But even a healthy animal—like a healthy child—cannot be perfectly guarded against every eventuality. Accidents do happen; emergencies arise in spite of every precaution.

Two things the owner *can* do. By exercising reasonable and humane precautions, he can avoid accidents resulting from carelessness. And he can learn how to cope with emergencies when they do arise.

Situations requiring first-aid treatment and emergencies requiring veterinary attention are closely related and often overlap. The problem may lie in your ability to decide what an emergency is and how you should respond in the best interest of your pet. Should you treat an emergency yourself or ask for professional help?

I will try to clear the gray areas by explaining how the veterinarian handles many emergencies, but ultimately you must make the choice: Do it yourself or ask for help. Fortunately, today, there are veterinarians in most areas who can be contacted day or night to help you make a considered decision.

Every year thousands of cats are lost needlessly simply because their owners have never taken the time to familiarize themselves with a few simple principles of first-aid and emergency treatment. Such owners become panicky and do nothing to help their injured pets—or do worse than nothing: the wrong thing. The person who has no understanding of the normal recuperative processes or powers of animals too quickly assumes that the best he can do for an animal that has been hurt is to put it out of the reach of pain and so destroys his pet when it might have recovered easily and completely.

Too many pet owners feel that since they prefer to have their veterinarian prescribe for all serious pet problems, there is no necessity for them to be able to handle difficult or unpleasant situations themselves.

Such owners should remember, however, that emergencies have a way of happening at inconvenient moments.

Any owner can, and should be prepared to, administer first aid to an injured pet. He should know how to restrain an animal that is frightened or in pain so that it will not harm itself or others. He should know how to stop the flow of blood from a wound, how to relieve as much pain as possible, and how to protect the pet until the veterinarian reaches it. He should also know *what not to do*. The skills and techniques are not difficult to learn or to apply. They are available to everyone—the cheapest and best insurance a person can get against the loss of his pet.

HOW TO RESTRAIN A CAT

Before you can attempt any sort of treatment for an injured animal, you must know how to protect yourself and how to prevent the patient from doing damage to itself or from escaping before you have taken care of it properly. Restraint of some sort is usually necessary to administer first aid and always necessary when surgery of any sort is involved. With some unruly pets it is even necessary when the animal is being groomed.

Since your cat's defenses consist of biting and clawing, it must be held so that it cannot reach the handler. An injured pet is often a panic-stricken animal. Under such circumstances even the most gentle animal may bite and scratch when you attempt to help it. Don't blame your pet and don't destroy *it* because it is vicious. Remember that biting is a normal reaction of a frightened or injured animal. Remember, too, that the pain may have subsided for the moment and that in handling the animal you may have caused it to recur with terrible intensity. Don't expect your pet to respond as it usually does. Expect it to act like what it is—an animal in pain.

Anyone who has tried to restrain a cat in order to execute a procedure disagreeable to the cat knows the problems and dangers involved. Those eighteen nails may seem like eighty and the strength of the animal is unbelievable.

Restraining a cat is ordinarily a simple matter, even though it defends itself with claws and teeth. The easiest method is to wrap a heavy folded blanket around the cat and grasp it firmly from each side. It usually requires no more than this to control the most vicious cat.

Because of an inherited reflex action cats almost invariably succumb to the firm touch of a strong hand that lifts them by grasping a large handful of skin on the back of the neck. Some of the most ornery old toms will curl up like little kittens when handled in this way.

Many ingenious devices are produced commercially for restraining and carrying cats. The heavy duck zipper bag is one. The cat is placed in it with its head resting through one end of the opening. The zipper is drawn from the rear, over the cat's body to its neck. The cat can't get its legs out or its head in. A stout laundry bag with a drawstring is popular with some cat owners.

For examining a cat that is badly frightened or in pain, two people are required. One person can hold the cat's head, with the fingers of one hand under the cat's chin and thumb behind its head; the other hand should hold both front legs. Both hands must hold tightly. The examiner holds the two hind legs in one hand and examines with the other. Let the cat squirm as it may.

The inept and often ineffectual attempts of the average person to control cats are amazing. Don't be afraid to hold and don't let go when the patient struggles. If either person fails to hold tightly, at least one will be scratched and the cat will probably get away. Be sure of your assistant and be sure the assistant has no cause to distrust you.

Perhaps the most inexpensive and one of the best ways to restrain a cat in order to take it to your veterinarian is to place it in a bushel basket with a top that fits under the handles; this can be wired together with very little effort. Since it is roomy, airy, and dark, the animal feels secure. Such baskets make ideal carriers and they are readily available in local produce stores. A cat should always be carried to a veterinarian in some type of container for very often the hand-held cat will see dogs in the veterinarian's parking lot when it is taken out of the car. Remember that this is not a happy place for a cat. It may struggle and attempt to get away from you.

A choking cat—one that is fighting for its breath as a result of a foreign object lodged in its throat—presents special problems. If you wrap it in a blanket, it may go into laryngeal spasms and die. In such cases, you should contact your veterinarian immediately, place the cat in a carrier, and run. A choking cat was rushed in to me one night at 2:00 A.M. His membranes were already blue and I had to explain to the owners the dangers of administering intravenous anesthesia even as I was injecting it. Had the animal had any less oxygen, he certainly would have died. Once under the anesthesia, however, he relaxed and, as his breath came more easily, his tongue turned from blue to pink. I sighed a sigh of relief. A needle was extracted from deep within his throat and he was out of danger.

With the sedatives, tranquilizers, and anesthetics available to the modern veterinarian, untold numbers of cats that previously would have been doomed are saved from death by asphyxiation.

The needle-in-throat case, however, had a tragic ending two weeks later. It seems that the owner, unable to examine his choking cat's throat, had done a very logical thing—he had used mineral oil to lubricate the throat and possibly to dislodge whatever was obviously present there.

In its desperate efforts to breathe, the cat had drawn some of the mineral oil into his lungs, which inevitably led to pneumonia. The owner failed to mention the mineral-oil treatment when he first brought the cat to me and I assumed that the pneumonia was due to infection caused by the needle. The post-mortem revealed, however, that the pneumonia was an aspiration pneumonia caused by the mineral oil. Only when confronted with the facts did the owner admit that he had administered that mineral-oil death warrant to his cat.

FIRST AID

The principles of first aid that the cat owner needs to master are simple and relatively few, but they are of vital importance in handling emergencies. Whether an animal that has been injured is to recover quickly or slowly, whether it is to be completely restored or marked or scarred—indeed, whether the animal is to survive at all—often depends upon the treatment it gets immediately after an injury. This chapter is intended to give the cat owner the general information he needs and at the same time provide him with a reference manual in which he may quickly find the specific way to handle any emergency that may befall his pet.

Shock. Any severe injury—an automobile accident, a burn, a struggle, a fight, or even a severe fright—may bring on this condition. The animal usually seems to be prostrated in a semioblivious state, yet apparently anxious. The nervous system is in depression, sometimes so severe as to cause complete immobility. On the other hand, an occasional animal may suffer the opposite effect, so that it seems to be in a state of nervous excitement. Usually, the pulse is slow and weak, the breathing shallow, and the temperature falls well below normal.

First aid consists in covering the cat with a blanket in order to raise its temperature to normal. Heat is helpful but *high* artificial heat is not desirable. Administer a stimulant, such as strong coffee (see page 156 for the lip pocket method of administering medications), then let the cat rest. Occasional fondling is often reassuring and helpful. Often, as the animal recovers, the pulse becomes too rapid and the temperature may rise well above normal. Recovery may sometimes take an hour or more. A cat in shock should be rushed to the veterinarian whenever possible. The suggestions above are strictly first aid.

Heat Exhaustion. Heat stroke occurs most often when a cat is left in an automobile that does not have sufficient ventilation and overheats in the summer sun. First aid may be lifesaving in such cases. Gently pour cold water all over an overheated cat, gallons if necessary, and as it appears to improve take it to your veterinarian.

We are all conscious of the refreshing sensation of a breeze in hot weather. This is due to evaporation of moisture from our bodies and the consequent cooling of the surface of the body. The bodies of animals are cooled by the same process; in addition, moisture evaporates from the throat and mouth as the pet becomes overheated and pants. Cats have few sweat glands in the skin compared to humans and horses, but they do have some. When an animal is sufficiently cooled by bodily and oral evaporation, it stops panting.

In itself, panting is a normal method of reducing body temperature. It may also be an indication of thirst or fever.

Accidents. A large proportion of the true emergencies seen by veterinarians involve trauma or physical injury very often caused by the automobile. If they were kept, the statistics on feline highway fatalities in our country would be shocking indeed.

When a cat is struck by an automobile, a certain sequence of action should be considered. First, if the animal is lying in the street, it should be picked up, preferably with a blanket or canvas, and removed to safety before it is struck again. Then quickly assess the animal's condition. If it is immobile, but still breathing, there are two possibilities: It may be seriously injured or it may simply be unconscious from a mild head injury. Many a cat, seemingly near death, suddenly regains consciousness and in fright leaps up and runs for the nearest cover. If it is at all able to do so, a cat will return home when its emotional state calms down. If respiration is abnormal and the tongue and gums are pale, the cat may have one of several conditions or a combination thereof: shock, internal bleeding, a crushed chest, to name a few. A veterinarian has a number of weapons at his disposal to combat any of these problems (oxygen, steroids, intravenous fluid, blood, and drugs, etc.), and one of your first decisions after an accident will be whether to seek out his help immediately or to treat the cat on the spot. If you decide on the former course, and if the accident occurs during normal veterinary hours, ask someone else to phone your veterinarian while you rush the animal to his office. Otherwise you yourself should phone first to ask for advice and to see whether or not he is available.

When a cat has sustained a serious injury many bodily changes occur (some, no doubt, that we don't understand), of which bleeding is the most common. Fortunately major internal and external bleeding is not as great a problem in cats as in many species, including man. Nevertheless, you should try to stop the bleeding as best and as quickly as you can. Sometimes a cat bleeds so much there is very little blood circulating to transport oxygen. The cat will be pale and unresponsive but does not die. Such a cat can be helped merely by adding fluid to the blood just to keep the volume up; a dramatic improvement in its condition will be evident in a short while.

If an animal does bleed internally in the abdomen, what becomes of the blood? When a clot forms, it is composed of red and white cells, plasma, and fibrinogen, which causes coagulation. As it forms, the clot squeezes out a fluid or serum. This serum can be, and is, soaked up by the peritoneum (the lining of the abdomen and covering of the organs). Obviously the serum gets back into the circulation and thus helps to increase the blood volume. Many of the red cells which transport oxygen through the body are in the clot. This clot does not persist permanently as a liverlike lump. Instead a process called lysis occurs. The cells simply dissolve into the fluid in the abdomen. Their covering disintegrates and releases the contents. The fluid is now circulated, but only a small amount is utilized by the body; most of it, including the red pigment, is passed out of the body through the urine as waste. When you see your weak but mending patient urinating what appears to be blood several days after an injury, don't presume that it is passing blood from its kidneys and bladder; the urine probably owes its strange tint to blood-coloring matter, hemoglobin. This fact is sometimes used as a diagnostic means of demonstrating internal hemorrhage that occurred several days before the red color is seen. Of course blood in the urine soon after an accident indicates a rift in the continuity of the blood vessels somewhere in the genito-urinary tract, which may then require surgery.

Some injuries, whether they involve bleeding or not, may lead to shock, which can be reversed or prevented by steroid injections. (Steroids are the family of drugs that include cortisone.)

With some individuals, the pain resulting from an injury is so severe that the victims will strain and struggle, and possibly cause further damage to themselves. In such cases, the veterinarian will administer sedatives or tranquilizers in addition to using other treatments.

Most seriously injured cats become quiet once they are home, which, in some instances, may be the best time to summon the help of a veterinarian. Even with an obviously broken leg, it is unwise to take the time for a first-aid splint, since cats, unlike dogs, will rarely cause more damage by struggling. Bear in mind, however, that some pets despise riding in a car and the fright caused by the ride can be the last straw for a pet, particularly if it is suffering from a respiratory injury. Since cats often hide in a dark place when frightened, your trip to the veterinarian can be made less eventful by placing the cat in a closed corrugated box or by wrapping the cat in a blanket (but keep the blanket loose around the face).

Don't assume that your injured pet will die of fright or loneliness in a veterinary establishment. If seriously injured, it won't care where it is until the crisis has passed. At this time, problems may arise, but by then your pet will be about ready to return to the security of your home.

Certain situations do not call for immediate veterinary attention. Bleeding lacerations, for instance, can and often should receive first-aid treatment from any Good Samaritan. A wad of cotton, pressed and firmly wrapped on a bleeding leg, usually stops even a bleeding artery. Cats are unique in their ability to clot blood quickly and the severed small vessels retract so that only severed major arteries and veins need such pressure bandages. Lacerations should be examined for the presence of glass splinters or other foreign material, which should be removed before bandaging.

For some reason the amateur is invariably unwilling to bind a wound firmly. In not one case of a badly cut foot have I ever seen a bandage applied by a client that was any more than a sop for the blood. Don't be afraid to bind a wound tightly. A good bandage will help the formation of a blood clot, and when the bandage is removed the clot itself will prevent more hemorrhage.

When in doubt about a possible emergency situation phone your veterinarian for advice, and, if necessary, get the patient to him as quickly as possible. If your veterinarian does not provide emergency coverage, do not hesitate to change doctors. And finally, bear in mind that the cat is an extremely resilient creature. Properly treated, cats can, and often do, spring back from seemingly disastrous emergencies, as the following true cases attest.

One such spectacular recovery concerned a three-year-old tiger cat crushed by two wheels of a trailer truck. I happened to be driving behind the truck and watched in horror as the cat, in its attempt to avoid a car heading in the opposite direction, ran under the truck. I pulled to the curb as the cat dragged itself over the curbing and sidewalk to a five-foot wooden fence, which it scaled with its forelegs.

I rushed to the fence expecting to see the poor crushed cat lying on the other side; instead I saw it disappear in the distance over a second fence. Back at the office a few hours later an emergency was announced and a tiger cat was brought in, paralyzed in its rear quarters. The address of the client was close to the accident I had seen. In spite of the multiple pelvic (hip) and femoral (thigh bone) fractures the cat recovered with virtually no aftereffects.

Another bizarre case involved a bloody, dirty pet with an unusual history. The previous evening the cat had been struck by a car and sustained a broken leg and lacerations. The owner, thinking the situation hopeless, dug a grave, shot the cat with his 22-caliber rifle, and buried the body. In the morning his wife opened the back door and there was the cat, bloody and dirty. The bullet had entered the skin over one eye and emerged behind the ear. The force caused unconsciousness but the projectile had not penetrated the cranium. The client decided that any animal that survived such an ordeal deserved a chance, and so we set the leg and patched up the wounds. Unfortunately, the day we removed the splint from the broken leg, the cat crossed the road and was struck again. This time the opposite leg was fractured and the owner came in with a request for euthanasia. We could not prevail upon him to give the cat one more chance.

In New Haven we have some high-rise apartments eighteen stories high, and it was on the window sill of one apartment on the top floor that the lady of the flat discovered her cat one morning. She approached the cat to bring it in but the cat leapt playfully away from her. When my client arrived at ground level there was the cat walking toward her. We bandaged one leg to support a minor fracture and found no other signs of that mishap.

In my opinion the domestic cat is one of the most resilient creatures on earth and deserving of the ancient adage "A cat has nine lives."

Breathing Problems. There are several emergency conditions that cause a rather sudden shortness of breath, not to be confused with panting from overheating. Anemia, for example, a condition in which there is an insufficient amount of oxygen-carrying material (hemoglobin) in the bloodstream, is caused by any number of factors and, although it develops over a period of weeks, can reach, very suddenly, a critical point at which the hemoglobin level has dropped below the level necessary to sustain life. In addition to short, rapid breathing, a pale tongue and gums are symptoms of critical anemia and a signal to seek immediate veterinary care.

Fluid in the chest, which compresses the lungs so that there is inadequate space for them to expand, may also result in rapid breathing and a depressed patient. These cases must all be treated gently since stress at this time can result in death.

As your veterinarian will tell you, it is a calculated risk to administer most anesthetic drugs to such patients, but there may be no choice. An oxygen mask or an endotracheal tube inserted in the windpipe may be necessary to administer oxygen. As the fluid is withdrawn and the lungs have room to inflate, breathing improves and the oxygen is no longer needed.

In sum, many breathing problems are true emergencies requiring immediate veterinary attention since there is no simple set of rules for distinguishing the true from the false emergency. Even pneumonia falls into this category since some untreated pneumonia cases die within two days from the onset of symptoms.

Rabies. The cry of "mad dog" is no longer heard as frequently in America as it used to be, though in Europe it is still fairly common. Nevertheless, it *does* occur. An animal that manifests any of the symptoms of rabies (see page 204) should receive immediate treatment. Here we need only concern ourselves with the problems of first aid—for the cat and for the animals or humans it has bitten—and the subsequent management of the incident.

For the suspected rabid cat, complete isolation must be provided. Shut the animal in a cage or room and call your veterinarian, and if a person has even touched the animal, call a physician immediately. Keep people and animals away from the rabid cat. Your veterinarian will diagnose its condition, and either the local authorities or the veterinarian will provide isolation until the diagnosis is clearly established. If an animal *is* infected, the local authorities will determine its disposition.

Any pet that has been bitten by a rabid animal should be quarantined. Since a high proportion of all animals—75 per cent of all uninoculated dogs, for example—are susceptible to rabies, no other course is safe. The period of isolation is long: An exposed animal must be confined for six months.

Although rabies is a horrible and fatal disease, a suspected rabid animal should never be destroyed. It should be allowed to die a natural death, even if it must be kept sedated by a veterinarian. Diagnosis of rabies is a difficult thing and the only way to be sure that an animal is rabid is to allow the disease to take its course.

Needless to say, if a human is bitten, call a doctor immediately. Only a physician is qualified to decide on the treatment or prophylaxis necessary for the humans involved.

Lacerations. Cats hustle through barbed-wire fences, step on broken bottles, scratch in ash piles, step on concealed metal scraps, and fight with other cats. As a result they come home gashed, bleeding, and torn. Yet, cats, because of their unique clotting ability, seldom bleed to death. Most of the cuts on animal skins are triangular tears, though some, of course, are clean, straight cuts. In either case, only a limited kind of first aid should be administered. Animal saliva contains an enzyme that digests germs; in addition, the surface of a cat's tongue is made up of small, tough barbs so strong that they can wear away flesh. All of which means that there is no better way of cleaning a cut than to allow the cat to lick it. Its tongue will wipe away all dead flesh or debris and kill germs in the process. Although a cat will heal its own wounds, blood clots, dirt, gravel, and any other foreign bodies, including hair, that retard healing should be meticulously removed with tweezers. Flush the area out with pure water and wipe it with a cotton swab. In order to further cleanse the area, wash it with hydrogen peroxide or any household antiseptic in weak dilution, according to directions on the bottle.

In cases of minor lacerations, there is no need to rush your pet to the veterinarian. Nor should you strap the cut together with adhesive tape or bind it up, unless there is persistent bleeding. Simply let the cat clean its own wound and then have the veterinarian take a look. In most cases, all he will do is cut away dead edges on the flap and suture it in place, so that when it has healed no ugly scar will remain.

There are times, however, when a cat won't lick a wound (this is especially true when an abscess is present) or can't reach a wound to lick it (for instance, cuts on the neck, head, face, and shoulders are out of the cat's range). If this is the case, cleanse the wound yourself and take your pet to the veterinarian as soon as possible.

The most dangerous cuts are those made by filthy objects. These cuts may heal by themselves or mat over with hair which then becomes part of the scab. Tetanus (lockjaw) germs occasionally infect such wounds. Since tetanus can develop only in a cut or puncture that cannot be aerated, wounds of this sort must be opened, cleansed, and kept open until they have been disinfected and sutured. Some wounds are best left unsutured for a considerable length of time. Flush these daily while they heal from the bottom out and have them sutured (to avoid unsightly scars) only when the healing process has reached the surface layers of the skin.

Bites. Animal bites and poisonous snake or insect bites need very different treatment, so we shall consider them separately.

Animal Bites. It is sometimes important to determine the kind of bite to be treated. The bite of a dog, cat, and even that of a rat can usually be distinguished by the number of teeth marks. A large dog's bite is usually characterized by four puncture marks. The distance between them, as well as their size, gives some idea of the size of the attacker. Little dogs sometimes open their mouths wide and leave impressions of their upper and lower canine teeth perhaps four inches apart, but the distance between the two upper canines will still be small. Large dogs may happen to get hold with only a small nip, but the distance between their upper canines may be as much as three inches in some breeds.

Because of their size and strength, large dogs inflict greater damage than do small dogs. Ordinarily, a dog attacking another animal does not simply attack, hold on, and squeeze; he shakes his head and thus drives his fangs in deeper. These teeth wounds can be cleansed by shaving the hair away and filling the wounds with antimicrobial agents. A veterinarian will probably administer antibiotics and perhaps give you some to administer at home. Such cuts usually heal in a few days.

Cats frequently fight among themselves: male cats have a predilection for attacking castrated males, and even queens fight at times. Cats are particularly prone to staphylococcic infections, which manifest themselves in abscesses (skin swellings that exude whitish or yellow pus when squeezed). When your cat comes home after a battle, watch the bites carefully every day and open any abscesses when they are still small. Often bites in or just above the paws, where many small bones and tendons are located, are neglected and infection creeps in all around the area, making it more difficult to cure.

"But," you may say, "look at all the old tramp cats; they get in fights and nobody bothers about them." Look at them indeed! They often have several patches of bare skin from these very abscesses, which, neglected, have broken and healed without hair to cover them. These cats bear scars from their battles and are so often infected with abscesses that they become hideous sights. Perhaps that is why they are tramps—nobody wants them.

One of the major causes of cat bite abscesses is the presence of hair introduced by the action of the adversary's canine teeth. An observant master should attempt to pluck such tufts from the puncture wounds in order to prevent abscess formation.

After some accidents, great pouches of fluid often develop under areas of skin that have been torn loose. Sometimes these areas fill with clotted blood and, if the injury is serious enough, bacteria may gain access to the pocket. In such cases, you should shave the skin, make an incision at the lowest part of the pocket, and drain the fluid and blood clots. Next, flush the area with antimicrobial agents and bind it tightly in order to press the skin against the underlying layers. Rebandage daily until healed. An anesthetic is sometimes used when a veterinarian performs this sort of surgery.

Snake Bites. First aid in snake bites is extremely important. When you suspect a rapidly increasing swelling to be the result of a rattlesnake, copperhead, or water-moccasin bite, there is usually sufficient time to reach a veterinarian. If you can't reach him, try your family doctor. Many physicians have saved animal lives in emergencies. If neither a veterinarian nor a doctor is available, and if the bite is no more than twenty minutes old, connect the two fang marks by a deep incision and then try to squeeze some of the venom out. The area will be so swollen and so anesthetized that the cat will not feel the presence of a scalpel. Undertake this procedure only as a last resort; it is really a job for a veterinarian.

Tourniquets are rarely used any more in snake bites, but when they are, make sure the tourniquet is a broad flat one and that it is released periodically. It should not be too tight since we are not concerned with shutting off the blood, but only the lymphatics.

Spider Bites. There are many spiders that are toxic to cats. The brown spider, the fiddle, and the black widow are all dangerous. Spiders are often found inside old skulls of horses and cattle that have died and been left unburied. (The black widow in particular has a predilection for old bones.) Cats prowl around such things and may be bitten by these poisonous insects, usually on the lips or face. Swelling occurs and increases in direct proportion to the amount of venom the spider injects. One bite may kill a cat, although this is rare. Usually very little can be done for a bitten cat at home. Take it at once to your veterinarian for treatment. In addition, if you know where the spider that bit your pet lives, make an effort to exterminate the culprit and, if possible, her young in order to save other pets and humans from being bitten.

Bee Stings. It is not uncommon to hear of pets being stung to death by bees. Cats frequently swell up from a single sting and come home drooling and in pain, particularly if they have attempted to swallow a stinging insect, such as a wasp, hornet, or bee.

The painful stings, the poisonous effect of the toxin, and worst of all, the sensitivity to foreign material common to cats that have been stung before may produce a severe shock. The treatment of choice is steroids administered intravenously by a veterinarian, along with other supportive treatment.

Foreign Bodies. No first-aid discussion could be complete without suggestions for the removal of foreign bodies.

In the Mouth. Cats sometimes overestimate their ability to manipulate certain bones. It is common to find such bones caught in various positions: wedged across the roof of the mouth between the back teeth;

driven down into the gum beside a tooth; driven through the soft tissue into the lower jaw; stuck between two teeth; stuck on top of a molar; or covering several teeth.

A T bone from a lamb chop is sometimes caught across a cat's mouth between the back teeth, with its sharp point sticking into the throat. The cat paws desperately at his mouth, and the owner often thinks that the end has surely come. Cats sometimes chew two- or three-inch shank bones from lamb so that the rounded bone slips down over their teeth and they can't close their mouths without forcing the sharp edges of the bone farther down against the gums. These cats become frantic.

Many other kinds of foreign bodies become wedged in the teeth or stuck in the mouth. No matter what the particular situation may be, the mouth must be opened and the object pulled out. Whenever possible, it is wise to rush the pet to the veterinarian, who has the instruments to remove the obstruction without difficulty.

One of the common foreign bodies in the mouth and elsewhere is a thread, on the end of which is usually a needle. Cats will eat the thread and then swallow the needle. Not infrequently, such a needle will pass through the cat and not cause any difficulty. But sometimes a needle will be turned so that the point wedges in the back of the throat, sometimes at the base of the tongue, in which case it is necessary for a veterinarian to enter the picture.

In the Stomach. If you do not actually see a cat eat a foreign object, you can never be sure that the cat does have it in his stomach. You may have seen him eat gravel or sand, or chew on an old doll. But circumstantial evidence is usually all that is necessary. If a small item the cat was playing with is missing and the cat begins to show evidence of stomach pain, it is time for action.

Suppose you suspect that your small cat has swallowed one of your child's iron jacks, the crisscross gadget the child picks up when he bounces a ball. The cat will probably show some evidence of stomach pain, and you should act at once. Your veterinarian may X-ray the cat to verify the presence of a foreign body and if feasible will administer an emetic.

You may be surprised sometime to pick up your cat and hear stones rattling together in its stomach. Actually you shouldn't be too astonished, for this is a fairly common occurrence. And it shouldn't worry you very much. Stones can usually be removed with an emetic. Cats with gravel impactions in their stomach can be relieved by the same means. Feed the cat a 1½ per cent peroxide solution followed fifteen minutes after vomiting by a dose of Vaseline to help move along the gravel that has entered the intestine.

Remedies of this sort for the removal of foreign bodies are properly classified as first aid. More difficult cases should be left to the veterinarian. With X ray he can locate bullets, needles, pins, and any of the hundreds of other odd and dangerous objects that cats have been known to swallow.

In the Rectum. If your cat squats, strains, cries, and possibly exudes a little blood from its anus, it may have a foreign body in the rectum. The squatting may be due to urinary tension, inflammation, and many other causes as well as a foreign object. A constipated mass may be considered a foreign body. Not infrequently the stoppage is caused by sharp bone splinters that were not properly softened and digested in its stomach. Poultry, pork, and lamb bones are the most likely to cause such difficulties. Since any movement of the sharp bones is extremely painful, the cat refrains from defecating. In time the fecal material piles up behind them and soon a solid dry mass with sharp bones sticking out of it precludes all passage. Sometimes even abdominal surgery is necessary to remove the mass.

First aid consists of enemas to soften the mass, though they often are not sufficiently effective to allow passage of the material. Humane considerations indicate a prompt visit to the doctor, who will probably first soften the mass and then gently reach in with an instrument and crush it into small particles. Occasionally an oily enema is sufficiently lubricating to permit the stool to be passed without great difficulty or pain. In difficult cases the veterinarian may have to pull out the sharp pieces with instruments to avoid lacerations.

Needles are frequently found in the rectums of cats. Often a thread hanging from the anus is a good indication of the cause of the pain. If the needle is just inside and can be felt, an ingenious person with a small wire cutter such as electricians use can snip the needle in half and remove the halves separately. Generally, however, this job is best left to the doctor, who will use anesthesia and a speculum to see clearly what he is doing. Frequently, X ray is necessary to locate a needle.

In the Skin. Foreign bodies in the skin or feet are usually splinters or bullets, although other objects, such as glass chips, porcupine quills, and fox tails (a weed seed) are not as uncommon as most people think. Common sense dictates the quick removal of such objects whenever possible. It also dictates the injection of an antiseptic into the wound. If a bullet has come to rest against a rib and it can be seen through the hole, you should do what your first impulse tells you: Pull it out with a pair of tweezers and cleanse the wound. More often than not bullets are diagnosed on X ray. Frequently these are not removed but antibiotics are administered to prevent infection.

Children may put elastic bands around the neck, leg, tail, or ear of their pets. The hair covers the band and it goes unnoticed until swelling starts. By that time it may have cut through the skin. There is little the owner himself can do after he has removed the band. If the skin gapes too widely, ask the veterinarian's advice. Ropes and small chains may also cut deeply through the skin. Most people have seen at least one animal with a hairless band of skin around the neck—mute evidence that some negligent owner left a rope, chain, or collar on until it cut the animal's neck. Having callously injured the animal, he failed even to have the gaping skin sutured.

Automobile-Fan and Fan-Belt Injuries. After a motor vehicle is run in cool weather, the motor remains warm for some time. Cats are attracted to the warm engine block and frequently curl up on the warm metal. The operator, unmindful of the presence of the cat, starts the vehicle, thereby frightening the cat, who, in an attempt to make a hasty exit, becomes entangled in the fan belt, which whips him around into the rapidly turning fan. The injuries from such an accident can be among the worst a veterinarian has to contend with. Some cats have their legs virtually torn from their bodies, but many are saved with prompt professional attention.

A selling point for many foreign cars may be that many have no opening through which the cat can gain access to the engine while others have protective devices covering the belts and fan.

If you discover your cat is attracted to your car's engine under these circumstances, sound your horn *before* starting the engine or set mouse traps on the engine block. The sting of a triggered mouse trap is minor in comparison to the hideous injuries of belt and fan.

Drowning. If a pet can be pulled out of the water while its heart is still beating, it can almost always be saved. Slow, steady artificial respiration does the trick, but the technique is somewhat different from that used on humans. Place the animal on its side and push with the flat of the hand on its ribs. Then pull your weight up quickly. Repeat at regular intervals about once every two seconds. The cat usually starts to breathe very shallowly, and gradually more deeply. Even when the heartbeat is faint, there is hope, and it always pays to try. Mouth-to-mouth resuscitation is not possible in cats but if the cat's tongue is pulled out and its mouth closed so that the front teeth hold the tongue forward, mouth-to-nose resuscitation is effective. A cat's nose is cleaner bacteriologically than our own.

Electric Shock. Since animals' bodies are such excellent conductors of electricity, the shock of 110 volts—which ordinarily merely jolts a human—may kill them. When shocked, animals sometimes stiffen so rigidly that they appear to leap into the air. There is a great temptation for a cat to chew a dangling electric cord, and many have been badly injured when they tried it. In such cases, always pull the plug out or throw the electric switch to an "off" position if the wire is still in contact with any part of the animal. One such experience is sufficient to teach a cat owner the hazard of loose electric wires—often at the cost of his pet's life.

Burns. If you are called upon to treat a burned animal, clean off all the hair that can mat down on the burned area. Then apply a solution of one part tannic acid to one hundred parts of water (strong, strained tea may be substituted). Then cover the area gently with Vaseline. Your druggist will furnish his best burn remedy and help in an emergency. Frequently the animal succumbs in spite of all treatment, depending on the area and the depth of the burn.

Your veterinarian should be called on for all except very minor burns. The anesthetic and treatment he can administer may save your pet. Burns scab over and heal under the scabs if left alone, but sometimes infections grow under the scabs. Tannic acid promotes healthy healing.

If half of an animal's skin is destroyed by fire, steam, acid, or any agency of burning, it is kindest to put it permanently to sleep. Burned areas usually fail to grow hair, and the period of healing is protracted and painful. Even the duration of shock that usually follows severe burns is long. The owner of any animal that has been badly burned must always decide quickly, "Is it worth it?"

Convulsions. The various kinds of convulsions, their causes, and the means of preventing them are discussed in later chapters of this book. They should be read carefully. Here we are concerned only with the first aid the owner should be prepared to administer.

The handling of a convulsion depends upon where it happens and also upon its nature.

You can't stop the convulsion, but you can reduce the amount of damage the animal may do. It probably won't bite you unless you get in its way. If you can guide the cat into a room where it can't do serious damage, by all means do so and close the door.

Let your cat alone until it has recovered from the convulsion and then look for the cause. Prevention of future attacks is the best first aid. Your veterinarian will help you to locate the cause and provide treatment.

A cat should not be handled while it is having a convulsion. Some leap up in a corner, others run for the darkest spot they can find. Let your cat be, and wait for the convulsion to be well over before you touch it.

However, if the convulsion lasts more than fifteen minutes, then gather the cat in a heavy blanket, place it in a stout box, and rush to the veterinarian; convulsions from poisoning may last until death.

Bruises. It requires a hard, glancing blow to bruise a cat. Even those cats that have been skidded along on a road until the hair is scraped off and the skin left bloody seldom swell as do some other species. Probably the looseness of the skin over the cat's body is one of its prime protections. When uninfected swellings are found on a cat, the only treatment called for is cleansing. The bruise will soon subside without further treatment. Under extreme conditions ice packs might be indicated, but if such is the case, professional help should be requested.

Teeth Extractions. Dangling loose teeth are so simply extracted—sometimes with one's fingers—that veterinarians wonder why they find so many in pets' mouths. Some teeth need special instruments to remove them in pieces, but the incisors and premolars are sometimes so loose that they can be pulled with small tweezers or forceps, or with clean electrician's pliers. If you are uncertain about how firmly set the tooth really is, better let the veterinarian attend to it even though you may have to wait as much as a week for an appointment since it is not an emergency. If a tooth can't be moved by the fingertip, it is a job for the doctor.

FRACTURES AND DISLOCATIONS

The most common disorders of the bones are fractures—all of which can be observed easily by the layman. Dislocations, too, are frequent. The causes of both breaks and dislocations are so varied that it would be of little use to list them; they range from the kick of a horse to catching a toenail in a crack between boards.

Before discussing specific types, let us consider the general categories of fractures.

Three different kinds of break are most often found:

In a greenstick fracture the bone breaks but stays in its natural position. Usually one side is broken but the other only bent.

A simple fracture is one in which the skin has not been broken.

A compound fracture is one in which there is an opening connecting the site of fracture to the outside of the body. This opening may be due to a wound inflicted from without or to a hole punched outward by the end of the bone being driven through the surrounding tissue and skin.

In addition there are other descriptive classifications. There are complete fractures in which bones are broken clear across; comminuted fractures in which bones are splintered; linear fractures in which the break is lengthwise; neoplastic fractures where the bone breaks as a result of a growth in its substance; sprain fractures in which a tendon tears away a piece of bone to which it is attached, and numerous other variations.

Besides learning a little about the kinds of fractures, it will be helpful at this point to review that part of Chapter 2 concerned with how bones heal. You will then have a clearer understanding of how fractures should be treated and why.

The owner should know how to treat his cat for shock, discussed earlier, when it suffers broken bones. If a veterinarian is near, the owner is well advised to call him immediately. The animal should be kept warm until the doctor can give the necessary treatment and set the bone.

Dislocations must be "reduced," i.e., slipped back into place, and this, too, usually is best left to the veterinarian. Breaks of almost any bone can be set. Some, like broken jaws, may need wiring; some may require complicated plating, or joining by grafting. These matters require specialized study and are definitely outside the realm of this book. A veterinarian

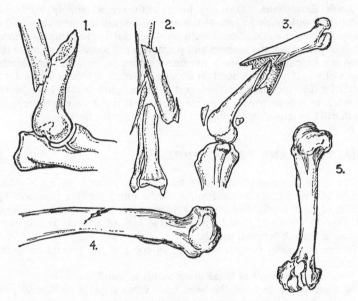

Common fractures. (1) Simple. (2) Compound, when some of the bones penetrate the skin. (3) Comminuted. (4) Greenstick. (5) Condylar.

will also decide what sort of splint to use (yucca, Stader, or Thomas) or whether a plaster cast (interspersed with cloth, with or without windows) or some other device is called for. If the fracture is compound, bone plates may be used. Even the cat's character must be considered. Some cats will chew almost any appliance off; others will co-operate as good patients should.

Every fracture case should be observed by your veterinarian once a week, so that he can check on the apposition, the healing, and the alignment, and remove the splint or cast at the right time. In growing kittens it is often safe to remove a splint three weeks after the break; in mature cats a month is the usual time.

Pelvic Fractures. Probably the greatest number of fractures are caused by automobile accidents, and, in my experience, pelvic fractures lead all other automobile-induced breaks in frequency. They are usually caused by the automobile tire running over the cat's hindquarters.

A fractured pelvis heals slowly, but much can be done to repair pelvic breaks and to hasten the natural process of reconstruction. Occasionally only one side is broken and the cat can continue to walk on three legs. More often the pelvis is fractured in such a way as to preclude walking until the usual numbness develops in the area. For several days after the fracture the animal may be unable to raise himself without help. Gradually he takes a few unstable steps and soon is waddling about. Don't expect him to run for at least a month after the fracture. Even after the healing is well started it may be necessary to help him up, carry him outside, and sometimes hold him in a position to defecate. Some animals learn why they are taken outside surprisingly soon, and, as quickly as they are placed in position, will void. Standing the animal up and putting pressure on the bladder from both sides usually causes urination, and it is not uncommon to have a cat so co-operative that just touching his sides is suggestion enough for him to urinate.

In order to examine the break, the veterinarian may lubricate a gloved index finger, place the anesthetized cat on its side, and insert the finger into the rectum. He may find that a bone edge has cut through the rectum, or he may be able to push a collapsed pelvis back into place by finger pressure and thereby relieve the cat considerably. He may also feel a break in the spine where the first tail vertebra joins the last sacral, which would account for a "dead" tail. Sometimes there is enough muscular strength left in such a tail to move it slightly. If it is set, it may retain its life; but more often the tail loses all its feeling and dries up. In this case your veterinarian will have to open the skin over the fracture and remove the useless appendage. If the cat can move its tail, it is conclusive evidence that the spinal cord is not severed.

Not all broken backs are hopeless. Many backs are set and wired so that the cats can live normally again. Palpation will usually determine where the tips of the vertebrae are out of line. Get your pet to the veterinarian as quickly as possible with as little jolting as you can. The spinal cord is a delicate structure. If the animal is to survive, the nerve damage must be held at a minimum.

A fractured pelvis may involve any of the six bones that comprise the pelvic girdle (three pairs of bones), and sometimes, as we have said, the spinal column. The bones of the pelvic girdle are the ilium, ischium, and pubis (two of each), plus the sacrum, that section of the spinal column consisting of five or six vertebrae ending where the tail vertebrae start. When the pelvis is fractured, any of the six pelvic bones may be broken or torn, or the injury may be to the backbone, the joints where the sacrum and the ilium join, one on each side, to make the sacroiliac joint, or the muscles and ligaments which hold this whole framework together. (See diagram of a cat's skeleton, page 18.)

Not infrequently fractures at the base of the tail result in nerves so damaged that the animal becomes incontinent of stool and/or urine, which means that it will not be able to control its bowel movements or urination. The excretory material will just come out at any time, even when the cat is not aware of it.

Fractured Femur. The examiner may find that nothing is wrong in the pelvis, that no bones feel as though they are broken, and yet the cat appears lopsided when viewed from behind. This may be an indication that the head of the femur—the thigh bone—is broken off. It may also mean that the hip is dislocated, a condition which we will discuss under dislocations.

In my experience, fracture of the femur is the second most common fracture. Such injuries are frequently surrounded by a pocket of blood because, as the cat trots home on three legs, the bone edges rub on the muscles and cut arterioles or venules—sometimes even a large artery or vein. An animal with such a fracture should be rushed to a veterinarian, who will have to anesthetize the patient to set the fracture. Anesthetics not only render the cat insensible but also relax the muscles and make the job easier for the doctor.

Many a well-set bone separates and slips so that it sets in a side-to-side position instead of end-to-end. If this should happen, the healing process will take longer and the broken leg will be shorter than normal. Even so, the cat may manage to get about with less of a limp than one would expect.

Fractures of the Toes and Tails. Dislocations occur in the toes and the tails of cats of all breeds. Kittens born with tails that bend backward actually have dislocated vertebrae, and bending the tail to straighten it usually results in breaking it or damaging it so severely that the end below the break dies and must be removed.

Toes broken at the joints usually are easily repaired by applying casts to the feet after reduction or setting. But when a ligament of the toes is cut or broken, it seldom regenerates and the nail bends upward. This is a familiar sight to veterinarians who see many steel-trap wounds. I have repaired feet where these little ligaments were cut on three of the four toes. Thereafter the cat may be unable to extend or retract her nails and her foot may appear dissimilar to the opposite foot. Sometimes repair of the tendons is possible to correct the problem.

Head Fractures and Concussions. Head fractures result from a variety of accidents—from being struck by a baseball to being hit by a truck. If the skull is cracked above the brain case, the cat may live, but generally so much brain damage occurs that the prognosis is unfavorable. If the skull over the brain case is not fractured, very often some other part of the skull is. A common spot is the bone covering the sinus in the forehead. The sinus itself may be penetrated and infection develops. Your veterinarian may have to remove infected pieces of bone, flush the sinus, and cover the opening with skin.

The arch of bone over the eye, which has a suture line (where two bones meet) through it, often breaks and presses inward, causing the eye to bulge. This necessitates pulling the arch back into shape, where it usually stays because the cat lets it alone after it learns that pressure against it occasions pain. The eye generally becomes inflamed and may even be damaged so that it has to be removed.

White Persian *Paul E. Robinson*

International News Photo

Short-Haired Black

Russian Blue *Casa Gatos Cattery*

Siamese *International News Photo*

Callavorn Cattery

Peke-Faced Red Tabby

Abyssinian *Chirn Sa-hai Cattery*

Dosing a cat is simple if you are quick. Tip her head back and straight upward. Have a pencil as well as the capsule or pill in your fingers.

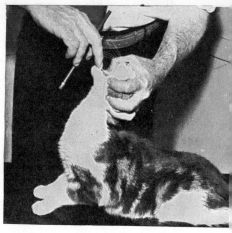

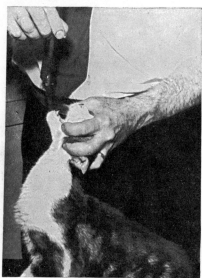

Drop capsule far back in her mouth. If she wiggles her tongue, it will slide over the back and she will swallow it if you close her mouth quickly.

If she doesn't swallow it, quickly push capsule down with pencil eraser and hold her mouth closed for a moment. In this way you won't be bitten.

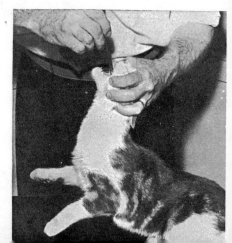

Restraining a cat can often be accomplished by merely grasping a large handful of skin on the back of the neck and lifting the animal.

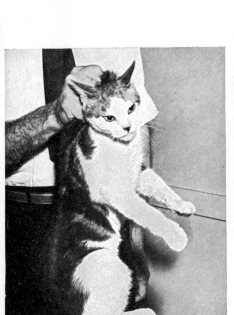

Another view. Even fierce cats may become subdued in this way. There is no pain. It's the way his mother carried him as a kitten.

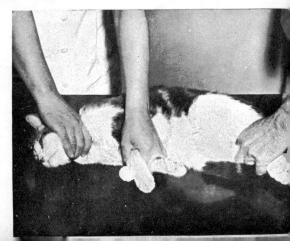

Two persons are needed to restrain some cats. Three hands hold, and one is free to examine or medicate.

Smoke Persian Kittens *Mrs. Bellows*

Manx *Marshall Clemeau*

Blue Persian *Purri-Isle Cattery*

Tortoise
Calico

Mollie Brennan

Black Persian *Hermscrest Cattery*

Burmese *Casa Gatos Cattery*

Persian *Azulita Cattery*

Jaw injuries are also common. Fractures in the center of the jawbone occur more frequently in my practice than fractures involving either of the bones (mandibles) that together make the jaw. The mandibles are joined by a cartilaginous attachment. When the fracture occurs here, it is obvious, because the jaw loses its firmness. If it is permitted to heal without attention, it often sets crookedly. The veterinarian may wire, pin, screw, or otherwise immobilize the bones to achieve a normal alignment. Frequently infection enters into these areas if the fracture is compound, in which case antibiotics are usually administered. Nursing is of primary importance. The saliva seems to prevent infection, so that no medication is required. The diet must be of a nature requiring no chewing—milk and mushy foods are indicated.

Hip Joint Dislocations. Cats' hip joints dislocate more often than any other joints. This ball-and-socket joint, like most others, is surrounded by a capsule. Ligaments and muscles, too, hold it in place. In spite of the fact that it is held very strongly in place, falls and blows such as those inflicted by automobiles somehow cause the ball to be forced out of the socket.

This dislocation may be such that the ball is above, below, or in front of the rim of the socket. Even the rim itself may be damaged so that it is extremely difficult to get the joint to stay together. Often the capsule, ligaments, and muscles that hold the joint together are so mutilated that the femur can be put back with ease, only to slip out again just as easily. It is often with great difficulty that this dislocation is corrected.

Shoulder Dislocations. These can be observed by comparing the feel of the two shoulders. Generally a quick forward pull while someone holds the cat firmly will snap a dislocated shoulder into place, with very little resulting pain. But a difficult dislocation should not be pulled more than once. There may be tissue between the two parts. If there is a fracture, a quick forward pull will sometimes sever vessels and can be a dangerous undertaking for the novice. Your veterinarian can locate the trouble quickly, and by anesthetizing the cat and then adjusting the leg, he will be able to replace it quite simply.

Wrist and Hock Dislocations. The many little bones that make up some joints are held together by ligaments that may be ruptured. The leg may hang sideways with skin and ligaments on one side torn away, and yet when it is straightened in a splint and held immobile, the joint heals and in time the animal will be able to walk as well as it did before the accident.

If an elbow is fractured, very often a frozen joint results, unless the fracture is reduced properly. This is one of the more difficult areas to treat.

Such injuries may require many weeks of careful nursing. Ligaments do regenerate and skin does grow across, but the spot will be void of hair. That is why the veterinarian tries to draw the skin as closely together as he can—and also because the skin makes the best and most natural covering.

POISONING

Pain, trembling, panting, vomiting, convulsions, coma, slimy mouths are all symptoms of poisoning. Any of these, except a caustically burned mouth, may also be a symptom of other maladies. But, if your cat should manifest any of these symptoms, you should investigate immediately to see if it has been poisoned.

Animals are very seldom deliberately poisoned. Usually they are poisoned either by chewing plants that have been sprayed, by gnawing at a piece of wood that has some paint pigment on it, by catching a ground mole that has been poisoned with cyanide, by consuming poison put out for other animals or insects, or by eating infected garbage. Since none of the poisons is easily traced, you ought to know the procedure to follow in case your pet may have been poisoned.

Call the veterinarian first, and if it is going to take any length of time to reach him, ask him if you should induce vomiting before you bring the animal in for treatment. If he says "yes," ask for instructions.

There are so many toxic materials in every household today, with all the new cleaning compounds, cosmetics, medications, paints, and so forth, that frequently the veterinarian will call the Poison Information Center (there is at least one in every state) to find out just how serious the toxic material is and find out the very latest information on treatment. The Poison Information Center will want to know the trade name of the product involved, the active ingredients that are listed on the container, and, if possible, the amount of toxic material ingested, as well as the weight and species of the animal. The Poison Information Centers of the United States have saved a great many animals from death by poison.

Plant Poisoning.   One of the reasons inside cats outlive those spending time outside is the lack of exposure to poisonous vegetation. True, the plant-poisoned cat is not common, and why a cat exposed to poisonous plants day after day, perhaps for years, suddenly decides to eat one is difficult to explain, but it does happen. Here is a partial list of dangerous outdoor plants, many of which are also found indoors.

English ivy	Yew	Bittersweet
Azalea	Privet	Holly
Lantana	Boxwood	Laurel
Delphenium	Andromeda	Rhododendron
Foxglove	Daphne	Hydrangea

Larkspur	Wisteria	Crown-of-thorns
Monkshood	Laburnum	Snow-on-the-mountain
Lily-of-the-valley	Lupine	Oleander
Choke cherry	Castor bean	Jerusalem cherry

These plants (as well as those listed below) may have either poisonous fruits, nuts, sap, blooms, roots, stems, or leaves. The accuracy of the lists is somewhat in doubt since one plant long listed as poisonous has recently been found to be nontoxic in animal studies. That plant is poinsettia. A partial list of common toxic house plants would include the following:

Philodendron	Mistletoe
Elephant ear	Daffodil
Dumb cane	Narcissus
Jerusalem cherry	Amaryllis
Lantana	English ivy

Of course the amount of the poisonous material ingested determines the severity of the reaction and since some plants contain small amounts they are not as dangerous as others.

Usually plant poisoning takes the form of a severe digestive upset (vomiting and/or diarrhea) accompanied by drooling and depression with loss of appetite. However, some poisons affect the nervous system, causing symptoms ranging from poor co-ordination when walking to sudden paralysis and death. Some cats convulse, although convulsions from all causes are rare in the feline.

Veterinary help should be sought promptly in cases of plant poisoning and of course the plant must be presented if possible for positive identification. Every phone book has listed in its white pages the number of a Poison Information Center, which is invaluable; but in some cases, an agricultural experiment station may be needed to identify the plant.

General Advice in Treating Poisoning.   Immediate action is essential, since some poisons are absorbed at once. If you have to take the cat to your veterinarian, get there with all possible haste.

Cats have a remarkable ability to determine when foods are contaminated with toxic materials and seldom ingest anything that is toxic. Of the specimens sent in to most toxicological laboratories with suspected poisoning, the actual verified cases are rare indeed.

Table VI—Household Antidotes for Common Poisons

POISON	ANTIDOTE
Acids (Hydrochloric; nitric; acetic)	Bicarbonate of soda; powdered eggshells

POISON	ANTIDOTE
Alkalies (Sink cleansers; cleaning agent)	Vinegar or lemon juice (several table-spoonsful)
Arsenic (Lead arsenate; calcium arsenate; white arsenic; Paris green)	Epsom salts (1 teaspoonful in water)
Hydrocyanic Acid (Wild cherry; laurel leaves)	Glucose (2 tablespoonsful dextrose or corn syrup)
Lead (Lead arsenic; paint pigments)	Epsom salts (1 teaspoonful in water)
Phosphorus (Rat poison)	Peroxide of hydrogen. (Peroxide and water in equal parts, 1 oz. to each 10 pounds of weight of animal)
Mercury (Bichloride of mercury)	Raw eggs and milk
Theobromine (Cooking chocolate)	Pentobarbital, phenobarbital
Thallium (Bug poisons)	Table salt (1 teaspoonful in water)
Food Poisoning (Bacteria from garbage or decomposed food)	Peroxide of hydrogen. Give water enema after stomach has emptied
Strychnine (Strychnine sulfate in rodent and animal poisons)	Sedatives such as phenobarbital, Nembutal (1 grain to 7 pounds of cat)
Sedatives (Overdoses in medicating)	Strong coffee (2 tablespoonsful)
Insecticides (Flea and tick powders or sprays; bug poisons)	Peroxide of hydrogen and enema. No antidote known

9. Drugs, Medications, and Their Uses

THERE IS an old adage in medicine which suggests that 50 per cent of everything we believe today will be proven false in twenty years. This adage may be accurate if we consider all aspects of medicine, but ten years would be closer to reality in the case of drugs. I am reminded of the old-timer who was asked if times had changed much during his lifetime. He replied, "Not much, we didn't have trolley cars when I was young and we don't have them now."

I used to keep gallon jugs in my office, each labeled, "That's where the money goes." In them I would toss dated and superseded pills, tablets, and capsules. It takes a surprisingly short time to fill one of those jugs. This doesn't mean that a gallon of pills and capsules are all bad; although some are still efficacious, many are not as effective as newer products.

In prescribing medications to cats one should have the pharmacological knowledge necessary to know which drugs are safe and efficacious when used in conjunction with other drugs. When two antibiotics are given they must not conflict with one another. There has been a great deal of research on combination incompatability in man but little in cats. When more than two drugs are given little is known as to side effects. It has been a trial and error proposition in both man and cats.

When the rat poison warfarin is fed to rats that have been fed DDT it requires four or five times the dose to kill them than when DDT is not involved. We know a cat fed dairy products will not benefit from the widely used antibiotic tetracycline.

I have no objection to home medication if an owner telephones and tells me what he plans to do so that I can at least warn of any unfavorable results. We know that a shameful number of people are admitted to hospitals to correct iatrogenic (medication-caused) problems. Many pet owners, unfortunately, seem to forget that animals are not immune to such problems.

Today we are able to treat many diseases with confidence. We have developed new uses and better methods of administering many of the older drugs. The discovery of the sulfas, antibiotics, and anti-inflammatory drugs has made it possible to cope with many of the most devastating diseases. We have developed new insect destroyers of great potency and seem to be on the verge of perfecting others in the near future. Equipped with a vastly improved arsenal of drugs and aided by an enormously expanded knowledge of the actions of those drugs, veterinary medicine has made astonishing progress even in the last decade.

The value of these lifesaving drugs is too often taken for granted by the cat owner. All of them are actually of the greatest importance to him, for in a very real sense it is they that have made it possible for him to own pets and keep them healthy and vigorous. If the owner is to take full advantage of this new science of health, he must know some of the fundamental facts about drugs and their actions so that he can use them more intelligently and more effectively. Obviously there is no need for him to understand the pharmaceutical intricacies of the various medicinal preparations, but he should certainly know the characteristics of the several general types of drugs and be familiar with their common uses.

The medical professions have changed so much that doctors (at least most of them) are now ready, willing, and able to explain the nature and action of their prescriptions, as well as any possible undesirable side effects. Most doctors have come to realize that your understanding of what is being given and why will make for more intelligent home care. And there is no reason why you should not be able to understand what your veterinarian tells you and what he has prescribed, especially since prescription writing is undergoing a small revolution. Latin names of drugs have been dropped and the metric system is being used instead of the old avoirdupois system with its minims, drams, scruples, etc. The U. S. Federal Food and Drug Administration insists that the simplest names or the exact chemical names be used on labels.

In order to understand the uses of drugs, you must first understand that drugs work in several different ways. Some drugs do not kill germs outside of the body as well as they do in the bloodstream; working in combination with the bacteria-destroying white cells in the blood, they are highly efficient. Without the white cells the drugs are of little value, and the cells without the drugs are helpless. This might be called a synergistic action. Phenols (such as creosol, thymol, tars) and mercurial salts, such as bichloride, kill by causing the protoplasm of the cells to precipitate. Other drugs, such as arsenic, prevent the multiplication of bacteria. Still others combine chemically with some constituent of the protoplasm of the organism. Some have oxidizing properties and some interfere with the functioning within the bacteria themselves. There are drugs that are incompatible with certain species; for example, phenol for cats. Still others produce odd side effects; for instance, an excessive dose of morphine when given to a cat causes convulsions and death.

The success of all drugs depends on their being used in proper concentration. They must be strong enough to kill or inhibit bacterial growth, yet weak enough to cause no harm to the tissues of the animal. The required strengths for the various drugs have been worked out by long study and testing, and your veterinarian's instructions should be followed explicitly. When he gives you pills or tablets with instructions to give them at certain intervals, he is usually calculating how fast the drug is eliminated, in order to be sure that your pet always has enough in his system to accomplish results. If you cannot give the prescribed doses at the prescribed intervals, it is better to leave the cat with the veterinarian, where the drugs will be given as they should be.

Which brings us to the question of body repair. Always remember that the body of a pet is composed of many delicate organs. Its potential length of life is more or less determined at conception. With good care and nonexposure to some diseases against which it may not be resistant, the pet should live its normal life span. But when it becomes sick there is no certainty that, with the jab of a needle and a dose of medicine, it will recover. Life isn't like that. Recovery takes care—and time. Think how long it takes for a cut on one's hand to heal. Cells slowly grow together, scar tissue forms and shrinks, and several weeks may pass before the area looks normal. Yet, too often, we expect pets to recover in a day or two from diseases more telling and debilitating than influenza is to humans. Drugs can and do have marvelous properties but they can't abolish the element of time.

Great care must be taken not to overdose, a common tendency on the part of laymen. If a teaspoonful cures, then three teaspoonful should cure in a third the time, he often reasons. Sometimes it kills. Doses have been worked out by pharmacologists with great care. The animal's size and the effect desired determine the dose. Overdoses are wasteful even when not dangerous. One most interesting fact is that the larger the animal, the less drug is needed proportionately. Doses are proportional to surface area rather than to weight, but weight is easier to measure. Whereas one might think that a smaller animal was tenderer and should have less than his proportional weight might indicate, the opposite is true.

ANESTHETICS, SEDATIVES, AND TRANQUILIZERS

General Anesthetics. A small revolution in general anesthetics has resulted in injectable and inhalable anesthetics that are safe and effective for cats of all ages. Of course their proper administration is a critical factor. If a tom has retained urine for an extended period he may be toxic and require a small fraction of the amount of injectable anesthetic necessary for a nontoxic tom. The same holds true for an animal in shock. When such anesthetics are given by the average veterinarian there is little risk to the animal.

I remember a twenty-three-year-old cat presented to me with a fist-sized growth on its side. The old-timer had been practically a basket case for two years. The owner asked me to try to remove the lesion even if the cat died. Since euthanasia was refused I agreed to try. I fully expected the cat to die while I administered the anesthesia and again while I performed the surgery, but it wasn't to be. The surgery went well and the patient recovered from the anesthesia more rapidly than many yearlings; healing was progressing splendidly in a week's time.

Many anesthetics are injected; others are given by inhalation. Each patient is carefully evaluated and from experience the method of choice is selected and the dose is carefully calculated.

How about the poor frightened cat who will bite and scratch if touched? These are often wrapped in a heavy blanket and eased into a container very much like a fish tank. One of several gases is introduced and the patient slowly relaxes. At the proper stage of drowsiness he is removed and either a mask is placed over his face or a tube is placed down his trachea and the gas administered through it.

Local Anesthetics. I find less and less use for local anesthetics since the general anesthetics are so safe. When a "local" is used even for the most minor surgery the cat is still aware that something is happening and we find ourselves with a moving target. We do use local anesthetics in eye problems and some to relieve superficial discomfort by external application.

Sedatives and Tranquilizers. Many veterinarians use an old and trusted sedative more than all others combined and that is phenobarbital. Given in both tablet and liquid form, it is one of the longest-acting of the barbiturate class of drugs.

Barbiturates, of which phenobarbital is a good example, have the following general actions:

Depressant. The size of the dose determines the degree of depression.

Sedative. Results are quickly accomplished, usually within an hour.

Analgesic. Barbiturates relieve signs of pain without causing unconsciousness.

Anticonvulsant. Occasionally near-anesthetic doses must be given to animals convulsing severely. Phenobarbital is effective even against the convulsions of strychnine poisoning, but for this purpose, other injectable barbiturates are preferable.

Anesthetic. Phenobarbital is seldom used for this purpose. When overdoses are given, the blood pressure falls and breathing becomes slowed.

If your veterinarian is planning to use a barbiturate for an anesthetic, there are several things he should be told about your cat, if you know them. If your pet has had an increased thirst, it may suggest kidney disease. Animals with kidney diseases require much smaller amounts of barbiturates given by any route of administration, since they are partially poisoned by the wastes in their systems. Liver disease and general debility also make a pet a poor subject for barbiturate anesthesia.

Animals terrified by thunderstorms, explosions from fireworks or blasting, or auto riding can be given small doses of pentobarbital with safety for partial sedation and to produce a temporary loss of fear and memory.

It may not be an important distinction but sedatives and tranquilizers are two separate classes of drugs. The effects of tranquilizers in cats must be carefully appraised to find the proper drug and dose. One tablet of a given tranquilizer may be ideal for one cat but another may require two or three tablets for the same results. Another individual may react so unpredictably that the same tranquilizer cannot be used. It is interesting that the first tranquilizer was discovered by a veterinarian.

Ethyl Alcohol. Clients are forever telephoning their veterinarians to say that they have just given their cats a dose of brandy or whiskey as a stimulant. Somewhere the layman has picked up the idea that alcohol is a great animal saver. Actually it has so few warranted uses in veterinary medicine that it need be mentioned only to emphasize the fact that it is actually a depressant, rather than the excellent stimulant that most people believe it to be. It stimulates neither the respiration, the heart and blood system, nor the muscles.

Alcohol irritates the skin, injures the cells, has an astringent action, and shrinks tissues; it causes irritation and inflammation to mucous membranes. When injected into tissue, it acts as an anesthetic, but may permanently destroy nerve tissue. Alcohol anesthesia, if given in large enough doses to anesthetize, is too near the fatal dose for safety.

Alcohol has very little germ-killing power, and only at 70 per cent by weight—a percentage difficult to approximate—is it worth using for this purpose.

Never give alcohol to "warm" a pet. All it does is lower the temperature by bringing the blood to the stomach and producing a false sensation of warmth. Nor should it be given as an aphrodisiac. I have known clients to use it in an effort to get shy breeding males to attempt copulation. They have found it often makes them worse.

Topical Anesthetics. Several drugs are also used to deaden pain simply by allowing them to soak through tissues. In addition to butyn, procaine, quinine, and benzyl alcohol are often used as topicals. Such anesthetics stop itching when they are incorporated in salve applied by being rubbed in, and relieve pain when they are ingredients of ointments used in cuts, sores, anal ills, or ear canker.

In using these drugs it is essential to keep them in contact with the tissue. If the cat persists in licking or rubbing them off, they must be replaced. Let me stress here an important warning: Phenol must not be applied to cats, *ever*.

Benzyl alcohol is a useful local anesthetic for surface application. It will dissolve in water one part to twenty-five. Its pain-quieting power is of short duration. When first applied there is a stinging sensation, followed by numbness. It is used in ointments to quiet skin irritation, in ear remedies to reduce the itching, and in salves applied to cuts or sores. Four per cent solutions are strong enough. It must not be used full strength.

PAINKILLERS

Acetylsalicylic Acid (Aspirin). "Doctor, how about an aspirin for my cat?" How many times I have heard these words over the telephone! The client sometimes goes on to tell me that she has already given Fifi three and the little thing seems to have a pain. Fifi is a six-pound Siamese.

A difference of opinion exists in the use of aspirin and related drugs in cats. There is no doubt that overdosing aspirin has killed many cherished animals. It seems to me that doses low enough to be safe in all cats are too low to be effective; so I don't recommend its use. Moreover aspirin is a cumulative agent in cats, so small doses over a period of time will eventually build to a toxic level.

The derivatives of salicylic acid, an ancient remedy obtained from the willow tree and synthesized from coal tar, are numerous, but only acetylsalicylic acid (aspirin) is of much interest to pet owners. The salicylates act to reduce fever slightly. No effect on heat production is noticed, but the heat loss is heightened by bringing the blood to the body surface where, in short-haired animals, it tends to dissipate. The dose should never be more than a grain for a seven-pound cat.

We can judge the effect of aspirin as a painkiller only by questioning human subjects. Students assure us it does not relieve sore throat, or toothache, or pain in the intestines. It does afford relief from neuralgia, rheumatic and headache pains. In some cat diseases with which we assume headaches are present, aspirin may be effective. Salicylates do not exert germ-killing power in the blood, so should not be given to cure disease.

You may have had any one of many painkillers prescribed for you—acetanilid, acetophenetidin, aminopyrene, or antipyrene. Don't use them on the cat. Veterinarians now have a large number of useful, efficient drugs to prescribe.

STIMULANTS

Caffeine. Besides having a slight stimulating effect on the peristalsis in the intestine, caffeine is useful because it (1) stimulates the general circulation by accelerating the heart, increasing its force, and raising the blood pressure. It affects the heart muscle directly. Overdoses cause such rapid heartbeat that blood pressure drops. (2) It increases the rapidity and depth of respiration. (3) It stimulates the nervous system. (4) It increases muscular strength and power. (5) It stimulates the production of urine by heightening the activity of the kidneys without irritating them. Thus it is a diuretic.

If an old cat can be taught to take coffee, it may be a lifesaver. Sugar and cream with it are not harmful. Very little coffee is required as a good-sized dose for a cat. The error most people make is in giving their pets too much. A Persian weighing fifteen pounds needs only one-quarter to one-third cup, while half that amount is enough for a small cat as the maximum dose. Yet an owner will often mistakenly give one cup to a cat if the cat is hungry for it. (One teaspoonful of instant coffee makes one cup.)

As a stimulant to counteract a narcotic or barbiturate poisoning, fairly large amounts of coffee should be given, but great care is necessary to prevent some from running into the lungs of the anesthetized animals. It is safer to give it via a stomach tube, or to let your veterinarian handle the problem. If coffee is not handy, strong tea is an excellent substitute. A cup of tea contains almost as much caffeine as a cup of coffee. Cocoa contains theobromine, whose action is similar to that of caffeine.

DIURETICS

Agents that increase the flow of urine are called diuretics. Several drugs incidentally increase urine flow, although they are used primarily for some other purpose. In addition to these, certain drugs, such as salines, by increasing thirst, cause the blood to absorb a surplus of water which later escapes through the kidneys.

Diuretics are occasionally useful to flush some circulatory toxin from the blood or to pull fluid from the abdomen and relieve pressure on the heart and lungs without resorting to tapping. Sometimes when cats have bladder infections, copious urine formation and elimination helps wash that reservoir clean. There are also times when abundant urine helps prevent formation of urine crystals and flushes out those that have formed.

Water. The basis of diuresis is water. Reducing the percentage of it in the blood is one thing that is striven for. This in turn creates thirst; more water is consumed, more eliminated. So your veterinarian may inject water with added salt to make a "physiological solution." Or he can inject a small amount of common salt in solution, or even give it orally so that the pet will drink copiously.

Urea, in its pure chemical form, is coming into greater and greater use. It is not necessary to administer it as an injection, and it may be given mixed with fluids such as meat broths. It is not advisable to give it to an animal with kidney disease. Your veterinarian will suggest the proper dose, if any is needed.

Sugar. Either glucose or cane sugar, or both, may be given, but in such large amounts that the pet can't utilize it all. It must be given intravenously, and when so given, especially in poison cases, helps detoxify some poisons. A 50 per cent solution is generally used. Cane sugar is used intravenously in double the dose of glucose and in some ways is preferable.

There are also proprietary drugs and mixtures which your veterinarian may favor. Probably the most effective diuretic is one called furosemide (Lasix), very well known to millions of human beings affected with fluid in their tissues.

HEART STIMULANTS

Digitalis.   Of the drugs whose action is specifically on the heart, digitalis stands first. The dried leaves of the lovely garden flower foxglove are the source of this remarkable drug. Several other plants produce the so-called digitalis principles: squill, a sea onion; strophanthus, a tree whose seeds are used; and even the bulb of the lily-of-the-valley.

Digitalis directly affects the muscle of the heart, whose force of contraction it greatly increases. The rate is also slowed. It is useful in many disturbances that result from heart failure—and heart weakness is heart failure. Dropsy and edema of the tissues may be due to heart, liver, or kidney failure. Digitalis gives relief in some cases. It is not, however, the universal remedy some people think. Digitalis is not a useful stimulant when a quick one is needed, because it takes too long to establish the desired effects. It is almost useless in some forms of heart trouble, in pneumonia, and in shock. The dose is such a tricky matter that it should be left to your veterinarian.

Epinephrine (Adrenalin).   When your veterinarian injects a small dose of epinephrine into your cat, to treat him for shock after an accident or severe intestinal bleeding, he does so because of certain lifesaving properties which the drug, produced by the adrenal glands, has demonstrated. Of its many effects, one of the most useful is that it contracts the capillaries and arterioles and encourages a firm clot on the injured tissue or organ. Some increase in blood pressure may occur to help the animal recover from shock; the drug also makes breathing easier, thus promoting oxygen absorption. The effects of epinephrine are of short duration—only a matter of minutes—but those minutes usually are all that are required to save the pet's life. This wonderful drug can be relied upon to produce all these effects.

Mixed with procaine and used as a local anesthetic in surgery, epinephrine helps prevent capillary bleeding. In cases of heart failure or stoppage, adrenalin, injected directly into the heart, may sometimes cause it to beat again. It also brings relief to victims of acute bronchial asthma. The dose is very small. Your veterinarian usually uses a 1:1000 solution and injects fractions of a cubic centimeter.

Rare though it is, a condition called anaphylactic shock may occur after an injection in the veterinarian's office. In such instances, adrenalin may save the cat's life.

Ephedrine. Another stimulant, this one of plant origin, has similar properties to epinephrine. Unlike epinephrine, however, it has the advantage of being absorbed from the digestive tract; it need not be injected unless quick action is required. Moreover, it has much longer effects. Practically everything said regarding epinephrine applies to ephedrine, except that it is sometimes harmful when used in shock treatment. It is very effective as a treatment for emphysema in old, wheezy animals. Animals that cough constantly, apparently trying to raise fluid from the lungs, are often benefited by a little ephedrine. A mixture with atropine sometimes works wonders.

Your veterinarian will advise you on its use and dosage, but it must be remembered that one tenth of the smallest human dose obtainable from drugstores is enough for large cats and should be divided to make the proper amount for smaller pets.

SECRETORY GLAND DEPRESSANTS

Belladonna is seldom used by companion-animal practitioners, but one of its derivatives, atropine, finds many uses. Atropine does almost everything that the parent product will do. It and similar drugs are given principally to cause dilation of the pupils, in eye examinations, to dry secretions, because they inhibit glandular secretions with remarkable efficacy, to aid in preventing car sickness, and to counteract overdoses of some drugs.

If a cat has been eating plants in a garden containing deadly nightshade (a rich source of belladonna), and you see it bumping into objects, trying to get into a dark spot; if you open its mouth and find it dry; if its temperature is high, heart very rapid, pulse weak, and gait abnormal; if it is restless and excited—call your veterinarian. He can flush out the offending herbage, inject medications repeatedly until the pet's mouth shows moisture, and thus save its life.

DRUGS TO KILL INTERNAL PARASITES

The drugs used to eradicate the worms that infest cats (the helminths) are called anthelmintics. Some of these parasites are flat worms (platyhelminths) and some are round (nemathelminths). The class of parasite-killing drugs is of vital importance to us all, since the most prevalent group of diseases to which pets succumb is caused by worms and external parasite infestation, with the consequent symptoms. The life histories of all of the common parasites will be considered in a later chapter. Here we will discuss only the drugs used in their elimination.

The evolution of drugs administered to cats is nowhere more evident than in those used for deworming. Most are prescription drugs.

Piperazine is the drug of choice for elimination of roundworms. It can be had as piperazine chloride, adepate, or hydroxide and other forms, all of which seem equally effective. Piperazine was discovered in Europe as a safe remedy for human pinworms. The dose for cats is 50 milligrams per pound of the cat's weight and is available in 250 and 500 milligram tablets or capsules which can be mixed with the food. No starving is necessary and its salty taste is not repugnant to cats. I suggest it be administered daily for 3 days. It is not a prescription drug.

Hookworms are seldom a serious problem in cats. If the cat appears "run-down," a veterinarian will usually discover eggs in the cat's stool. He can supply you with the newest drugs or he can inject the cat with preparations which will eliminate the hookworms with almost no inconvenience to you or the cat.

Medication for tapeworms and the rare case of whipworms should be obtained from your veterinarian along with detailed instructions for its use. Perhaps his hospital should be the place for its administration so that your pet can remain under observation.

DRUGS TO KILL EXTERNAL PARASITES

Rotenone. This drug (and related resins), obtained from the roots of tropical plants, notably derris in the East Indies and cube in South and Central America, is one of the most potent insect killers known. It kills animals by paralyzing their respiratory tracts, though pets can eat it in small amounts usually with no ill effects. It is more poisonous if inhaled, and is especially so if it gets into fresh open cuts.

Rotenone also kills fish. If you use it, don't allow rotenone to blow onto the water in a fishpond. And don't dust your cat close to the home aquarium.

Probably rotenone in dusts, diluted to 1 per cent, is as safe for flea and louse powders as anything one could ask. While other powders are dangerous to cats, which lick themselves, rotenone is not. No cat should be put in a closed box and dusted, since it is then forced to breathe the dust. It is hard to believe that pets could be so mistreated, but they often are— by people who want to keep the powder off their clothes.

Incidentally, with some people—not all—rotenone causes numbness of the lips and tongue tip. The sensation soon passes. If you are sensitive, dust the pet in the open where the breeze blows the dust away from you.

Rotenone is an ingredient of some of our best dips and rinses. A 1 per cent solution in pine oil to which an emulsifier has been added kills all feline insects except ticks.

Pyrethrum. Chrysanthemums contribute pyrethrum to our store of drugs. In pure form, the chemical agents made from it are called pyrethrins. They are mentioned here because they are so often ingredients of flea powder, but the fact that they are included here is not an endorsement, since they merely stun the insects. The early powders were sold with the advice that you dust the animal, brush the fleas and lice onto a newspaper, and burn the paper. You burned it because the insects usually refused to "stay dead" and manufacturers knew it.

Pyrethrum has a wonderful psychological effect on the cat's owner. When it is used as an ingredient of a powder or rinse, the insects appear to die instantly. They drop off, and that is what the owners love to see. Mix in some rotenone and the bugs not only drop off but they stay dead! The combination of the two drugs makes a fine treatment for the owner as well as for the pet.

A host of insecticides have come and gone in the past fifteen years. Many were efficient and safe when used as directed but they had their drawbacks. The greatest of which was the pollution of the environment. Some would kill for twenty years and one, DDT, all but caused the demise of several of our native birds.

Most of the more dangerous ones fortunately are not available for use on cats and have restrictive use in any capacity. One, Chlordane, is available to kill ticks, fleas, and lice but, being a poison, it must be used with discretion. It is also used in the treatment of mites.

DRUGS APPLIED TO THE SKIN

Possibly because vanishing and other creams are thought by many to be essential aids to beautify the human skin, many pet owners have come to the mistaken conclusion that there must be similar lotions for animals' skins. Some think there are miracle drugs or vitamins that may be given to make an animal's skin and coat shine and its eyes sparkle. There are no such lotions, nor does a healthy animal need any.

What we are going to consider here are vehicles, skin remedies, drugs used in burn treatments, antiseptics for cuts and scratches, and liniments.

Vehicles for Drugs Applied to the Skin. Wool fat, also called lanolin, forms an excellent vehicle because it holds most drugs and, when it is absorbed into the skin, carries the drugs with it. It is adherent, sticking even to moist surfaces. Wool fat of the ordinary variety contains about 25 per cent water. It can also be obtained in an anhydrous form (without water).

Petrolatum is available as a liquid (mineral oil), or as a jelly (Vaseline). When used as a vehicle, it is not absorbed, and drugs used with it remain more or less outside the skin. Depending upon whether a liquid or solid nonabsorbable preparation is desired, one or the other form is used.

Propylene glycol is used in many remedies. It is a solvent and dissolves wax, hence finds its use in ear remedies. It resembles glycerine in consistency and is soluble in water.

Vegetable oils: Cottonseed, soybean, and other edible vegetable oils make vehicles for drugs to treat skin diseases.

Skin Disease Remedies. Almost every veterinarian has his favorite remedy for skin diseases. Some smell so unpleasant that the cure is almost worse than the disease. Some require such frequent application that treatment becomes a great bore. Some irritate. It is unfortunate that one general remedy for all such diseases is not available, but since some of these diseases are caused by mites, which require special drugs, others by fungi, and probably still others by bacteria and viruses—not to mention occasional cases resulting from some allergy—no one remedy can be suggested. Here are some of the common effective drugs and chemicals used today:

Sulfur. This is one of the oldest and still one of the most reliable of skin remedies. Sulfur should not be used alone—as such it is useless. But when oxygen in the air combines with sulfur it forms sulfur dioxide, a gas deadly to some fungus diseases and to some insects. It is this constant gas formation that cures. Sulfur, to be of value, must therefore be kept in position by some base that holds it in place and yet does not cover it to such an extent that air cannot reach it. The old lard-and-sulfur or axle-grease-and-sulfur treatments had some virtues, but they cured very slowly because the grease coated the sulfur particles.

The fineness of the sulfur particles, too, makes a great difference. Coarse sulfur crystals are not as effective as sulfur that is close to the colloidal state. Colloidal materials are so fine they will stay in suspension as if they were in solution and never settle out. It is possible to obtain colloidal sulfur, but it is expensive and its results are not sufficiently greater than those obtained by the finest air-floated, mechanically ground product to warrant the additional cost.

Sulfur mixed with vegetable oils produces better results than that mixed with heavy greases, but other drugs can be added which help materially, as we shall see.

Recently a dermatologist told me if he had his choice of only one material to use for dermatological problems in people it would have to be sulfur.

Calamine Lotion. Some mild forms of skin disease are cured by this white liquid, which needs shaking each time before application. Calamine itself is a 98 per cent zinc oxide preparation with a little iron rust mixed in it. Calamine lotion contains 8 per cent calamine. It is effective in certain cases where only the surface layers of the skin are attacked. The ear is part of the skin, and rather good results have been obtained by pouring calamine lotion into the ear canal and allowing as much of it as possible to stay in after the pet has shaken its head.

The family medicine chest contains a number of preparations that tempt an uninformed owner to apply them to his cat. Calamine lotion, zinc oxide ointment, and boric acid to name a few are all toxic to cats when ingested. If applied to areas that a cat can reach with its tongue or with its front feet, which the cat can then lick, these and many other drugs are dangerous. Telephone your veterinarian for advice before using such home remedies. He may agree to the use of a toxic substance if an Elizabethan collar is applied (see Chapter 10).

Boric Acid. The medical profession has prescribed boric acid for so many years for so many millions of people that the first thing the layman thinks of to cure almost anything is boric acid or boracic acid (different names for the same substance). In skin disease its value is questionable. It does not kill germs, but does retard their growth.

Salicylic Acid. One of the reasons salicylic acid is useful in skin remedies is that it destroys the outer layers of skin but does not destroy the growing layers. Corn removers, most of which contain salicylic acid and collodium, are examples of this drug. When applied, the skin swells, becomes soft, and the outer layers slough off. Like boric acid, it slows the growth of bacteria but does not kill them. Salicylic acid seldom makes up more than 10 per cent of any solution or ointment.

Tannic Acid. This is an astringent—an agent which causes shrinking and stops discharges. Considerable difference of opinion exists among veterinarians as to whether it is preferable to apply an astringent, and dry up an area affected with dermatitis, or to inflame it with some substance and, with the aid of the inflammation, cure it with other drugs.

In a 5 or 10 per cent solution, tannic acid is effective over raw areas such as those eroded by disease organisms or sore from constant scratching, since it causes a film of protective protein to form. But there is a question whether, except in the case of burns, this is always desirable. Cats may bite and scratch the film off as fast as it forms.

Burn Remedies. When a cat is burned either by fire, scalding, or corrosion, by acids, caustics, or other chemicals, the capillaries of the skin become dilated in all the burned area. You will remember that any skin burn seeps a moist substance. This seepage goes on and on until, in cases of large burned areas, so much plasma escapes that the animal's blood-volume loss becomes extremely serious. That is point one to remember. The second point is that all of this area affords an excellent growing medium for bacteria, whose toxic by-products may cause death to the burn victim. The third is that supportive treatment for the animal is essential because one often finds a temporary improvement followed by prostration, due to shock.

Tannic acid is the first thought of many doctors when confronted with a burn victim. When a fresh 10 per cent solution is used, a thick scab forms over the burn and to a large extent prevents the loss of plasma, although under the scab the tissue may remain moist.

To prevent growth of bacteria, most veterinarians use antibiotics. Some favor salves containing combinations of drugs, but spreading salves over painful burned areas adds to the pain. In first aid, however, it's a case of any port in a storm, and salves may be the only available remedy.

After the burn itself has been treated, supportive treatment is often necessary. If the pet seems to be in shock, an infusion with saline solution and glucose can save its life. Clients often want their veterinarians to give sedatives in such cases, thinking it is the pain that causes the shock. If sedatives are administered, the dose must be small or the drug may cause death.

Drugs for Cuts and Scratches. Does it sound unprofessional to say that any ordinary cut, scratch, or scraped area that the pet can reach to lick is better left untreated? If the injury is so small or unimportant that it does not need suturing, it does not need medication—if Dr. Cat can reach it. The scales on our pets' tongues can clean a wound beautifully, and clean wounds heal well. There are, however, many wounds in places our pets cannot reach, such as those on the head, neck, and shoulders, abscess formations under the skin, and wounds under long hair. There are also many cats that will not lick cuts, wounds, or surgical incisions as dogs do, and such cats will have their abrasions, too. Many of these wounds may be cared for by the owner. The variety of drugs available for treatment is wide, and the list is growing. Here we need discuss only the most important ones.

Disinfectants, germicides, antiseptics, bacteriostatics, fungicides, bactericides all play a part in treating minor cuts and scratches. Disinfectants overcome infections by destroying bacteria, fungus organisms, viruses— all kinds of infective organisms. Antiseptics inhibit the growth of bacteria or other infecting agents, but do not necessarily kill them. Germicides and bactericides are agents that kill germs. Contrary to what you may have thought, there are not very many that will kill germs and not injure tissues as well. Bacteriostatics arrest the growth of bacteria. A viricide is an agent that kills viruses. Fungicides are agents that destroy fungi.

As medications become more specific we find a greater variety available. The problem we face with new preparations is twofold: (1) they are available only on prescription, and (2) the selection of the best medication or the problem at hand is complicated at best. John Q. Public, as well as all branches of the medical profession, is constantly bombarded with literature claiming that the latest medication is the best. "It ain't necessarily so." Some of the older medications are often every bit as good as the newer models, which usually cost five times as much. But there is less profit in the older medications and so little motive to advertise them.

Normally, I resist using brand names, but since it is effective for the prevention of superficial infections and may be purchased without a prescription, Bacitracin ointment is helpful. Dozens of helpful medications containing antibiotics are available on prescription only.

Tincture of Iodine.   One of the mainstays of veterinarians a few years ago (and commonly used in the average household as well), tincture of iodine still has its uses. It destroys all bacteria and many fungi and viruses, regardless of their race, creed, or color. Since a number of applications to the same area may result in burning, it is better to use the tincture diluted by an equal amount of water when several treatments are indicated. Iodine discolors, and animal hair, once discolored with it, may retain the stain for months. This, plus the fact that the treated area burns and smarts when it is applied, makes its use of limited value for pets.

Hydrogen Peroxide.   When you apply this product to raw tissue there is a fizzing, and a white foam appears. This means that the peroxide is decomposing into water and oxygen. And only while this decomposition is progressing is the treated area being disinfected. But this fizzing helps wonderfully at times to loosen debris in wounds. As a germ killer, it is less efficient than many others, and is best employed to cleanse wounds and to flush out the sheaths of male cats when they become infected. The drugstore strength is 3 per cent, which has been found best for all such tasks.

THE ANTIBIOTICS

When researchers learned that some bacteria and molds give off substances toxic to other bacteria, a new branch of bacteriology was born. When further research demonstrated that these substances would kill bacteria and not poison animals, a lifesaving blessing of inestimable value was bestowed upon both us and our pets. And we are told that wonderful as penicillin and the other antibiotics of the "first generation" were, they were but heralds of far more wonderful drugs to come. Several, still in the experimental stages, have a specificity for certain types of bacteria.

Most of the antibiotics are prescription drugs. At first they were given in quickly absorbed doses, mostly intramuscularly and at very frequent intervals. Later a way was found of combining them in vehicles from which they are slowly absorbed, so that daily injections now suffice to furnish a high enough concentration in the blood to control effectively the germs against which they are being used.

The list of useful antibiotics for cats grows larger and more costly with each passing year. But there is good reason for developing so many of these microbe-killing agents. When exposed to an antibiotic, pathogenic bacteria may be completely destroyed or inhibited so that the cat's immune system can destroy them. In any event, the "survival of the fittest" mechanism eventually rears its head and a few microbes survive the unfavorable environment created by the antibiotic and eventually thrive in it. Another, more potent, antibiotic must be used to suppress the new strain of microbe, until it too ceases to be effective. Of course, it may take years for this evolution to take place, but many scientists believe that one day we will run out of effective antibiotics and have to find a better way to control disease.

When your pet develops a bacterial infection the ideal approach to a cure is to grow the offending microbes in containers of food for the bacteria, and to add small disks of antibiotic. If the bacteria cannot grow around a disk, the antibiotic in it may well help your cat to cure itself of the disease. However, we rarely perform a "culture and sensitivity," as it is called, on the first visit since with experience a veterinarian has learned he can cure perhaps 90 per cent of bacterial infections with an antibiotic that has helped correct similar problems in many other animals. The 10 per cent or so that do not respond may be candidates for this laboratory test.

Fortunately for cats, their bacterial infections (unlike man's) still succumb to even the older antibiotics. Cats are also lucky in that one life-saving antibiotic, chloramphenicol, has caused major problems and even death in humans, but has not had serious side effects in cats.

Penicillin, streptomycin, tetracycline, and chloramphenicol are the most widely used antibiotics in feline medicine. All are prescription drugs, which for some strange reason are available without a prescription from pet shops for use in treating fish. The pet shop charges more for these drugs than a pharmacy requiring a prescription. Conversely, the same drug when packaged for a large animal, such as a cow or horse, is usually much less expensive per unit than for cats or even humans.

If cost is any indication it would appear the lives in a fish tank are more valuable than the life of a creature that needs a prescription.

THE SULFA DRUGS

The person who did not own cats B.S.D. (Before Sulfa Drugs) cannot imagine what their discovery has meant to pet owners. True, most are outdated, and all are being replaced for some purposes by the antibiotics, but veterinary medicine is now a far happier profession because of them.

The first to be discovered was sulfanilamide. Instantly hailed as a cure-all, it was said to be a specific for coccidiosis, viruses, including distemper in dogs, and all kinds of bacteria. But genuine study showed that its field was very narrow: it killed only a limited number of bacteria and was ineffectual against viruses, coccidiosis, warts, bad disposition, or ingrowing toenails!

Laymen cannot obtain sulfa drugs without prescriptions. If you are interested, your veterinarian will tell you why he prescribes the sulfa drug he prefers for your cat.

In spite of all their wonderful effects, no drug and no combination of them has yet been found that will kill all bacteria, and few affect viruses.

EMETICS

Hydrogen Peroxide. Used at half the ordinary drugstore strength, which is 3 per cent, this drug probably is the best emetic yet discovered for cats. Mix equal amounts of peroxide and water and either make the animal swallow it, by the lip-pocket method (page 156), or administer it with a stomach tube (page 156). Vomiting occurs in about two minutes and continues at intervals of about thirty seconds for several minutes thereafter. Dose for a cat is two tablespoonsful.

In a stubborn cat the dose may be repeated twice over a ten-minute period until vomiting occurs.

Mustard. This is difficult to administer orally and is best given via a stomach tube. One quarter of a teaspoonful will cause vomiting fairly effectively for a ten-pound cat. Larger doses may prolong the vomiting for too long a time.

Ipecac. Although many laymen try to use ipecac to make cats vomit, it is about the slowest-acting emetic of any and therefore of little use in emergencies. Drugstores carry syrup of ipecac. The dose is generally ten to fifteen drops for a ten-pound cat.

Salt. Common table salt may be used, but it is difficult to administer. A strong solution is required—about a half teaspoonful of salt for a ten-pound cat. It is the poorest emetic of those mentioned.

CATHARTICS AND LAXATIVES

These drugs, which promote defecation, may be classified in a variety of ways: according to their severity (mild, medium, violent); according to their natures (oils, salines, metals, glandular stimulants, etc.); according to their action (lubricants, bile-flow stimulants), and so on. I shall simply list the most easily available cathartics and laxatives and a few of those prescription drugs that your veterinarian uses or prescribes. The order of their listing is no indication of their value.

Castor oil is a fairly quick-acting cathartic. Cats usually defecate about two hours after dosing. The stool is not fluid but only slightly softer than normal, unless overdoses are administered. Castor oil should be given on an empty stomach for the best results. The dose for a ten-pound cat is one-quarter teaspoonful. Remember that castor oil does not lubricate the intestinal tract, but rather acts as an irritant acid which causes a speed-up of evacuation. Racinic acid does the physicking; the oil is partly digested. Sometimes well-meaning cat fanciers give large doses to their pets. This is a mistake because overdoses can be extremely toxic. As in the use of any oil, you must be careful not to get any into the cat's lungs. Use the lip-pocket method of administering (see page 156).

Vaseline. In contrast to castor oil, the oral dose of Vaseline acts as a lubricant and almost all of it is deposited with the feces. A cat takes one-half to one teaspoonful without discomfort. Larger doses may be given, but overdoses are inadvisable because the Vaseline tends to leak out, and cats will lick themselves and thus take feces into their stomachs. Unfortunately it is not uncommon for owners to give a cat a tablespoonful, which would be equivalent to the owner taking more than a glassful.

Long-continued use of Vaseline is not recommended, since it dissolves the fat-soluble vitamins in food, preventing their absorption.

Milk of magnesia, a 10 per cent solution of magnesium hydroxide, is one of the mildest of laxatives. Doses of a teaspoonful produce laxation in a ten-pound cat in about six hours. Overdoses do little harm but do re-tard digestion because of their reduction of stomach acidity. In cats the pill form is seldom satisfactory.

Epsom Salts. This would be the perfect cathartic for cats were it not so intensely disliked, even in solution, because of the bitter taste. Several theories have been advanced as to how the salts accomplish their results. Probably they do it by drawing large amounts of water into the intestine (osmosis) and, by thus filling the intestine, soften the contents and me-chanically stimulate its action.

The dose for a ten-pound cat is a half teaspoonful, usually partially dis-solved in water. Try to give at least that much; you generally lose some in the process. Its action is fairly rapid, and evacuation occurs in two to four hours after dosing.

Phenolphthalein. For those who want a mild laxative for pets, phe-nolphthalein is among the best and deserves much wider use. It is com-bined with chocolate to form some of the more common human laxatives. It has a slightly irritating effect on the intestine, but, interestingly enough, exerts its principal action on the colon. Generally five or six hours elapse before the pet wants to defecate. Despite the fact that it is a phenol deriva-tive, it is reasonably safe for cats. The dose is one half the children's dose.

VACCINES

Vaccines are biologics, either bacterial or viral, for preventive inocula-tion, i.e., they induce the body to produce antibodies against disease-producing agents.

Vaccine may consist of several different materials. It may be bacteria, live or dead; virus, live, dead, or attenuated. For vaccinating against a bacterial disease, live bacteria of a less intense strain of that disease are used. The animal is given the real disease, but of a strain which has proved from long study to produce mild symptoms. The animal actually becomes sick, recovers, and is henceforth immune. Autogenous vaccine, on the other hand, is made from the very organism affecting an animal.

Dead bacteria in suspension form a common type of vaccine used for several diseases of pets—always as a preventive. Sometimes several species of bacteria are mixed in one vaccine in order to immunize our pets at one time against all the diseases these bacteria cause.

Virus vaccines may consist of live virus, so the animal actually is given the disease. Attenuated virus vaccines are those which have been attenuated (weakened) either by passage through a different species grown on tissue cultures or by chemicals. A number of cat vaccines are produced by inoculating chicken eggs with a virus, a process that attenuates the virus.

STEROIDS

This group of drugs, of which cortisone is a member, has had wide and effective use. Some steroids encourage healing, while others retard the healing process. Intense itching may be controlled by certain steroids, which do not, however, cure the cause of the itching. Some depress the immune system and are valuable in organ transplant cases to prevent rejection of the transplant. If used with the correct antibiotic for a given infection, they are helpful in reducing inflammation, but if used with the wrong antibiotic for a given infection, the results can be disastrous.

So we may call steroids a mixed bag in treating infections—they can be lifesaving or disastrous. A good example of this dichotomy is the treatment of a fresh scratch to the cornea of an eye. Healing is spectacular, but if the same steroid is used to treat an ulcer of the cornea caused by herpes virus the cat can be blinded in a day or two. An evaluation of each problem is necessary before using steroids. On the other hand most skin infections, when treated topically with steroids and the proper antibiotic, will show improvement in a matter of hours.

ANTIHISTAMINES

Most antihistamines have limited use in feline medicine but can relieve some of the signs of upper respiratory infections and are effective when given to a cat with an insect sting reaction. If your cat has been sensitized to insect stings you should consult your veterinarian, who may want you to have medication on hand for a future reaction. Fortunately cats seem to lose their sensitivity over a much shorter period of time than a human or a canine.

ANTIEPILEPTIC DRUGS

In spite of many newer drugs, my first choice to treat epilepsy is still phenobarbital. The trick is to give the maximum dose of this cumulative drug without producing side effects. The main side effect is a staggering gait similar to that of a human with too much holiday spirit. Initially I prescribe enough to make the cat drunk and then reduce the dose slightly. Another widely used drug is diphenylhydantain, also known as Dilantin. This drug is converted to phenobarbital in the liver and unlike phenobarbital has long-term side effects. Your veterinarian will have to evaluate an epileptic cat to decide which drug or combinations of these and others to use to help control seizures.

STOOL SOFTENERS

If a change in diet does not prove effective, dioctyl sodium sulfosuccinate is helpful in keeping the stools soft in a chronically constipated cat. Another, more natural, approach involves using psyllium seed, either whole or in powdered form, to accomplish the same end. Metamucil, available without a prescription from pharmacies, is mixed with the food. Usually one teaspoonful in each meal is sufficient but, since it is nontoxic, more may be added. If the patient is used to eating dry food the diet will have to be changed to a food in which you can mix the powder.

Finally, in summary, here are a few points you should think about when medicating your pet:

1. There may be undesirable interactions when more than one drug is given.

2. Long-term antibiotic therapy may lead to a fungal growth in the intestines which can be difficult to correct.

3. Any animal can be sensitive to a drug, in which case the cure may be worse than the disease.

4. Insecticides may lower fertility in both queens and toms.

5. Steroids may cause fluid retention, obesity, and reduce healing time.

6. Some drugs cause respiratory depression and are dangerous before anesthesia.

7. Antibiotics, steroids, antihistamines in combination with other drugs can cause serious side effects.

8. When oil preparations are forced some may enter the windpipe and lungs causing pneumonia.

9. If a cat takes dairy products the tetracyclines are not effective.

10. Some drugs predispose a cat to thrombosis (blood clots).

11. Some alter liver function and bile flow.

12. Some cause heart problems during anesthesia.

10. How to Administer Medicines and Apply Accessories

*A*LL cat owners should know how to administer the common drugs used with animals, how to give their cats medicine in liquid, capsule, and tablet form, how to apply the standard bandages, how to take the temperatures of animals—in short, how to handle all the little problems of caring for a sick or injured pet.

Your veterinarian will diagnose your cat's condition, prescribe the proper medication, and tell you the kind of care and attention your pet needs. That alone is not enough to restore the animal to health. In most cases you will treat your pet at home, and it is your responsibility to carry out the veterinarian's instructions. The most effective drug ever prescribed will not help your pet if you cannot manage to get more than 5 per cent of the dose down his throat. If you allow the animal to remove the bandage the veterinarian has applied and permit him to expose an open wound to infection simply because you don't know how to reapply it so that it will stay, you can hardly expect a quick and satisfactory recovery.

Your veterinarian will outline a course of treatment for your sick cat, but the way you carry out his instructions and the care you give the animal will usually determine how effective the treatment will be. If you can give the doctor the kind of intelligent co-operation that he has a right to expect, your pet's chances for recovery will be greatly increased.

METHODS FOR ADMINISTERING MEDICINE TO ANIMALS

Liquids. When done properly, dosing a cat orally with liquid requires less skill than many think. Whenever a liquid is to be given, you should always remember that if certain of them enter the lungs they can be very dangerous. The first question you should ask yourself is: What would happen if the animal inhaled some?

Pure water solutions of quickly soluble drugs are least dangerous. Hydrogen peroxide turns to water and oxygen when it decomposes in the fizzing effect known to everyone. On the other hand, milk, which is sometimes used as a base or vehicle for drugs, contains solids. Fat is one of them, and fat in the lungs is especially dangerous. If the drug used is harmless when inhaled into the lungs—that is, if it is a water solution—it is fairly safe to fill the animal's mouth and throat and force it to swallow the medicine. If some of the medicine trickles down the windpipe, the only unfortunate thing that can happen is a blast in your face or on your coat sleeve when the patient coughs. But when a solution dangerous to the lungs is to be administered, a little at a time is the rule you should follow.

This is particularly true of mineral oil, or baby oil as it is sometimes called. Such oil is not readily coughed up since it is rather thick and once in the trachea (windpipe) it will descend into the lungs causing a mechanical pneumonia. Countless cats have inadvertently been killed slowly by this oil. If small amounts are given at a time there is rarely a problem.

In either event there are two practical ways of giving a liquid medicine: the lip-pocket method and by stomach tube. Let's see how and when each of these is used.

The Lip-Pocket Method: Although an experienced person can accomplish this alone, you will probably find that two people are necessary for satisfactory results. Place the animal on a table broadside to you and make it sit. Tilt its head back so that it is looking at the ceiling. With your right hand hold its chin in this position. Slide the finger of your left hand under its lip, at the angle where lower and upper lips join. Pull this out and upward away from the teeth. Now you have a cup, or pocket, which will hold a considerable amount of liquid. While you hold the patient in this position, your assistant holds both front paws firmly with one hand so that the cat can't pull them loose, and with the other he pours the medicine into the lip pocket. As it runs between its teeth and onto the back of the tongue, the cat will swallow it. When this is gone, pour more of the medicine in until the whole dose is administered. A word of caution: The assistant should stand out of the line of fire, for if the animal coughs, he or she is liable to be thoroughly sprayed.

Some cats will shake their heads violently and lose some of the medicine. For that reason it is best to set the medicine container down quickly and place your hand about the cat's head to hold it until it has swallowed all the medication.

The Stomach-Tube Method: What seems a great task is in reality a simple and safe method if two people co-operate to dose an animal. A piece of tubing, one-eighth-inch inside diameter and six to twelve inches long, depending upon the size of the animal, is large enough for a cat. You can get both the tube and a plastic syringe from your veterinarian. The syringe should be filled with the medicine and left within reach. When you are ready to insert the tube, hold the animal as described above with the head straight up. As the tube is pushed over the back of the tongue into the throat, the patient will gulp and swallow it down. If it has been moistened, it will slide down with reasonable ease.

There is a danger that the cat will chew the plastic tube off and swallow it, in which case you and it are in trouble. To prevent this, bore a hole large enough to emit the tube through a stick of wood six inches long and one-half-inch square. Place the stick across the cat's open jaw and run the tube through it. The cat cannot close its mouth and the tube will be safe.

There is one other danger to guard against. You must be extremely careful not to get the tube into the windpipe, for if fluids are forced down the tube into the lungs by mistake, the results may be tragic. By holding the upper end of the tube close to your ear, you can tell whether the other end is in the windpipe by the purring sound of air rushing in and out of the tube with each breath. If the tube has been inserted properly, you will not hear any sound at all. Another method of being sure where the tube is is to feel the throat. The windpipe is in front and closest to the skin, and in animals that are not too fat you should have no difficulty in feeling the tube in the esophagus behind it.

When you are certain that the tube is where it should be, have your assistant—who needs both hands for the job—connect the syringe to the tube and squirt the medicine or liquid food down the tube. In mature animals the stomach tube may be left in for several minutes without causing distress; the patient goes right on breathing normally.

You should never try to squirt a drug into your cat's mouth, snap it shut, and expect the animal to swallow it. Most of the solution will run out as the animal shakes its head. You can sometimes overcome the patient's dislike for some drugs by disguising them in sweet syrups, thinned down. Glucose (dextrose) is often administered to advantage to sick animals, but if given in the form of corn syrup or honey, it is difficult to pour and must therefore be thinned. If any sweet substance is given carefully and without a struggle, the subsequent dosages will be simpler.

Some veterinarians dispense a disposable hypodermic syringe without a needle to administer fluid medications. The tip of the syringe is placed between the back teeth from the side of the cat's mouth and the plunger is pressed slowly to allow for swallowing before more medication is introduced.

When a drug is prescribed for certain intervals, remember that very often there is an attempt to build blood levels and maintain them. If one dose is missed, sometimes the whole treatment must be started again. So it is imperative to follow instructions.

Pills and Capsules.   It doesn't require sleight of hand to get a pill or capsule down the throat of a cat, even when the cat resists. It's all in knowing how. Opening the animal's mouth, dropping in the medicine, closing his mouth, and rubbing his throat may work now and again, but it's not a sure enough method to rely on.

Some capsules contain bitter drugs that, if bitten, can frighten or suffocate your cat, or give off a taste so obnoxious that it will try for many minutes to cough or scratch them out. If you are giving your pet medicine of this sort, you will want to be certain that no capsules are dropped between its teeth or insufficiently pushed down its throat.

Giving pills to cats is actually quite simple. After you have had a little practice, you can do it so quickly that before the cat has time to think about scratching the job is done. With the cat sitting in front of you on a table, facing toward your right, grasp the whole head in your left hand, with your thumb and fingers pressing from opposite sides of the upper jaw. Pull the cat's head gently backward until its nose is pointing straight up and hold it in this position. With your right hand pull down the lower jaw and, as you do so, with your left hand push the lips between the teeth so that the cat can't close its mouth. Now drop the pill or capsule on the back of the tongue, where it touches the palate, and as the tongue wiggles watch the pill slip over the back of it. It will slide out of sight. Let the cat close its mouth. Seldom will a cat spit up the pill. If you find that your cat is inclined to do so, then hold a pencil in the right hand as well as the pill. The moment the pill lands on the cat's tongue, give it a gentle quick push with the eraser end of the pencil and it will surely be down so far the cat will swallow it when you let go of its head. I use my finger rather than the eraser end of a pencil on all but the most aggressive animals and have been bitten only once using this technique.

If one person holds a cat by the nape of the neck off the floor (chest height) and the other one goes through the dosing routine, it is sometimes even easier because many cats tend to relax in this position.

When All Else Fails. Among many tricks for the administration of capsules or tablets, one that often works is the mixing of the medication with butter or margarine and smearing it on the cat's lips and between the teeth and even on the front of the forelegs. Unless deathly sick a cat will lick all such material off to clean itself. Of course a capsule is emptied into the butter and a tablet may be placed on a hard surface and rolled with a round bottle to powder it first.

Some cats have a particular fondness for sardines and for such animals medicine may be mixed with the sardine oil. Vaseline may be mixed with an equal amount of sardine oil and fed as a laxative or as a hair-ball treatment. If your cat enjoys a particular food such as thick chicken soup you may find it a good vehicle for medications.

A word of warning: Some medications are not compatible with some foods, so before attempting mixtures consult your veterinarian.

BANDAGES AND THEIR USES

Applying bandages of various dimensions to the outside of the body is truly an art if it is done properly. A few simple basic directions will be useful to those who have never bandaged an animal. Not that these instructions will make an expert nurse of the beginner, but they should make it possible to apply most of the common types of bandages securely and with reasonable facility.

Cats need bandaging to keep them from licking or tearing at newly sutured wounds or surgical incisions, to hold dressings in place, to prevent them from chewing their skin when skin irritations itch, to hold broken limbs straight in splints before they are set, and most important of all to control bleeding.

Of the many kinds of bandage used by physicians and nurses, only a few are very useful in veterinary work. Rolls of muslin and gauze, many-tailed bandages, and adhesive are those usually needed. Anyone can rip an old sheet into three-inch-wide strips to make a bandage in a pinch. But those strips should be rolled tightly before applying. A four-foot gauze or cotton bandage, two inches wide, serves nicely in bandaging a cat.

Many-tails are simply strips of cloth as wide as the area to be bandaged on the patient and torn in the same number of parallel strips from each end toward the central area.

Adhesive tape one inch wide should serve almost any purpose. To cover a wide area it can be lapped, and if a narrower strip is desired, it can be ripped easily.

Most bandages will be applied by the concerned owner for minor cuts and blemishes, or as stopgap measures before taking the pet to the veterinarian, who will then instruct the owner on the proper way of bandaging in the future.

The most common use of bandages in pets is to prevent self-injury. Suppose a cat has been caught in a steel trap, but is found before the part of the leg below the trap jaws has died. The skin has been cleaned and the veterinarian has sutured it. If the cat is not prevented from licking it, it may remove the stitches and open the wound. Moreover, after the bandage is applied, there will be considerable weeping from the wound and, despite antiseptics, an odd odor will develop. This is not necessarily a bad sign. The cat smells it and becomes frantic to lick it, since there is something about the odor that animals are attracted to and that excites them to lick. At any rate, they may rip bandages off, necessitating application of new ones fairly often.

In covering such an area, several things must be kept in mind. The bandage cannot be wound too tightly or circulation will be impeded and the area below it will swell from the pooling of blood and lymph. But it must be wound tightly enough not to slip. If swelling occurs, the bandage may be cut but not necessarily removed. New adhesive must then be wound around it.

First some surgical dressing (powder, solution, or salve) is applied, and usually a sponge of several thicknesses of gauze put over it. The bandage is unrolled about the wound firmly until several thicknesses have been applied. The end is torn lengthwise to make two tails, which are tied in a knot at the bottom of the tear and then wound around the leg in opposite directions and tied in a knot again. When the bandage fails to go on smoothly, or when it is necessary to go from a thin place on the leg to a thicker section, twist the roll occasionally and it will go on with professional smoothness. If one layer of adhesive tape is then applied it will hold the bandage material in place and be sufficient protection against the patient's efforts to remove it. Adhesive tape must be wound around the gauze or cotton bandage so that none of the bandaging is observed. If on an extremity, it must extend up perhaps an inch or more above the bandage on the hair or skin for it to stay in place. Otherwise the cat will just flip its foot around and off comes the bandage.

The only time you would make two tails on a bandage is when you are tying one around the neck or the body, because if you're going to cover the bandage with adhesive tape you don't need to tie the knot.

Bandages are used very frequently to check blood flow, and in this case they are called pressure bandages.

To stop the flow of blood from an extremity, apply a small cloth sponge directly to the cut and quickly wind a bandage tightly about the area many times. It may become red from blood soaking through it, but it will slowly stop bleeding.

Tourniquets are so often recommended to stop bleeding in human beings that pet owners sometimes resort to them injudiciously. With a pet, a strong elastic band can suffice, or even thumb pressure over the cut artery. If a tourniquet of any sort is applied to a whole limb, it is important that it be released every ten minutes to let blood in and out of the part below the tourniquet.

Many-tailed bandages are usually used about the body. When cats scratch and chew holes in themselves because of skin infections, there is often no better accessory treatment. Skin remedies and the bandage are applied. Depending upon how much of the body must be covered, the bandage generally has two or four holes cut to allow the legs to go through. Then a row of knots is tied along the back and left in bows, so that it can be untied to remove the bandage, which may be used again. Long surgical incisions on the sides, back, or abdomen can be satisfactorily covered in this way and the bandage will stay in place if snug.

USING THERMOMETERS

Ordinary rectal thermometers, which one can purchase in any drugstore, are adequate for taking the temperatures of our cats. It is a simple matter to shake one down, then dip it in Vaseline or mineral oil and insert it three quarters of its length into the rectum. The time for use will be indicated on the thermometer container. It should then be removed, wiped clean with a piece of cotton, and read. (Don't wash it in hot water.) Anyone can read such a thermometer by twisting it slowly until the wide silver stripe appears and noting the figures opposite the top of the column. Some thermometers are graduated in fifths, and since each fifth equals two tenths, the reading is usually expressed in tenths, i.e., 102⅕ degrees F. is 102.2 degrees F.

The arrow at 98.6 represents the normal human temperature, and this of course is disregarded, since the average normal temperature for the cat is 101 degrees. However, many cats vary a few tenths of a degree and usually the temperature is lower in the morning than it is in the evening. Frequently, the excitement caused by presenting a cat to a veterinarian will cause the temperature to be elevated.

Feline temperature taking for the novice is usually a two person job— one to hold the cat and the other to insert the thermometer.

DEVICES TO PREVENT SELF-INJURY

After any operation, or even to prevent a cat from chewing or scratching at an area of skin infection, it may be necessary to apply one of several devices designed to permit healing without interference.

Boxing Gloves. To prevent a cat from scratching itself, "boxing gloves" may have to be applied to its feet. These consist of a wad of cotton around the foot, gauze wound over the cotton, and the whole covered with adhesive tape. The tape should be started an inch above the gauze in order to fasten it to the hair and prevent it from slipping off. Batting itself with such soft devices discourages a pet from scratching.

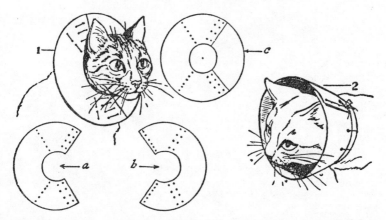

Devices to prevent self-injury. (1) An Elizabethan collar, improvised from thin plywood or extra-strong cardboard, is helpful in preventing an animal from chewing on cuts or sores or removing bandages. a., b., and c. show how collar is made and put together. (2) Head funnel of plastic or heavy cardboard prevents an animal from scratching sores or irritations on its head or ears.

Tying the Legs.   When a cat refuses to leave its face alone and insists on scratching with its front paws, and if only a day or two of prevention is required, the front legs may be crossed and taped together at the wrists with adhesive tape. The tape is, of course, removed when the owner takes the cat outside.

Elizabethan Collars.   These may be made, easily enough, from two pieces of heavy, stiff cardboard or plastic, held together with shoelace or cord ties. (See illustration.)

The Cone Collar.   A variation of the Elizabethan collar, this is a piece of flat, flexible plastic used to make a partial cone. The edges are punched and the device is brought together around the head. The small end of the cone may either be fastened to the collar or left free; the larger end of the cone (the base) is a little beyond the cat's nose. (See illustration.)

Another way of improvising an Elizabethan collar is to obtain a child's inexpensive plastic sand bucket, cut a hole in the bottom large enough to accommodate the cat's head, and fasten it to a collar that fits snugly around the cat's neck.

11. Problems of the Reproductive and Urinary Systems

KIDNEY DISEASE

*D*ESPITE the large amounts of meat and organs consumed by cats, kidney disease, even kidney stones, is rare in any except old cats. It does occur, of course, as a result of infections, poisonings, injuries, and leukemia. Abnormal thirst is one of the first signs of the disease and a urinalysis is essential for a diagnosis.

Taken in the early stages, infective kidney disease is often curable. One should not delay in taking the cat to the veterinarian for treatment at the first sign of loss of appetite and a sharply increased thirst. In chronic incurable cases there is dehydration and a smell of urine on the breath.

Feeding ice cubes, which the pet can lap, often overcomes the thirst, and absorption of the water from the body cavities can still be encouraged. Very little meat, organs, fish, skim milk, cheese, eggs may be fed to a cat with kidney disease. But as you have seen in the section on feeding, cats can be fed low-protein diets and still thrive. Cereals, vegetables, and fats must be the mainstay of the diet in some cases. After you think the animal is cured, a visit to the doctor for another urinalysis is necessary to determine whether a higher protein diet is safe.

Stones rarely develop in the kidneys, but when they do, their presence can be determined only by X ray. Small gravelly stones which move from the kidneys down the ureters to the bladder cause pain to the cat as they do to humans.

The kidney pelvis may be inflamed, even when the bladder is not. Stones may dam up the urine and cause a larger pocket to develop in the kidneys. Bladder inflammation may be spread forward to the kidneys, and when this occurs the cat may suffer pain under the loin, run a fever, void urine containing blood and pus, and even have diarrhea. If the inflammation is not treated, it may in time result in enlargement and finally destruction of the kidneys.

Kidneys long infected lose their ability to function and shrink so that a chronic condition is produced.

One result of malfunction of the kidneys is dropsy. The abdomen distends and the tissue along the belly and the legs fills up with blood plasma. Quite often heart weakness is associated with this disease.

BLADDER AND URETHRAL PROBLEMS

The correct name for one of the more common and devastating conditions in cats is urolithiasis, which means the formation of calculi in the urinary tract. Calculi are solid aggregations chiefly of mineral substances and salts. Although both toms and queens can be affected, the tomcat suffers more serious consequences when calculi build up in his urethra preventing normal urine passage. This is due to the greater length and smaller diameter of the tom's urethra. When the passage is completely blocked the poor cat tries as he will but cannot urinate. When his urinary bladder is fully distended he will continue to strain, often making yowling or growling sounds as if he were in great pain, and so he is. Normally the abdomen of a cat is soft and pliable with no large firm objects palpable; but this situation changes dramatically in the presence of a distended urinary bladder, which can grow to the size of an orange. Every groan should be interpreted as a call for help, a call that often develops into an emergency situation in the wee hours. If the internal pressure of the urine in the bladder is not relieved in time the lining of that organ is compromised and the cat dies. The veterinarian usually administers an anesthetic, flushes out the urethra, and expresses the bladder.

At this point there are many possible treatments. If the blockage is toward the end of the penis that organ may be amputated and a new opening created. Some surgeons perform an abdominal operation to open the urinary bladder and flush it out, thereby removing any deposits that may cause future blocking. My choice has been to flush the urethra, place a catheter into the bladder, and suture it into place for one week. It takes that long to stretch the urethra so that it will remain stretched for the future passage of calculi. Most tomcats will remove a catheter if given the opportunity so an Elizabethan collar (see page 161) is applied for the week. Being an extremely adaptable creature, the cat adjusts to the awkward collar with grace.

The question "What causes it, Doctor?" is a logical one which must be answered "We don't know." There are many theories, one of which is that a virus or perhaps more than one virus grows in the bladder, opening the way for bacterial infection. Some of the normal salts in the urine precipitate on clumps of bacteria into fine sandlike particles. The normal bladder opening to expel urine is high up on the posterior end of that organ so the sandlike material gravitates to the bottom. When there is a significant amount of sand some overflows with the urine and irritates the urethra, resulting in straining, which causes more sand to descend. If the irritation is sufficient, the small urethral opening becomes even smaller as a result of the swelling that accompanies inflammation. The sand, mixed with mucus, blocks the passage, resulting in an emergency situation.

The next question is how to prevent the problem. There is evidence that the sand or crystals do not develop well if the urine is acid. Normal cat urine is usually acid (while the opposite is often true in cats with cystitis, i.e., their urine is alkaline). As a preventative, many veterinarians suggest urinary acidifiers, one of which is vitamin C, also called ascorbic acid. Even when 250 milligrams of vitamin C are administered three times daily, the urine should be checked regularly to be sure it is acid.

Although the theory suggests a virus as the cause, we regularly prescribe a sulfa or antibiotic to treat this type of cystitis and urethritis. The medication is used to treat the secondary bacterial invaders.

In my experience once a tom has had this problem he may have bouts off and on for over two years. But eventually most cats develop an immunity or in some way adjust to the condition and remain free of the problem for the remainder of their lives.

The queen's anatomy precludes her suffering from the life-threatening attacks of the tom; instead, she indicates the problem by frequent urination of small quantities of urine. Queens are usually affected so mildly that most are not taken for veterinary assistance.

Much has been written about the advantages of a low-ash diet to help control urinary infections; but it should be noted that the cats in colonies fed high-ash diets have no higher incidence than those fed low-ash diets. If you wish to try a low-ash diet, bear in mind that most canned foods with the water removed have more ash than most dry and semimoist foods.

A good home-prepared low-ash diet would consist of 50 per cent beef, fish without bones, or poultry with 25 per cent rice and 25 per cent canned tomatoes. I suggest that all commercial cat food, whether dry or moist, be mixed with enough water so that its consistency is that of a stew. It will take a few days for a cat to adjust to the new consistency, but once it does, the risk of a urinary infection is considerably lowered.

UTERINE INFECTIONS

It is not uncommon for female cats to develop infections in the uterus (pyometra) which can be treated only by removal of that organ. If this is done, it is advisable to remove the ovaries also, since there is no point in having a female cat repeatedly coming in season and attracting males if she can no longer produce kittens. A queen with a uterine infection usually leaks a sweet-smelling pus from the uterus that keeps her soiled about the vulva and backs of her legs. Her abdomen, in a severe case, is distended sufficiently to make the owner suspect pregnancy. She will also run a fever.

At birth kittens are sometimes too large to pass through the pelvis, and at such times, if action is not taken to help the delivery, all the kittens may die, causing decomposition and rupture of the uterus.

CRYPTORCHIDISM

Next to urine retention, the failure of the testicles to descend constitutes the most common defect of the genitourinary tract in males. The cryptorchid (animal with hidden testicles) needs attention. He may be a monorchid (one testicle hidden) or a complete cryptorchid. It is better for cats to have hidden testicles removed since they often become cancerous.

Most animals with one or both testicles undescended have abnormal temperaments. If your cat does not behave as a normal, gentle cat should, examine the scrotum and, if you can feel only one testicle, take the cat to your veterinarian for a thorough examination. The testicle may be located in the canal under the skin, but if the veterinarian can't feel it at all, the inevitable conclusion is that it is still lodged in the abdomen.

NEUTERING

It is the consensus among cat fanciers that the altered tom and queen make far more satisfactory pets. We have heard many of our clients with wide experience in handling cats say bluntly that breeding cats are definitely unsatisfactory. Some people think otherwise.

Generally speaking, the altered cat requires much less care. It stays home, is more carefree and affectionate, is safer to handle, costs less to keep, lives longer actuarially speaking, and seldom is made useless as a mouser as so many believe.

The toms specifically lose their potent and—to most people—obnoxious odor, stop spraying and use their pans or boxes, and stop howling, fighting, and staying out all night. If castrated at an early age, they never develop these undesirable traits and tend to grow larger than their whole brothers.

Queens, after the spaying operation, attract no more males and cause no more cat concerts outside the house. In addition, the neighbors cannot blame the spayed female if their tomcat must be taken to the veterinarian for wound treatment. The queens stop calling and rolling, a type of behavior abhorrent to many owners. They use their food to better advantage, have no periodical weight losses, and have no kittens with the occasional complications and nuisance this entails. To many owners, just the task of having to find homes for unwanted kittens is reason enough for spaying a cat.

One should think ahead and ask, at the time of taking in a kitten, "Do I want a breeder, or do I want a pet?" If the answer is a pet, then neutering is the ready-made solution.

12. Problems of the Digestive System

THE MOUTH

*T*HE MOUTH, which is properly considered as part of the digestive tract, is perhaps exposed to more infection than any other part of the body. Although the tissues are particularly resistant to infection, the several parts of the oral cavity are subject to a number of diseases.

Lips. Where the long upper "canine" teeth rub on the sides of the lower lips there occasionally develops an infection that produces a sickening odor. The lips develop sore spots and the cat drools copiously. Even a few drops of the saliva dropped by the cat is sufficiently malodorous to make a room unpleasant. Though the putrescent odor might lead one to think that the animal is about to die, actually the condition is easily cured with a few drops of tincture of iodine, full strength, daubed on the infected spots with a small cotton swab. Sometimes two or more treatments on consecutive days may be necessary to do the trick. Antibiotic creams and ointments are less irritating but usually require more applications.

Injuries to the lips commonly cause difficulty. Sometimes an upper lip becomes impaled on an upper canine tooth. It must be freed, and this often requires considerable manipulation.

Occasionally the upper lip thickens with a raw area, a condition aggravated by the cat's constant licking with its rough tongue. This has been referred to as "rodent ulcer," and is a condition that must be corrected by a veterinarian. Injections, ointments, irradiation, hormones, and even surgery may be necessary.

Stomatitis. Stomatitis is infection of the mouth. Some doctors think that it may be indirectly due to a niacin deficiency, although the one vitamin that cats usually have in ample amount is niacin. Whatever the cause, cats' mouths often develop infections of this sort, and injections of niacin do help greatly in relieving the condition. The spirochete of Vincent's angina (trench mouth) is present in some of these infections, but whether it is the primary cause of stomatitis has not been determined, since the mouths of normal cats frequently harbor this spirochete. It is probable that this infection more or less destroys the victim's sense of taste and causes pain whenever food is eaten.

Treating a cat with an infected mouth is difficult. Sodium perborate can be obtained in any drugstore and used as per directions for humans. But the cat will soon learn to fight off attempts to swab its mouth. When it does, it is best to soak a ball of cotton in the solution and hold it so the cat bites it. The squeezing of its jaws will swab the mouth thoroughly. Medication should be continued twice a day until the infection is cleared up. It is not difficult to tell when the patient is cured, for when the pain and soreness have passed, the cat will stop looking wistfully at food and really eat it with a voracious appetite.

A troublesome problem occurs when the body itself rejects patches of the inner lips, gums, or the tongue, resulting in ulcerations. This is called an auto-immune condition and is often incurable.

Diseases of the Teeth and Gums. Although cats' teeth are generally uncommonly sound until old age, sometimes minor dental ailments do arise. Occasionally a tooth will be broken and will require anesthesia and extraction.

Whereas humans frequently need dental care for cavities in their teeth, cats develop very few such painful defects. Nearly all their tooth troubles are due either to bacterial infections or to defective diet. Chewing on hard foods cannot be the reason for a cat's relative freedom from tooth decay, since many pets are fed on soft, mushy food all their lives, and their teeth, while becoming covered with tartar, do not decay. The true reason is to be found in the structure and perhaps the chemistry of the mouth.

Cats are susceptible to gum disease caused by the build-up of tartar and the subsequent receding of the gums. Infections work between the tartar and the gums until the teeth loosen and even fall out. Check your cat's teeth at least every six months, and if you notice excess tartar, seek professional help. An accumulation on some of the large back teeth can be snapped off with your thumbnail placed under the edge at the gum line. We often see tartar accumulations larger than the teeth they have formed on.

Cats on deficient diets can lose their teeth in their youth. Those that get off to a poor start frequently develop such bad teeth that they have to be extracted by the time the cat is eight years old. One warden tells of examining the teeth of over four hundred wild cats killed while preying on a pheasant ranch far out in the country. Not a cat among them had a missing tooth, and none had an excessive amount of tartar. Apparently cats on natural, complete diets have beautiful teeth, in contrast to the pampered house pet that is so often given meat, meat, and more meat. The owner usually shrugs and says, "That's all he will eat." The cats-gone-wild prove otherwise.

It is only humane to have all loose teeth extracted, even if it means the cat must be fed mush the rest of its life. Many canned cat foods are excellent and all of them are mushy in consistency, so that a cat can thrive on them.

THE ESOPHAGUS

Troublesome conditions in the esophagus are chiefly the result of burns from irritants; injuries by foreign bodies such as bones, pins, needles, and wood splinters; and inflammation caused by infections from bites or accidents.

In the section on upper respiratory infections the role virus plays in ulcers (including those in the esophagus) is discussed.

Symptoms of trouble in the esophagus are cessation of eating and vomiting, sometimes with blood in the vomitus. The cat may sit with its head and neck stretched out. It may drool and gag. If you press its throat, the cat may react by pushing your fingers away with a paw.

Removal of foreign bodies necessitates anesthesia and veterinary treatment. Injuries may so nearly close the esophagus by the inflammation they cause that only passage of a soft stomach tube, or intravenous medication, can save a cat so afflicted.

THE STOMACH

Inflammation of the Stomach. In humans we speak of dyspepsia. The feline equivalent is a simple inflammation of the stomach (gastritis) that interferes with digestion. It may be caused by accidents, such as a kick or blow when the stomach is filled; by distention of the stomach wall from overeating; by food that is too coarse or indigestible; by poisons, including food poisoning; by foreign objects such as chips of broken glass, tiny sharp bones, or porcupine quills; by parasites and diseases.

In poisoning, the stomach lining reddens, thickens, and may even slough off in areas. The inflammation often extends through the entire wall. A doctor performing a post-mortem examination may see the normally white stomach wall with great red blotches, usually along the lower curvature where food settles and where most of the damage is done.

One of the earliest symptoms of gastritis is nausea. Loss of appetite is to be expected also. Temperature is a poor index, because, while disease may raise it, poisons or toxins may depress it. In many cases the cat will let out agonizing cries easily recognizable as expressions of pain. Depending on the cause, the bowel movements may be normal or of a diarrhea consistency. Since stomach inflammation associated with disease ordinarily affects the whole intestine as well, diarrhea is usually present.

Whether treatment will save a cat with gastritis depends on the cause. Large foreign objects can be surgically removed. Ground glass is not so dangerous, and if the pieces are small enough to be swallowed they will usually be found in the feces. Hair can be helped out slowly, as we will explain later. Porcupine quills work themselves out, and whether they will kill the cat is a matter of the direction they take after leaving the stomach. Sometimes administering stomach sedatives, which a veterinarian can give you, helps greatly. Since rectifying an injured stomach is simply a matter of removing the damaging agent and waiting until the body heals itself, there is always the danger that the owner will lose patience. If any kind of treatment requires patience, this is surely it—this waiting for the slow regeneration of injured tissue. There is no quick cure, but in the long run the waiting pays.

Ulcers. In cats ulcers are produced in a number of ways, the most common being the administration of excessive amounts of drugs, such as aspirin, which is not recommended for cats; or caffeine. Aside from such external causes, ulcers also seem to develop spontaneously. Regardless of what causes ulcers, they are always difficult to diagnose. Usually they are discovered by X-raying after barium has been introduced into the stomach or on post-mortem examination. They might be suspected if a cat eats very little, loses weight, occasionally passes dark blood in the feces, and shows pain when examined in the vicinity of the stomach. Perforating ulcers usually cause incurable peritonitis.

For minor gastritis, in cats and in humans, there are a host of coating agents that are often helpful but I would at least consult a veterinarian as to the proper product and dose.

Hair Balls. Actually these are usually not balls at all. It would probably be more accurate to call them hair ropes. I have removed several surgically in which the hair accumulation had taken a spherical shape. One had a sort of handle which protruded up the esophagus and the lump itself was as large as a tennis ball. In most cases there is a large clump in the stomach and attached to it there is a hairy rope which may extend several feet along the intestine. Cats normally rid themselves of hair in the stomach by vomiting it, if it does not pass out of the pylorus—the exit valve of the stomach. But when the lump becomes so large that it can't be regurgitated it causes serious difficulty.

There are two facts to be remembered about hair balls. The first one is that nature's way of eliminating hair in the intestinal tract is by decomposition. The lump fills with bacteria which in time decompose it so that it can be sloughed off. While this is going on—the process may last a month or more—the cat is absorbing the bacterial toxins. It gets thin, and in many cases shows a definite rise in temperature as a result of autointoxication. As soon as the lump has decomposed and passed out in sections, the cat becomes ravenous and recovery is rapid and complete.

The second fact to remember is that there is never any reason to allow the hair to accumulate. It should be a matter of prevention—and prevention is such a simple thing! It consists of administering Vaseline once a week, or giving the cat some edible oil in amounts too large to be digested. Some people add mineral oil to the food, but it is not as effective this way as when given on an empty stomach. Others open a can of sardines, eat the fish, and set the can with the fishy oil on the floor and let the cat lap it up on an empty stomach. This is an excellent method of preventing hair balls.

A bile-salt pill can also be given once a week to prevent hair balls. There are several proprietary mixtures, containing laxatives and oils, which are very effective preventatives.

Once sizable hair balls have developed, difficult and complicated procedures are sometimes necessary for their removal. Surgery may have to be employed. Your veterinarian will usually decide to operate only when he can palpate a lump too large ever to be eliminated by drugs or natural means. Such a step is much better than doing nothing, on the assumption that the cat can live long enough without nourishment for the lump to decompose. This starvation treatment is inhumane, even though many cat owners, through inertia and thoughtlessness, allow it to go on.

Decomposition can be used sensibly as an ally. If drugs are given that kill the bacteria in the hair lump, the cat may feel better but the lump will be even harder to dislodge. It is usually wise, therefore, to give oils or drugs that cause a slimy mass in the stomach, in which the tangled hairs will gradually disintegrate. Sometimes a dose of hydrogen peroxide (page 151) will bring up a large-sized hair lump. This treatment is most likely to be successful after oil has been given for a long enough time to thoroughly lubricate the mass in the stomach.

Bile-salt pills can sometimes be used to rid cats of large accumulations. If one pill is given every four or five hours until three have been given, a single series may move the hair that is causing the cat's sickness. However, it is usually advisable to repeat the treatment after a few days.

In some cases the veterinarian may be able to pass a small tube into the gullet of an anesthetized cat, insert instruments that grasp the hair, and pull it out. There are other methods that may prove feasible in certain cases. If your cat does not respond to home treatment within a reasonable time, it would be best to seek professional help.

Whatever method is used to eliminate the hair balls, it is unnecessary to see the cat starve during treatments. Its appetite may be nil, but in this case forced feeding will have a considerable sustaining effect. A few tablespoonsful of corn syrup, thinned to facilitate pouring and fed daily, are very helpful. If powdered dextrose is used, it must be made into a solution thin enough to be swallowed easily. A small amount of brewers' yeast powder mixed with the syrup or dextrose furnishes B complex vitamins. A syrup containing vitamins and minerals is also a worthwhile addition.

Foreign Bodies in the Stomach. Aside from hair—and occasionally grass—it is rare to find other foreign bodies lodged in the stomachs of cats. In my experience the most common cause of this kind of digestive difficulty has been insects. Large meals of crickets or grasshoppers may gather into balls with the legs of the bugs intertwined and the sharp points of the mass scratching the tender stomach wall. This results in severe discomfort until the skeletons have been softened by long exposure to digestive fluids. In some areas Japanese beetles are particularly troublesome to cats eager to eat insects. If you will look at a beetle's legs with a magnifying glass, you will understand the danger of allowing a cat to eat too many. Obviously a cat may eat a few insects of any kind along with other food without harm. The indigestible residue is mixed with the other material and passed off in the feces. When too many are eaten, however, it may be necessary to dose the cat with Vaseline to help move the crusty insects along the digestive tract.

String and even thread with needles on the end are sometimes swallowed. There is something about ordinary dry string that seems to entrance a cat. Generally the interest that starts with play ends in swallowing. Strings two or more feet long have been pulled out of cats while others pass unnoticed with the feces. Nevertheless, the sight of a foot-long piece of butcher string dragging after a cat quite naturally causes the owner alarm. It need not. It is a simple matter to catch hold of the string and gently pull it out. If you reach a point where it does not "pull" easily, cut it off, leaving two to three inches, and wait. In 99 per cent of such cases the cat will pass the remainder in the next movement.

No matter in what part of the cat's body a needle is ultimately found, it is safe to assume that it originally found its way into the mouth on the end of a piece of thread. If you attempt to pull a thread out of the cat's anus and it refuses to budge, veterinary attention is called for. The needle on the end of the thread may be located across the lower bowel. The same applies to a regurgitated thread found hanging out of a cat's mouth; it is probably attached to a needle embedded in the tissue of the throat.

THE INTESTINES

Diseases of the Intestines. Much of what has been said of the common ailments of the esophagus and stomach applies equally to the intestines. They are exposed to the same organisms that affect the esophagus and stomach. Parasites, however, do more damage to the intestines than to the stomach. Hookworms attach themselves to the intestines and suck blood; the larvae of both the hookworm and the roundworm bore through the intestines; and coccidia live in the intestinal walls. Tapeworms hold on to it and whipworms sew their whiplashes under its lining.

Rough, coarse material may chafe the delicate villi and cause diarrhea. But aside from these special conditions, the ailments of the intestines are largely extensions and complications of those arising elsewhere.

The Colon.   There are a host of problems that cause inflammation of the lining of the lower extremity of the intestinal tract. When inflammation is present the debris left from digestion in the upper or small intestine further irritates the lining and the resulting fluids cause loose stools. Normally, the colon extracts excess fluids from the debris rather than add to it.

If the colon is sluggish, spent food passing through it will be dehydrated and difficult to eliminate, a condition otherwise known as constipation.

When nerves leading to the colon are not functioning normally, it may overdistend, producing an impaction that may call for oral medication or enemas. The condition is called megacolon and if persistent your veterinarian will suggest surgery.

JAUNDICE

It has been said there are over two hundred functions of the liver, one of the most important of which is the production of bile, necessary in food digestion.

When bile does not enter the intestinal tract the digestion for which it is responsible does not occur and a fetid gray-colored stool results.

If the bile is blocked from entering the intestine by disease, parasites, cancer, stones, or injury the bile "backs up" in the liver and enters the bloodstream causing obstructive jaundice. Jaundice is a sign of a problem, not the problem. Certain poisons, when ingested, will damage the liver, causing the bile to enter the bloodstream, with jaundice as a result.

The same may be said of disease conditions, the most common of which in the cat is probably leptospirosis (discussed elsewhere).

Jaundice caused by poisons or by diseases such as leptospirosis is usually accompanied by normal-colored stools since some bile does enter the digestive system.

When administered to a cat, magnesia (or one-half teaspoon of Epsom salts) effects an outpouring of bile in the small intestine, which in excess acts as a laxative. A fatty meal will accomplish similar results.

I mentioned poisons as a cause of jaundice but remember cats are uncanny in avoiding toxic substances and laboratory-confirmed cases of poisoning are rarities.

Two diseases that produce jaundice and that used to be confused with jaundice produced by leptospirosis are infectious peritonitis and leukemia. Both are discussed in the following chapter. Even before tissues become yellow with bile, the urine, if observed, will be dark yellow. A laboratory test identifies the presence of bile pigments.

Cirrhosis of the Liver Cirrhosis occurs only rarely in cats, usually as a result of a disease that scars parts of the liver, thus interfering with circulation. This causes the liver to contract, leaving a shrunken organ incapable of performing its functions and eventually incompatible with life. We may be entering the era of liver transplants, which would be the only hope for such a patient.

Enlargement. Liver enlargement may result from improper circulation, or from an excess of toxins, produced, for instance, by diseased kidneys that cannot excrete waste materials. Tumors are also prime suspects in liver enlargements. The victim slowly loses weight and becomes emaciated but with some abdominal distention.

13. Contagious Diseases and How Your Cat Catches Them

$\mathcal{I}$F YOUR cat contracts pneumonia you will know that it is sick. But unless you know more than that, there is little that you can do for the animal. On the other hand, when you know something about the types of diseases and their causes and your pet becomes ill, you can handle the situation much more intelligently. You may be able to recognize the symptoms well enough to diagnose the condition and treat it yourself. If you do not recognize the symptoms, or if it is a serious disease that you cannot treat, you will realize the importance of having the pet properly cared for by a veterinarian. You will also be much better able to give the veterinarian the specific, accurate information he needs to have to treat the animal quickly and effectively.

A knowledge of the causes of the diseases to which your pet is subject and of the ways he may contract them is even more important from the standpoint of prevention. Many diseases can be avoided by observing a few simple precautions. Some of these maladies, once contracted, are difficult or impossible to cure. To the pet owner and to veterinary medicine, the prevention of disease in animals is as important as it is in the case of humans. A pet that is kept well is a good pet—a lively, active companion.

A simple understanding of the basic facts about disease is sufficient for the pet owner. He doesn't need to learn and remember a series of medical names or technical terms. He should know the broad general classifications into which all diseases are divided, he should be familiar with the common characteristics of each, and he should have a general knowledge of the way each affects animals. This is hardly too much to expect of any person who is really concerned with his cat's welfare.

To most pet owners all animal diseases are more or less alike—the result, they think, of some vague thing called "germs." Actually, of course, there are a number of distinct types of diseases, classified according to their causes. Some are caused by bacteria, some by viruses, and others by fungi, or parasites, or growths, or deficiencies. To understand the diseases themselves it is necessary to know something about these causative agents.

There are thousands of these agents, most of which live in harmony with us and all of nature; but a small per cent of them can cause disease. New disease-causing organisms are being described regularly but not without intense effort. A good example is Legionnaires' Disease, which required the work of countless scientists and millions of dollars before the causative agent was identified and a treatment developed.

Contagious diseases, as discussed in this chapter, are those that spread from cat to cat and should not be confused with communicable diseases transmitted from cat to man and perhaps vice versa. The latter are discussed in Chapter 16.

In order to cause disease an organism must fulfill certain criteria:

1. It must be capable of causing disease;
2. It must enter the animal;
3. It must enter in sufficient numbers;
4. The animal must be susceptible.

BACTERIA

Bacteria are single-celled organisms; those that cause disease are called pathogenic. Of these there are many forms, and all are, in some way, transmissible from one animal to another.

Since bacteria are too small to be seen without magnification, they must be studied through the microscope. There they appear as different from each other as the various farm animals. Some are spirals, some are little balls, some have whiplike attachments, and some look like baseball bats.

(1) Streptococci (grow in chains). (2) Staphylococci (grow in bunches). (3 and 4) Bacilli.

Coccal bacteria are round. Streptococci (pronounced strep-toe-cox-eye) are round bacteria that grow in strings. They produce such diseases as pneumonia and pus infections. Staphylococci are round forms that grow in groups like bunches of grapes. They are notorious pus producers and abscess formers.

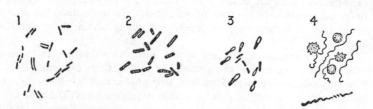

(1) Bacilli (rod-shaped). (2) Bacilli (rod-shaped). (3) Mycobacteria (club-shaped). (4) Spirochetes (among blood cells).

Bacilli are rod-shaped bacteria, many of which are mischief-makers, sometimes complicating other diseases. Bacilli come in many different forms and cause a myriad of diseases such as bubonic plague, tularemia, and some poultry diseases. Salmonella organisms cause food poisoning in man and other diseases in animals. Shigella cause dysentery in kittens, and bird typhoid; clostridia cause lockjaw, food poisoning (botulism), gas gangrene; mycobacteria cause tuberculosis.

Spirochetes are corkscrew-shaped organisms that cause diseases such as trench mouth and leptospirosis.

Since these are all comparatively large forms, too large to enter the cells of the body, bacteria float or propel themselves about in body fluids or remain stationary. Some invade the bloodstream; some are specific for certain tissue, such as pneumococcus types for lungs; others are found only in the stomach and intestines.

RICKETTSIAE

Rickettsiae are different from bacteria. They are smaller—so small that they have been found inside of cells. They are responsible for such diseases as Rocky Mountain spotted fever, which is spread by the parasites of rodents, dogs, and humans.

FUNGI

A third class of infecting organisms most interesting to the veterinarian and to the cat owner is the fungus (plural, fungi or funguses). Fungi are plants of a low order that produce seedlike spores. Spores resist drought, heat, cold, and other environmental factors. When conditions of moisture and temperature are right, they grow into mature forms.

Many skin diseases in cats are of fungus origin. Ringworm, which grows in individual cells, is a fungus. Molds are fungi. There are a great many kinds of fungi—good, bad, and neutral types. Penicillin, one of the most extraordinarily effective drugs ever discovered, is made from a mold.

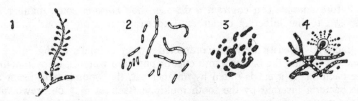

(1) *Yeast*. (2) *Rickettsia* (*greatly magnified*). (3) *Fungi* (*grow by budding*). (4) *Fungi* (*grow in threads*).

VIRUSES

Viruses live *in* the cells. They are so small that they are invisible through an ordinary microscope. Photographs of them made through the electron microscope indicate that, like bacteria, they grow in various forms. Their exact nature is not understood, and few cures for the diseases they cause have been discovered. If your veterinarian diagnoses your cat's disease as a virus disease, and tells you that he has no medicine with which to cure it, believe him. Don't run to another doctor expecting him to cure it with drugs. If he does effect a cure with drugs, your pet probably did not have a virus disease. At least this is true on the basis of what we now know about viruses. There are exceptions, however: Psittacosis, caused by a large virus, can be treated successfully with antibiotics. But such cases remain rare.

Viruses, even more than bacteria, have affinities for certain tissues in the body. Rabies, for instance, is neurotropic, which means that it attacks nerve tissue. Distemper has an affinity for the epithelial tissue (skin and mucous membranes). Some viruses attack the lining of the nose and throat, and others attack lung tissue.

One of the tragic facts about viruses is that they so weaken tissue that bacterial diseases can get a start and develop. Certain bacteria are such constant companions of viruses that scientists once believed bacteria to be the cause of a number of virus diseases simply because bacteria were constantly present. This was true, for example, of distemper, which scientists thought was caused by a bacterium called *B. bronchisepticus*. Bacterial pneumonia can be a secondary complication of cat distemper. Of course veterinarians should and do try to cure any part of the disease they can. If antibiotics or sulfa drugs will destroy bacteria that complicate virus diseases, they should be used, *but not to treat the virus,* because they are worthless against it.

DISEASE TRANSMISSION

Before animals can contract a disease, they must in some manner be exposed to the infecting organism. Exposure can come about in many ways.

Bacterial diseases may be contracted by an animal's eating infected food, by getting the bacteria into cuts or puncture wounds, or by inhaling the bacteria. If a cat is bitten by another cat, the wounds may fester as the bacteria inserted by the tooth multiply. Bacteria may be drawn into the system, or they may be present in air passages, waiting for a virus or general loss of resistance to weaken tissue and set up conditions favorable to their growth.

Some virus diseases can be passed from one animal to another by inhaling one brief sniff of a sick animal's breath, or even by inhaling air in a room in which a sick animal has sneezed and left minute droplets floating about carrying the virus. Other virus diseases can be transmitted by bites, as in rabies.

Fungus diseases are spread in several ways: by contact, by wind, by water. Suppose your Siamese develops a concentric bare spot on his nose. How did it get there? Well, he may have pushed his nose against a spot on your infected dog, or he may have rested on a couch where the dog had been lying previously, or a breeze may have blown spores on him. Somehow they settled on his nose and grew. Some of the worst skin diseases a cat gets can be contracted by his lying on a lawn, or rubbing against another cat, or from dust blown on him containing spores that find entrance to his skin through fleabites.

IMMUNITY

Some knowledge of the body's defense against diseases and of immunity is necessary in order to understand methods of prevention and cure.

When a cat that has been bitten develops an abscess, his body builds a dam around the area and walls it off from the rest. The next time he is bitten other infections may develop from the same bacteria. But if, instead of developing a localized abscess, the bacteria invade the bloodstream, a different condition develops. *If the cat survives by its own bodily mechanism or chemistry,* it will be immune to that species of bacteria for a long time afterward. But if the cat is treated with medication that destroys every bacterium of that type in the body within a few days, then solid immunity may not be developed. Why?

Because the body builds up defenses to overcome bacteria or viruses in several ways: white cells may engulf them, or the body may develop antitoxins that counteract the toxins elaborated by the bacteria. All animal bodies have the power to develop specific counter-chemicals that will act to destroy invading bacteria. We call these defense chemicals antibodies.

It is amazing how specific they can be. The antibodies against one disease organism are seldom of value against another. If a cat recovers from virus pneumonia, for instance, he can still contract feline distemper. If he recovers from one species of coccidiosis, he can still contract another form. But if the cat is to develop immunity, he has to recover without medication. If the recovery from a bacterial disease is due to chemicals added to his blood, he does not always develop the antibodies that will solidly protect him against that form of disease in the future.

There are different kinds of immunity. Passive immunity is conferred by additions of biologics to the blood to ensure temporary protection. Inherent or inherited immunity is transmitted from parent to offspring. Acquired immunity is acquired after birth. Active immunity is produced by an animal's own tissues or fluids. It may be produced:

By having a disease and recovering.
By constant mild exposure to the disease-producing organism.
By injection of dead bacteria, or products of dead bacteria.
By injection of dead viruses or viruses that have been attenuated
    (a) by the addition of chemicals to live virus;
    (b) by passing the disease through another species;
    (c) by growing the virus in cell cultures.
By injection of toxins.

PARASITIC DISEASES

External Parasites. Parasitic diseases from which our cats suffer are real diseases, often tragic in their consequences. Have you ever thought of lice infestation as a disease, or hookworms, or mange? Fortunately these are the easiest diseases to manage, as long as we remember that the cure is only half of the job; the important part is to prevent reinfestation. For this reason every pet owner should know, in a general way, the life history of all of the common parasites.

The Flea. Those little elusive insects that jump so far and those big, brown, long-bodied insects that crawl about on our pets are fleas. The big ones are always females; the little jumpers may be either males or young females. Fleas are a serious threat to the health of animals. They carry and spread tapeworms, bubonic plague, and other diseases. They also help spread summer skin diseases, cause loss of weight and poor coats on their hosts.

There are four common types of fleas: the human flea, dog flea, cat flea, and the sticktight flea. The human flea may breed on cats as well as on humans. The dog flea and the cat flea infest either dogs or cats, but prefer their specific hosts. When they bite humans it is only because they lack a dog or cat to feed on. The sticktight flea is most often found infesting the rims of the ears of animals but may also be found attached to other parts of the body. There are dozens of other fleas that are more or less host-specific.

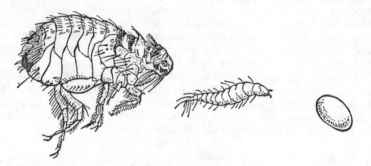

Stages of the flea, enlarged fifty times. Left, adult; center, newly hatched larva; right, egg.

Dog and cat fleas produce large numbers of white eggs, which drop off the host. The eggs sometimes get into cracks in the floor, into a sandbox, or into the furniture where the pet sleeps, and lie there in a dormant state for many months before conditions become right for their development. Some eggs hatch very soon after they are dropped. Moisture and heat are essential for hatching. Since flea eggs are deliquescent, that is, they absorb water from the air, they hatch whenever the weather becomes warm and humid. In excessively dry climates and high altitudes fleas are almost unknown.

Out of the egg comes a worm, the larva, which grows quickly. When it reaches the size of a very small maggot, it spins a cocoon and pupates like the caterpillar. Out of these cocoons come males and females, which, at this stage, look very much alike. They are able to jump prodigious distances and are remarkably well protected against pressure. If you roll one tightly between your fingers and let it go, it will jump about as well as it did before.

After they hatch, fleas crawl up anything vertical and wait there, about a foot from the ground or floor, for a host to pass. If your pet is taken out of the house for the summer, you may find after a few weeks that the fleas are attacking you instead. The fleas you find in the house have developed from eggs dropped from your pet, and since the original host has been removed, they use you as a substitute. Nor are the fleas confined to the house or cattery. You may easily be flea bitten in the garden if your pet has the run of the grounds and eggs are dropped there.

During their life on the cat, fleas excrete a blackish substance that looks like tiny cinders. This material falls from the cat and is eaten by the developing larvae; it should not be confused with flea eggs. If you find these tiny black crusts on your cat's skin, they are an indication of fleas even when you can't find the fleas.

Recognizing the life cycle of the flea helps us to understand the problems involved with eliminating this parasite. If we discover fleas only after the cat has been infested for a few weeks we can assume there are eggs on the premises that will hatch over a three- or four-week period if the temperature is warm and the atmosphere not too dry.

Therefore, if flea powders, sprays, or collars are used and every flea on the animal destroyed there will still be newborn fleas that will leap on board as the cat passes. So, if you depend on flea killers applied to the cat you must recognize that it will take many weeks to rid the premises of these unwelcome insects.

Spraying overstuffed chairs, couches, and all your cat's favorite resting places is helpful, but it is usually not possible to spray all the areas of a home where a cat wanders. Furthermore the outside cannot be sprayed and many eggs develop outside.

Persistence in treating a cat in an infested location will be rewarding but prevention is obviously the proper approach. I prefer the flea collar and have observed excellent results, particularly where it is applied before the warm flea season. The chemical in the first collars available caused an unsatisfactory number of neck rashes and even open sores. New collars rarely cause a problem.

Sticktight fleas do not move about or jump, but cling to the skin, often in large clusters. The female burrows into the skin and lays her eggs in the ulcers she produces. After the eggs hatch, the larvae fall to the ground, where they complete their development within four weeks, when conditions are right. This flea is more prevalent in warm climates than in cold. Not only dogs, cats, and other four-legged pets are infested by sticktight fleas, but birds as well. Such an infestation is far more lethal to birds, especially those in the chick stage.

In some regions of the country, ticks are called sticktights. This is a colloquialism, since they are not at all the same thing.

The Louse. The louse lives all its life—embryonic and adult—on an animal or bird. All species of pets may be infested, and it is believed that no type of louse can live for more than three or four days off the animal or bird on whose body it depends for sustenance. The biting louse of cats is subclassified into several species. Some are red, some gray, some bluish, but in spite of obvious differences their life histories are very similar.

A louse hatches from its egg, called a nit, which the female has fastened to a hair. The little louse, if it is a sucking type, crawls onto the body of the animal, fastens its mouth in the skin, and sucks blood. A large number can suck so much blood and give off such a powerful toxin that the host often becomes anemic and dies. The biting louse, on the other hand, feeds on skin scales and organic matter as well as on blood. After the males and females copulate and the female's body fills with eggs, she lets go of the skin and, crawling on the hairs, attaches to them tiny silvery eggs large enough to be seen. The eggs of the biting louse hatch in five to eight days. The young mature two or three weeks after hatching. Lice do not drop off their hosts spontaneously. In general, infestation is spread by contact and by close association. Apparently lice move from one host to another of a different species quite easily. For example, dogs and cats kept in close proximity are usually infested equally.

Lice are frequently a cause of death for whole litters of kittens. The owner may be unaware that the queen is infested with lice, but, when the pet has kittens, the lice tend to leave the mother and gravitate to the kittens. Apparently the latter are more tender morsels. Before the owner knows it, the kittens have developed a leathery feeling, fail to thrive, and die. Every litter of kittens should be watched constantly for the presence of lice.

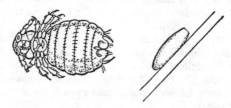

Louse and nit, enlarged twenty-five times. Left, biting louse; right, nit glued to hair.

Scratching by cats is one of the means by which lice are spread. The cat's skin itches when infested, and its scratching will naturally remove a small number of the parasites. It is believed that this is one of the chief means of transferring lice from one cat to another, provided, of course, that the next cat comes along within three days. If nits are attached to the hairs that the cat breaks off in scratching, they may lie around for a considerable period before hatching.

One type of human louse, *Pediculus capitis,* can live on cats. In many cases, pets which have been treated for lice have become reinfested by lice from human beings. Fortunately, not all types of lice are able to infest both species.

Chiggers (also called harvest mite, chigga, chigre, jigger, red bug). Adult red bugs, which are quite large, do not bother humans or pets. Nor does the second, or nymph, stage. The larvae alone attack animals, and then only shortly after they have hatched. Like ticks, they suck blood and drop off to molt. After this molt the nymphs may even feed on plants, but not on mammals. The tiny larvae annoy pets a great deal. They often cause severe scratching and sometimes loss of weight, without the owner's understanding the cause.

Destroying lice is a simple matter. I prefer using rotenone products since they lose their potency in a few days and do not pollute the environment. Powders, dips, and sprays all are effective but the treatment should be continued until all the nits have hatched and this should be weekly for a month.

The Tick. Ticks are rapidly becoming a problem to cat owners and they are often a nuisance in the house, even in a home where no pet is kept. Ticks feed on many species of domestic animals as well as on wild ones, and some are found on birds. One characteristic of the most common ticks found on pets and man is the necessity for each to feed on blood at some stage of its life.

Dog ticks, wood ticks, spotted-fever ticks, Pacific Coast ticks, brown dog ticks, lone-star ticks, Gulf Coast ticks, blacklegged ticks—all are common names for the several kinds of ticks. Some ticks are known by several names. All of them are very much alike, have similar life histories, and all are infrequent visitors to cats.

Ticks pass through four stages: egg, seed tick, nymph, and adult. The female lays enormous numbers of eggs in a mass on the ground or in a clump of grass. There may be as many as three thousand to six thousand eggs in one such mass. When the American dog tick hatches from the egg as a seed tick, it has six legs. It attaches itself to a rodent that carries it about for from two to twelve days and then drops off after it has become

Ticks, enlarged six times. Left shows adult female before feeding; right, adult male.

engorged with blood. By this time the tick has eight legs, has molted, and is called a nymph. It again attaches itself to a rodent and for three to ten days rides and engorges blood, then drops off and molts again. It is now mature and, in order to attach itself to a larger animal, gravitates close to a path through the woods and climbs a bush, where it is rubbed off onto its new host. It is an interesting if unexpected fact that studies made of these pests show greater concentrations along paths than in the pathless woods.

After the female has attached herself to a host, the male crawls under her and mating occurs while the female is filling with blood. If you look under the big beanlike body of female ticks on an infested animal, you will almost invariably find a male—a small creature which does not grow nearly so large as his mate. The female engorges on the host for from five to thirteen days, then drops off, falls to the ground, and, being enormous and practically helpless, lays her eggs and dies.

Some ticks are not quite so discriminating as the American dog tick. Some spend their seed-tick and nymph stages on birds and even reptiles, and one, the Gulf Coast tick, spends its immature stages on birds that live on the ground, such as quail, turkeys, and pheasants. Still others feed on birds exclusively, notably *Argas reflexus*, whose host is the pigeon.

The brown dog tick, which is becoming the most widely distributed tick in the North, prefers to pass its early life inside dwellings. It is often found under picture moldings, behind baseboards, and in furniture. Even adult ticks can be found in such hideaways. Fortunately they rarely suck human blood as some other species do and they do not require an intermediate host.

It bears repeating that ticks are not as attracted to cats as they are to dogs and rarely pose a serious problem for cats.

Ticks are removed with a little effort just by pulling with fingers or forceps. Two common fallacies come to mind concerning these creatures. One is that they "screw" themselves into the skin clockwise and must be unscrewed counterclockwise. The second is the fear of leaving the head buried in the skin. The tick's head does not enter the skin, only the mouth parts, and there are no screwlike threads to "unscrew."

Tick bites usually cause swelling and some inflammation, which heal without treatment unless the tick is removed with scissors, in which case the embedded mouth parts are left behind and cause more swelling and an extended period of healing. So, instead of cutting them off, pull the ticks off and then dispose of each one by burning or flushing them down the toilet.

I prefer to pick ticks from cats myself rather than using strong insecticides, which are more dangerous to the cat's health than the parasites. The premises may be sprayed with tick spray, which is not dangerous after it dries, but keep the cat out of the area in which you are spraying until the spray does dry.

MITES: Mange on cats is caused by mange mites, which are so small that they cannot be identified without a microscope.

Red mange mites (*Demodex cati*). Also known as demodectic mange mite and follicular mange mite. When a cat shows a baldish area under the eyes, on the cheeks, on the forehead, or on the front legs, it may have red mange. If it is not checked early, it may soon have serious consequences. One of these is the bacterial infection that often develops, causing pustules and intense reddening of the skin, with violent scratching from the irritation.

The young mites, as they hatch from the eggs, appear to be elongated globs, but they mature very quickly to look like minute eight-legged worms. They live in sebaceous glands and in hair follicles, so that when

an animal has been infected the hair soon drops off the infected area.
They reproduce prodigiously. In eight days a thousand female mites may
have increased to twelve thousand. In eight more days these may have
become 132,000.

Cat mites (*Notoedres cati*) produce a disease called scabies in humans. The mite is round, with four pairs of short legs. The female tunnels
into the skin and lays from twenty to forty eggs, which hatch in three to

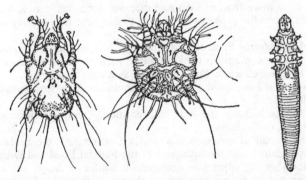

*Mites that attack mammalian pets, all greatly enlarged. Left, ear mange mite;
center, sarcoptic mange mite; right, demodectic mange mite, also called red and
follicular mange mite (extremely rare in cats).*

seven days. One female can easily produce 1,500,000 descendants in
three months. The newly hatched larvae have three pairs of legs. They
molt to become nymphs, which molt still again before they become
adults. This process requires two to three weeks for completion. Only the
adult female burrows beneath the outside layers of skin; males and immature forms live on the surface under scabs or skin scales.

Ear mites (*Otodectes cyanotis*). Ear-mite infestations are second only
to fleas as far as cat problems are concerned. They live primarily in the
ear canal and produce a dark brown to almost black crumbly wax. We
often see thousands of mites in an ear, which for some strange reason appears to cause little more than occasional shaking of the head in some animals. Others will all but scratch their ears off with the nails of the hind
legs.

Kittens are frequently presented with advanced cases that they acquired from their mother and, having never known life without them,
show, in their actions, no sign of discomfort.

Two other external signs of ear mites are accumulated blood between
the layers of skin of the ear called a hematoma (see page 244) and an
open abraded area behind an ear. This is caused by scratching.

Flooding the ears with mineral oil or baby oil every other day will de-

188 THE COMPLETE BOOK OF CAT CARE

stroy mites over a three-week period. The object is to drown the adults and young as they hatch. Your veterinarian can prescribe more effective medication that will also destroy bacteria that may have entered the damaged tissue of the canal. After you apply the medication, massage the base of the ear before the cat shakes the medication out. Since mites live for some time in the area around the ears, it is wise to treat the hair with a flea powder, spray, or rinse as described previously in this chapter. Furthermore, when a cat sleeps, the tip of the tail may rest against the infected ear and it too may need treatment.

If you have more than one cat and discover ear mites in one, treat all of the cats, since the problem is difficult to diagnose in the early stages.

Control of External Parasites. Bathing in itself will not eliminate parasites, as many people seem to think, but a number of preparations used with the bath are effective. Some are used as a rinse or dip following the bath, as described previously; others are liquid soaps or soap cakes with insect killers added.

After the bath keep the cat well powdered with a nonpoisonous powder, spray, or flea collar.

With the advent of government-supervised advertising, the banishment of dishonest claims, and the insistence of the Federal Food and Drug Administration that ingredients be declared on bottles of drugs, any ingenious person can make his own household remedies by reading the percentages of the contents of bottles he has bought. And it is amazing how much money can be saved. This is especially true in the field of grooming. You will find mineral oil and pine oil mixed selling under a trade name at many times the cost of the ingredients, which can be bought in any drugstore. You will find derris root or cube root mixed with dried clay (recommended as a flea powder) selling at high prices. It is an excellent flea powder, but, if you have many cats you might just as well buy derris root or cube root and use less of it, undiluted.

There seems to be a constant barrage of criticism directed toward the Federal Food and Drug Administration, but I for one believe they do a tremendous job in safeguarding the health of our animals.

Resin strips are available that are impregnated with a volatile insecticide called vapona. At first they were marketed under the name of Vapona Bars. Later they appeared as No Pest Strips. They can be hung in any room and will kill all sorts of flying insects. One strip is sufficient for 1,000 cubic feet of space. In catteries they destroy mosquitoes and flies, but also insects that do not fly, such as fleas, lice, and mites.

The life of the strips is said to be four months but the life can be greatly extended by hanging one up for a week or two, after which the strips can be placed in a jar with a tight cover and kept until they are needed again.

A so-called invisible collar is also available in pet stores. This is a stick in a tube containing a long-lasting flea killer, which is rubbed around the cat's neck once a week.

I have placed cats with hundreds of fleas in cages in a room with one fly bar to find all the fleas dead on the paper in each cage in twelve hours.

A questionable treatment, suggested by an old-timer, consisted of rubbing the cat's coat with drinking alcohol and then sprinkling sand into the coat. The fleas get drunk drinking the alcohol and kill each other throwing stones.

Internal Parasites. Many pets suffer from parasites that damage the inside of the body, in contrast to those we have previously considered, which attack from the outside.

ROUNDWORMS: These include all worms under the classification of nematodes, such as hookworms, whipworms, esophageal worms, heartworms, lungworms, and kidney worms, as well as the large roundworms, which most pet owners recognize. In this section, the term "roundworms" refers to the whitish or ivory-colored worm that grows up to five inches long in the stomach and intestines of pets, is pointed at both ends, and inclined, while alive, to curl up. When dead, it straightens out so that it may appear to be simply bowed at the ends.

Although there are several kinds of intestinal roundworms, their life histories are much the same. The eggs pass out of the animal with every bowel movement. In less than a week, if the temperature and moisture are propitious, a little worm forms in the egg. In other words, it has to incubate before it can hatch. Now this egg is in the infective stage and, as such, it will live for years, waiting to be picked up by a suitable host. It may enter the host in any one of dozens of ways. A queen may walk in a spot where feces have entirely disintegrated but where the eggs remain. They stick to her feet; she licks herself and becomes infested. Even cats that live all their lives inside homes, are pan trained, and never make mistakes, are frequently infested for the simple reason that the material in their pans is not changed often enough. Pans should be changed once every five days or oftener.

The egg enters the stomach, and the shell, or coat, is digested, liberating the embryo. If it happens to be an egg of *Toxascaris leonina* the larva moves along into the intestine, where it penetrates into the lining, remains there for ten days, and grows. Finally it returns into the lumen, or hollow part of the intestine, and continues to grow to maturity, feeding on the animal's partially digested food.

If the roundworms are of the *Toxascaris canis* or *T. cati* varieties, they are much more harmful to their host. In the intestine the little larvae bore through the intestinal lining and enter the bloodstream, where they grow. Many may be found in the liver and spleen while on their way to the lungs. In the lungs they penetrate through from the blood vessels into the air spaces and are moved on to the windpipe. Up this they move in mucous secretions until the irritation causes the animal to cough and gag as if clearing its throat. The small amount of mucus with the worms in it is

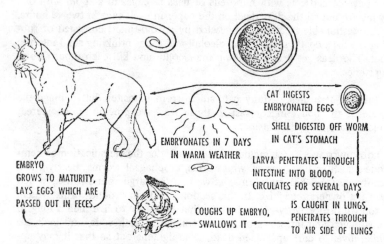

CAT INGESTS
EMBRYONATED EGGS

SHELL DIGESTED OFF WORM
IN CAT'S STOMACH

EMBRYONATES IN 7 DAYS
IN WARM WEATHER

LARVA PENETRATES THROUGH
INTESTINE INTO BLOOD,
CIRCULATES FOR SEVERAL DAYS

EMBRYO
GROWS TO MATURITY,
LAYS EGGS WHICH ARE
PASSED OUT IN FECES

COUGHS UP EMBRYO,
SWALLOWS IT

IS CAUGHT IN LUNGS,
PENETRATES THROUGH
TO AIR SIDE OF LUNGS

Life history of a common roundworm. Above, left, mature worm; right, egg magnified four hundred times.

swallowed. Down the gullet go the parasites, which from then on, until old age overtakes them, or worm medicine kills them, live in the intestine, migrating up and down at will, copulating and laying thousands of eggs.

Not only do roundworms give off a toxin, but the migrations of the larvae in the body, especially in the lungs, frequently cause death. The pneumonia they cause is called verminous pneumonia.

The incubated eggs of these parasites, when ingested by a human, cause visceral larval migrans, a very serious disease; so cleanliness and care in disposing of cat excreta are essential.

Piperazine is the drug of choice for roundworms—it is safe and efficacious in all but tiny kittens or weak older kittens and may be found where pet supplies are sold. Follow the directions on the package. For weak or very young kittens ask the advice of your veterinarian—don't take chances.

Hookworms are like minute leeches in that they live on blood which they suck from the intestine, to which they cling with a set of hooks or teeth about the mouth. Hookworms cause anemia and loss of condition. A heavy infestation causes death.

The animal hookworm is not the same worm that causes so much hookworm anemia in humans. No animal hookworm is over five eighths of an inch long for females and slightly less for males. Three types are found distributed in different geographical areas. *Ancylostomum caninum* has a very wide distribution, while *A. braziliense* is more or less confined to the South and tropical regions. *Uncinaria stenocephala* is a northern hookworm.

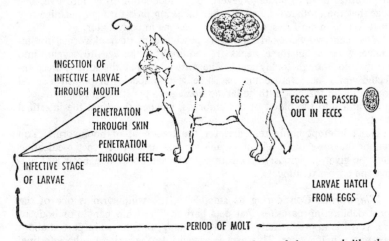

INGESTION OF
INFECTIVE LARVAE
THROUGH MOUTH

PENETRATION
THROUGH SKIN

PENETRATION
THROUGH FEET

INFECTIVE STAGE
OF LARVAE

EGGS ARE PASSED
OUT IN FECES

LARVAE HATCH
FROM EGGS

PERIOD OF MOLT

Life history of the hookworm. In the body, the larvae behave much like the roundworm larvae, spending their early days in the cat's blood and lungs. They are coughed up and swallowed. They then attach themselves to the small intestine by their hooks. Above, left, hookworm life-size; right, egg enlarged four hundred times.

The life history of the hookworm is interesting. The eggs, passed out of the host in the feces, need warmth to develop. Therefore the warm months are the hookworm months in the North, whereas the whole year is hookworm time in warmer climates. After the eggs have incubated from three to six days, larvae emerge. These are called the first-stage larvae. Three days later the larvae molt and become the second-stage larvae. Eight days later they molt again to become third-stage or infective larvae and then lie waiting for a host. Hookworms can bore through the skin to reach the bloodstream. More often they are ingested through the mouth and are sometimes inhaled with dust kicked up in a place where stools have disintegrated and become mixed with soil.

If the larvae have reached the bloodstream by boring through the skin or internal tissues, they eventually reach the lungs, bore into the air sacs, are finally coughed up, swallowed, reach the intestine, and molt two more times. Three weeks after they first entered the body as larvae, hookworms are large enough to lay eggs. Sometimes hundreds cling to an animal's intestinal lining. They are very debilitating. A hookworm can suck an appreciable amount of blood in a week. A thousand can suck one and a half tablespoonsful *in a day*. No wonder hookworms cause anemia!

With these facts in mind, two questions can now be answered:

How can mother animals lick their offspring clean of feces without becoming infested with intestinal parasites? The answer is that all the eggs of parasites have to undergo several days' incubation to be infective. The eggs that the mother cleans from her offspring pass through her digestive tract and lie in her feces, unharmed, to become infective later.

How can two-week-old kittens be passing eggs of hookworms, for instance, when about three weeks are required for the eggs to develop into worms old enough to lay eggs? The answer is that the kittens were infected while they were embryos. Since several species of parasites spend some time in the blood, these larvae manage to penetrate through the placenta and into the blood of the embryos, whence they find the intestinal tract.

Don't attempt home remedies for the treatment of hookworms. You cannot diagnose them without a microscope and the correct medication must be given judiciously. Let your veterinarian do the diagnosis and suggest the proper treatment.

Whipworms. Considering its small size, the whipworm is one of the most debilitating parasites that pets harbor. The whip handle or body of the worm is approximately half an inch long, but the whip part is about one and a half inches. This part is sewed into the lining of the intestine, but the pest can withdraw it to move. The worm is very thin; even the body is no thicker than the diameter of coarse sewing thread. Whipworms lay yellowish eggs of a lemon shape. Incubation in the soil requires about three weeks at a fairly high temperature before the embryos are infective. So far as is known, upon being ingested, the larvae are liberated and fasten themselves at once along the intestine, chiefly in the large bowel or colon.

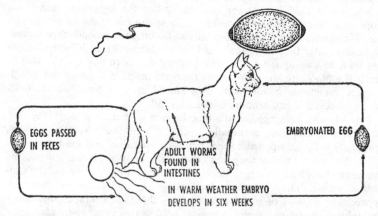

EGGS PASSED IN FECES

EMBRYONATED EGG

ADULT WORMS FOUND IN INTESTINES

IN WARM WEATHER EMBRYO DEVELOPS IN SIX WEEKS

Life history of the whipworm. Above, left, whipworm; right, egg, enlarged four hundred times.

Fortunately whipworms are extremely rare in cats, though their eggs are occasionally found in laboratory fecal examinations.

Here, too, your veterinarian needs a sample of stool in order to make a microscopic identification of whipworm eggs and to prescribe the proper treatment.

Trichinella spirales may be found in large numbers in cats, usually after the cat has eaten an infected rodent. Symptomatic of this parasite is a sudden onset of bloody feces.

Stringyloides spercoralis is a minute worm of the small intestine that until recently was thought to be contagious to humans. Parasitologists no longer believe that these canine and feline parasites are the same as those that affect man. The major symptom of the malady is a protracted loose stool which may contain blood.

Lungworms. These tiny worms, about a quarter of an inch long and very slender, are found all over the United States in cats with persistent coughs. If your cat has a stubborn cough—not a sneeze—let your veterinarian examine it for lungworms. The cough is not due to the presence of worms in the lungs, but rather to their migration through the respiratory system.

Cats contract lungworms by eating snails or slugs that have become infected with eggs. The eggs hatch and the larvae migrate much as hookworm larvae do, taking about forty days to mature to the egg-laying stage.

The adult worms live in the branches of the pulmonary artery for as long as ninety days. Cats kept in back yards where slugs and snails abound constantly become infected during warm months. Usually the cat's coughing stops toward the end of winter.

This disease must be treated by a veterinarian.

TAPEWORMS: It is comparatively easy to remove tapeworms from cats. The hardest part in their control is in the prevention of infestation. This requires a knowledge of tapeworm life history.

There are two general kinds of tapeworms—the armed and the unarmed. The armed have suckers and hooks with which they cling, while the unarmed are equipped with only a pair of grooves that hold to the intestinal lining. A large armed tapeworm has powerful devices that enable it to hold fast despite all of the pull exerted on it by the passing food. It seems almost impossible that the little head can hold all of the worm, yet that is what it does. Besides the host in which they spend most of their existence, all tapeworms require an intermediate host and, in some cases, two such hosts. All are composed of a head to which are added a series of flat segments, joined one to another.

The Flea-Host Tapeworm (Dipylidium caninum). This is the most common tapeworm in dogs, foxes, and cats. It is about a foot long. The head is smaller than a small pinhead and the segments close to the head are stretched to the thickness of a thread. This section is called the neck. As the worm grows, the segments become wider and shorter. The last few segments are again longer and contain eggs. When ripe, these segments are shed and passed out with the stool. If no stool is present, the segment is moved downward to the anus, where it may cling until it dries into a small, brownish, seedlike grain, which drops from the pet.

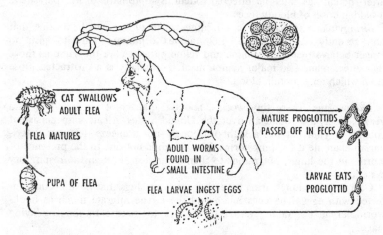

Life history of the flea-host tapeworm. Above, left, tapeworm, which often grows to be eighteen inches long. Right, capsule with eggs, enlarged one hundred and fifty times.

The eggs are not extruded without considerable pressure to the segment; then they appear in capsules and look, under a microscope, like bunches of grapes. When your veterinarian makes a fecal examination and tells you that your cat is free of worms, do not blame him for not detecting the presence of tapeworms. After you have seen a dozen segments, you may have an examination made and receive a negative report. Your veterinarian studies the stool for eggs, and if the tapeworm has passed no segments (proglottids) before the examination, he won't find any. Finding segments is the only effective way to determine the presence of this worm. The segments, when freshly passed, often appear alive and move like tiny leeches or slugs, raising one end until they dry up. At first they are off-white, but once dry, they turn a tannish color and shrink down to about a quarter of the size of freshly passed segments. Clients often tell veterinarians of finding grains of rice under their pets' tails.

Fleas and biting lice are the intermediate tapeworm hosts. When fleas are in their larval stage, they feed on tapeworm segments, among other foods. The eggs from these segments develop into tapeworm larvae as the flea matures. If an animal ingests the flea, the tapeworm larva is released and attaches itself to the intestinal wall, where it remains and grows.

There is no over-the-counter tapeworm medicine worth much and garlic, which the misinformed think destroys them, seems to nourish the worms so that they produce more segments. Veterinarians have satisfactory medications, although they may have to be repeated once or twice before all the tapeworms are eliminated. If the medicine destroys the body of the worm, leaving the head, it will develop to the segment-shedding period in about three weeks. All intestinal tapeworms are treated with the same medications.

The Rabbit-Host Tapeworm (*Taenia pisiformis*). This is a coarser worm than the flea-host tapeworm. Sometimes five to six feet long, it has larger and more active segments. The intermediate host is the rabbit or hare. This tapeworm lays many eggs, which pass out of the cat in his stool and cling to vegetation. Rabbits eating the vegetation become infested. The larvae work into the liver of the rabbits to develop, and from there into the abdominal cavity, where they attach themselves to intestines in small cysts. When a cat eats an infested rabbit, it too soon becomes infested.

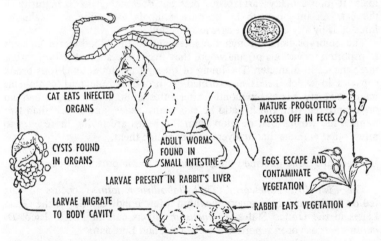

CAT EATS INFECTED ORGANS

MATURE PROGLOTTIDS PASSED OFF IN FECES

CYSTS FOUND IN ORGANS

ADULT WORMS FOUND IN SMALL INTESTINE

EGGS ESCAPE AND CONTAMINATE VEGETATION

LARVAE PRESENT IN RABBIT'S LIVER

LARVAE MIGRATE TO BODY CAVITY

RABBIT EATS VEGETATION

Life history of the rabbit-host tapeworm. Above, left, worm. Often grows to be two or three feet long. Right, egg, enlarged four hundred times.

Cats seldom kill adult rabbits and never kill adult hares. Baby rabbits, which are often killed by cats, are not likely to be infested with the cysts. How, then, do cats acquire the rabbit-host worms? It would seem by eating rabbits or hares shot and lost by hunters or killed by dogs or foxes. A healthy, hungry cat will not eschew so delectable an item. Since dogs, foxes, and cats have so many parasites in common, dogs and foxes often help spread parasites to cats and vice versa. This kind of tapeworm is an excellent illustration.

The Pork, Beef, and Sheep Tapeworms (*Taenia soleum, T. saginata, T. marginata, T. ovis*) have been reported as long as fifteen feet. It is rare to find these tapeworms in city pets. In country animals, which may feast on carcasses of dead animals, these infestations may occur. Hogs, cattle, or sheep that have fed in pastures where human excreta has been deposited can eat grass to which tapeworm eggs cling. The cat or other pet eats flesh from these animals and becomes infested from the cysts containing the tapeworm heads.

The Rodent-Host Tapeworm (*Taenia taeniaformis*) is a widely distributed form that probably does its worst damage to cats. Rats, mice, squirrels, muskrats, and other rodents may act as intermediate hosts. The heads in the cysts develop in their livers and remain dormant until eaten by an animal. Cats are the most likely pets to suffer from this parasite, since they feed on the host.

The Hydatid Tapeworm (*Echinococcus multilocularis*). This unique parasite is dangerous because it does damage to so many species of animals. It infests many carnivorous pets but does not grow to maturity in the cat. As intermediate hosts, most animals, including man, can be infested if by any chance the eggs are ingested.

The embryos bore through the intestines to the bloodstream and are transported to various organs where they become cysts that may measure three inches in diameter. The lining of the cyst produces numerous brood capsules in which heads are formed. A brood capsule may contain as many as forty heads six months after infestation. If an animal eats an organ infested with the hydatid he eats many heads, and in less than two months the worms that develop from the heads are laying more eggs to infest other animals that inadvertently consume them.

There are three unarmed tapeworms that are important to pet owners:

The Fish-Host Tapeworm (*Diphyllobothrium latum*) occurs in cats fed on fresh-water fish, generally within a few hundred miles of the Great Lakes in the United States. *D. mansoni* affects cats in Puerto Rico. *D. mansonides* has been reported in New York and Louisiana.

A human harboring the tapeworm passes out the eggs in feces that are dumped via sewers into the lake. Small crustaceans eat the eggs. In the first type, fish eat the crustaceans; in the latter two types, amphibians, such as frogs, or mammals that swallow the crustaceans, can be the second hosts. Cats that eat the infested fish, amphibians, or mammals become infested in turn. Raw whitefish, trout, salmon, pike, perch have all been incriminated as passing the cysts of these huge worms to pets.

Some of these worms have three thousand to four thousand segments and at their widest may be half an inch or even more across.

Taenia serialis. This is an intermediate worm between two and three feet long which dogs and foxes frequently carry in their intestines, and which they contract by eating cysts and their inhabitants—the heads, which may number a dozen or more—when they eat hares, rabbits, or squirrels. Some cysts may be an inch in diameter and cause the intermediate host great discomfort. The rabbits or squirrels become infested from eating grass, nuts, or other vegetation to which eggs of the worm are sticking.

It should be noted in passing that many pets that are only intermediate hosts can be made very sick by the cysts of tapeworms developing within their organs and muscles as well as in their intestines. Rabbits are the most common hosts.

Flukes. Several species of flukes have been reported in cats but only rarely. All flukes need intermediate hosts in order to spread to cats. These may be raw fish, snails, crawfish, or lizards.

The liver is usually affected so that liver ailment symptoms are those observed. The flukes get into the bile duct and also inflame the pancreas. The animal shows pain and loss of appetite. In severe cases there is bloody diarrhea and sometimes undigested fat in the feces. Some cats become yellowed with jaundice.

Diagnosis requires an examination of the stools, so take some stools to the veterinarian, who can then make a positive diagnosis and prescribe treatment.

PROTOZOA

The protozoa, the lowest form of animal life, are responsible for a number of very serious pet diseases. There are several forms, of which the sporozoite named coccidia are most important. These one-celled minute organisms live among the cells of the intestinal lining. Their life history is exceedingly complicated, and the damage they do is accounted for by the enormous numbers that develop before the body eventually overcomes them. Three other types, toxoplasma, piroplasma, and anaplasma, cause considerable damage as parasites of pets.

Coccidia. Each species of animal and bird is infested by specific types of coccidia, but some have more than one. Dogs and cats have three principal forms affecting both species. Rabbits, poultry, and even reptiles are afflicted. All types of coccidia are extremely prevalent, the year round in warm climates and in the summer in the cooler areas.

In size, coccidia are microscopic. The form found in the feces, the egg or oocyst, is roundish with a nucleus inside. Some oocysts show divided nuclei. The forms infesting cats are *Isospora rivolta, I. bigemina,* and *I. felis.* Rabbits are principally infested with *Eimeria perforans.* Birds may be host to at least a dozen species. Some are residents of the cecum and some are found in the intestine. Guinea pigs, rats, and squirrels each have specific types. *I. bigemina* may be the same organism as toxoplasma.

After it has been outside of the host for several days, the coccidia egg form develops into the infestive stage, provided conditions are favorable. Flies carry it to feeding pans or animals pick it up by licking their feet or by getting feces into their mouths. Inside the animal the coating of the egg form is digested and the infestive forms that have developed in the egg are released. These bore into the cells lining the intestine and develop until they divide into other bodies.

Coccidia. Three common types as they appear when enlarged through a microscope. Left, Isospora bigemina; *center,* Isospora rivolta; *right,* Isospora felis. *Each is magnified about four hundred times. Coccidiosis caused by* Isospora bigemina *may be confused with Toxoplasmosis.*

This division and growth damages or destroys the cells, but these new forms now enter other cells and repeat the cycle. This goes on through several divisions and attacking of new cells, until at length male and female forms are produced. The males fertilize the females and thus produce the egg form that is passed out with the feces and deposited with the loose stool to infest other animals or birds.

Coccidiosis is a disease of self-limiting character. Once recovered from a specific species of coccidia, the animal can no longer be infested, but this does not apply to all other species of the disease. A cat recovered from *I. rivolta* can be infested with *I. felis* just as though it had never been infested at all.

There are many suggested treatments but, in my opinion, since coccidia are self-limiting, good nourishment and cleanliness are as effective as any medication. A high-fat diet appears to be helpful in severe cases but many infestations are so mild that no signs of the disease are observed, although the oocysts are visible under the microscope.

Toxoplasmosis. Two excellent studies indicate that *Isospora bigemina,* the smallest coccidia of cats, and *Toxoplasma gondi* are one and the same organism. If true, one name will be dropped in favor of the other and I presume toxoplasma will be retained.

In 1971 a great interest in toxoplasmosis was manifested in several national magazines and newspapers, as a result of a series of articles in *Science* magazine. A number of unwarranted scare articles stressed the danger to pregnant women of contact with an infected family cat. The stories omitted to tell all the other ways toxoplasmosis could be contracted.

It is now known that a high percentage of human beings have had the disease without knowing it. Probably a high percentage of cats have had it too and are immune. The following symptoms should alert one to the possibility that the cat has the disease but these same symptoms are those of many other diseases: loss of appetite, diarrhea, lethargy, shortness of breath, fever, sniffles, tremors, depression. A cat would have to be very sick with the disease to exhibit all of these symptoms and this is rare. Few die from it.

Toxoplasmosis can be determined by fecal examination and it can be cured by antibiotic administration. Consult your veterinarian if your cat has loose stools and be particularly careful in handling the contents of the pan since the disease is thought to be spread by contact with stool containing the infecting organism, *Toxoplasma gondi*. Probably the danger from the cat exists for only a few weeks after the animal has recovered. The pan should be cleaned daily and the feces burned wherever possible. Putting them in the garbage is a danger to feral cats that feed from the pail.

Treatment consists of ordinary feeding and patience. Let your veterinarian prescribe the suitable drugs after he has diagnosed the disease. When you take the cat to his office, take a teaspoonful of stool to aid in his diagnosis.

Piroplasma and Anaplasma. These are carried by ticks. They are minute animals that live in the red blood cells and produce diseases called piroplasmosis and anaplasmosis. Of course the disease is due to the enormous numbers of organisms that develop, and to their effect on the efficiency of the red cells in transporting carbon dioxide and oxygen.

Two or three days after infestation the first symptoms appear. The number of red corpuscles is reduced and the white increased. The color from the broken-down red cells being thrown off by the body causes reddening of the urine. The parasites multiply by division. New ones attack other red cells.

An intermediate form does not develop in the vector of this parasite as in the case of tapeworms; injections of infested blood into a susceptible animal will be all that is necessary to start the disease.

So far the disease has been confined to the warm climates where ticks are prevalent, but with the increase of ticks in cooler climates, piroplasmosis may become a cool climate problem as well.

Babesia is another red-blood-cell parasite, transmitted by ticks, that may cause problems for cats. This parasite is rarely diagnosed. Wild raccoons in many areas have a high incidence of babesiosis.

Infectious Anemia or *Hemobartonella* is not a deficiency disease in the usual sense but does result in a deficiency of red blood cells. *Hemobartonella* is the name of a parasite of the red cells that causes anemia in cats. It was once thought to be the major cause, but with the separation of many anemia-producing viral diseases, we now think it accounts for only 10 per cent of the anemic cats.

There is a higher incidence in young adult males due perhaps to injuries sustained in fighting and hunting before they are proficient at these activities.

The signs of this disease are those of any anemia: weakness, loss of appetite, and general malaise. The diagnosis is made by stained blood smears, which may have to be done daily until the parasite is identified.

With concerted effort most cats are saved from the effects of the parasite, but untreated the mortality rate is high. Blood transfusions and antibiotic therapy often save even the advanced cases.

There are no protective inoculations for this parasitic disease.

VIRUS DISEASES

Panleukopenia (Feline Distemper or Infectious Enteritis). This is the most disastrous disease in the feline world. It has in the past killed more susceptible kittens than all other ailments put together and its control is in large part responsible for the feline population explosion. Panleukopenia can destroy 90 per cent of the kittens exposed to it; however, the inoculation against it is among the most effective ever developed.

The virus is transmitted either by direct contact or by exposure to the excrement, vomitus, or saliva of an infected animal; even fleas may spread this malady and the virus lives for months in the environment. An exposed susceptible cat develops a fever of 104 to 105°F. and may die suddenly after a brief period of depression and vomiting. These are the animals so often presented to veterinarians by owners who insist they died of poisoning.

Cats that survive the initial fever, depression, and vomiting appear to improve for twenty-four hours or so with temperatures returning to normal for that period but returning to about 104°F. for an extended period thereafter. With the second rise in temperature diarrhea develops. The stool is foul-smelling and may become dark with digested blood as the disease progresses. With intensive care, including antibiotics, intravenous fluids and tube feeding, many cats can be saved. As they dehydrate with vomiting and diarrhea the cats become thirsty but will not drink since the virus causes a painful throat; however, they go to water and hover over it as if they were going to drink. They may nod and dip their chins in the water but that's as far as they will go.

To treat this disease at home is often a disaster and many veterinarians cannot take such a patient with so highly contagious a disease into the hospital. This dilemma is solved either by finding an establishment equipped with isolation facilities or one willing to treat the cat as an outpatient. If such an afflicted cat lives for five to six days it usually survives.

It is interesting to note that when cats raised in a germfree laboratory environment are exposed to the virus of panleukopenia, they never die and rarely show any symptoms of disease.

The virus of this disease has been found to persist outside of a cat for as many as six months, so it behooves owners to carefully disinfect areas where the sick cat has been kept before a susceptible cat is brought in. It is not known how long a recovered cat can transmit the disease. It is reasonable to expect that a new cat will be susceptible and to treat its drinking water with certain antibiotics at the first signs of the disease. Once a cat has recovered from even a mild attack, it is probably immune.

Infectious Respiratory Diseases.   Although great strides in the prevention of many respiratory infections have occurred in the recent past we nevertheless have poor tools with which to treat these diseases. Most are caused by viruses and to date we have few approved viricidal preparations. Most of the virus diseases are not in themselves killers but so weaken the cat that secondary bacterial agents are the cause of the fatalities. These are called opportunist organisms. When your veterinarian prescribes medications for a viral disease it is hoped that these opportunists will be controlled and that the cat will develop immunity to the virus and recover.

To support the sick cat, hydration and nutrition are critical, and in many cases your veterinarian will suggest intravenous and stomach-tube feeding. On the other side of the coin it seems feasible to me that some disease-causing organisms may have nutritional requirements that are not necessary to the host. I believe that one day we will treat some diseases either by feeding diets that lack a nutritional element or by administering agents that remove the nutrition needed by the infection to tip the scales in favor of the cat. Indeed this may be part of the success of some of the present-day cancer chemotherapeutic agents used in man and other mammals.

A large percentage of infectious respiratory disease falls into one of two categories. The first is called feline viral rhinotracheitis (FVR) and the other feline caliciviral disease (FCD), also called in the recent past, feline picornavirus infection (FPI).

Other viral respiratory infections are feline pneumonitis (FPn) and feline reovirus (FRV). Also included in this category are a group of diseases caused by mycoplasma, the smallest free-living organisms known; several conditions caused by bacterial organisms; and even certain allergy-like conditions.

FVR produces copious discharges from the eyes. The third eyelids are usually raised and make the eyes seem to be rolling back in their sockets. As the disease progresses, the nasal passages are affected with a discharge similar to that in the eyes, and the corneas, which are the exposed surfaces of the eyes, often become ulcerated and blindness may eventually set in.

The ocular discharge of FCD may resemble that of FVR in the early stages but in a few days the FVR discharge is thick and tacky whereas that of FCD remains watery and less severe. Similarly, the sneezing and nasal discharge is more pronounced in FVR than in FCD. Ulcers of the tongue are seen in both infections but FVR affects the tip of the tongue whereas FCD is more apt to affect the sides of the tongue and the roof of the mouth.

It should be noted that feline rhinotracheitis is caused by one member of a large group of viruses called herpes virus. Most of us have had "cold sores" (caused by a herpes virus) and some may have suffered from a condition called herpes simplex. One form of the virus, which causes a fatal encephalitis in man, does not affect cats as far as we know.

Table VII

SYMPTOM	DISEASE
1. Clear eye discharge	Early FVR FCD
2. Mucous eye discharge	FVR
3. Sneezing	FVR and slight in FCD
4. Coughing	FVR
5. Mouth ulcers	FCD Less in FVR

FVR = Feline Viral Rhinotracheitis

FCD = Feline Caliciviral Disease

Another factor that must be mentioned is that allergies, bacterial infections, and caustic agents may account for similar respiratory symptoms also seen with viral diseases.

Feline pneumonitis has been a catch-all term for certain cat diseases and according to most experts the name is misleading. I think many mild viral infections and irritants are unfairly placed in this category. It is caused by a specific organism, Chlamydia Psittaci. Although its name implies a lung problem, this is rarely the case, since the symptoms are usually confined to the head. Unraveling these problems is a job for your veterinarian and not always easy for him; the treatments vary with the disease and its intensity in a given animal.

Inoculations. The available preventive inoculations for FVR are effective for from six to twelve months. (A recovered cat is immune for about the same period of time.) Although there are many strains of FCD, inoculation of a vaccine prepared from one strain protects cats against all strains for an extended period of time.

The low incidence of feline pneumonitis and the limited protection of either recovery from natural infection or vaccination has resulted in doubts about the value of preventive inoculations. Since feline reovirus causes a mild disease and is rare, no preventive vaccine has been developed.

Infectious Peritonitis. Feline infectious peritonitis (FIP) appears to be increasing in incidence with each passing year. It is a wasting fatal disease with an unfortunate name. Unfortunate since peritonitis refers to the abdominal cavity and the disease affects the chest as frequently.

With an incubation period often in excess of a month, it is considered a slow virus disease.

When the chest is involved, fluid accumulates, resulting in difficult breathing; when the abdomen is involved there is usually an obvious swelling also from fluid accumulation.

Since only a few cases have been cited in the literature as having been cured, we must consider it a fatal disease. Numerous cases have been treated with both conventional and less conventional methods at the New Haven Central Hospital for Veterinary Medicine, with uniformly poor results. In my opinion once a diagnosis is made the cat should not be permitted to suffer to a miserable death.

Leukemia. One of the great scientific accomplishments in recent history was William Jannett's discovery in 1964 of a virus that caused spontaneous cancer in mammals. The disease is more properly called lymphosarcoma in man and beast but there is no evidence that the feline virus affects mankind. Moreover, when left untreated in humans, it is thought to be fatal, whereas many felines recover spontaneously without signs of disease other than positive blood tests.

The symptoms of this malady are many and varied since the virus affects any organ or combinations of organs in the body. Usually a loss of weight and activity is noted, as well as pale gums and tongue, since anemia is one of the more consistent signs. Weight loss follows a loss of appetite and reduced fluid intake.

It would appear that this is a slow virus since it takes months, often over twelve months after exposure, before the cat is clinically ill. Thus, if one cat of several in a household is diagnosed it is common for another to develop the signs months later. Fortunately we do have a blood test for leukemia in cats and when one in a household is diagnosed it is wise to test the others, since a positive test will reveal a normal-seeming cat to be a potential carrier. In my opinion a potential carrier cat should be eliminated to protect the healthy pets, and yearly tests should be undertaken until all signs of the disease are gone.

There may be an inoculation for feline leukemia in the future and when it arrives it will prevent a great deal of suffering since this is one of the major causes of death in the domestic feline world.

Perhaps it should be emphasized that no case of human leukemia has ever been traced to an infected cat, although the virus will grow on human tissue cultures. There is no higher incidence of leukemia in those of us who handle these sick animals than in the general population, and therefore I see no public health problem from feline leukemia.

Rabies. Because of the many popular misconceptions concerning rabies, it seems advisable to review a few general facts about the disease and its spread before taking up the specific symptoms.

CAUSE AND DISSEMINATION: Rabies is a virus disease, transmissible to almost all kinds of warm-blooded animals and many kinds of birds.

In the past the dog was the principal agent of dissemination. This is no longer true. Rather, the skunk is the number one animal to spread the disease. Due to the efforts of the veterinary profession in inoculating dogs and cats since 1953, the present incidence of rabies has been reduced by more than 50 per cent. During this period of time rabies in dogs has diminished from over five thousand to slightly over one hundred per year, and in cats, from over five hundred to about one hundred cases a year in the United States.

Not all cats bitten by a rabid animal develop rabies. In one study, only about 15 per cent of the humans who took no treatments to protect themselves after being bitten developed the disease. In the past, when rabid wolves bit humans, a higher percentage died. Of dogs bitten by rabid dogs, 40 per cent died; of horses, the rate is also 40 per cent; hogs, 30 per cent; cattle, 30 per cent. The percentage of cats is not known.

Rabid dogs bite dogs, but they can't catch cats as easily. A rabid cat does not run about trying to bite other cats and dogs, although there are exceptional cases where they have been known to attack anything in sight —even cows. Rats may have rabies and infect the cats that kill them.

It is the saliva of the rabid cat that is dangerous. The bite drives the virus in the saliva deep into the tissues, where, being a neurotropic virus, it attaches itself to nerves and grows. It is not dangerous on the unbroken skin, although it is dangerous in the eyes. When an animal is bitten, there is no certainty about how long the virus will take to progress along the nerves until it reaches the huge mass of nerve tissue, the brain. The location of the bite has some effect. If a cat is bitten on a back foot, the virus will have quite a distance to travel before it reaches the brain, while with a bite in the jaw the elapsed time would be much less. From fifteen to 285 days are the extremes found in a study to determine how long this process takes.

If the virus is able to attach itself to a nerve after the cat has been bitten, the cat has rabies. If his body is capable of destroying the virus, the cat does not have rabies. The time that elapses until the virus grows to the brain is not an incubation period in the true sense.

What we think of as rabies is merely the manifestation of brain inflammation—encephalitis—and the animal may exhibit any of several typical forms of that malady. Thus present-day ideas about rabies are completely different from those of our forefathers. Even the old name, hydrophobia, is no longer used. The terms dumb and furious rabies have also been dropped because the symptoms these terms describe are only two manifestations of encephalitis. Once the symptoms appear, it is a downhill drag until death.

Periodically, information is disseminated by some well-meaning groups to the effect that rabies is overplayed by money-hungry veterinarians. It even has been claimed that there is no such thing as rabies. This is dangerous talk and when you run across such claims, you must not only doubt the statements, but you should also doubt everything else the authors say.

SYMPTOMS: The earliest sign may be what seems to be a perverse appetite, due to hunger coupled with such a dimming of the sense of taste that anything will be chewed and swallowed. A rabid cat will usually hide. It will lose its normal voice and cry in a subdued, hoarse voice indicative of paralysis of the larynx. Since it cannot drink, it will soon show evidence of dehydration.

Complete character reversals are frequent. In its hiding place the seemingly timid animal may have a change of personality, springing out at people, more often children, and inflicting scratch and fang wounds. Children have had their faces disfigured by rabid cats, and adults, bending over to succor the cat that won't come out of a hiding place, have sometimes suffered severe lacerations about their hands and arms.

In all forms of rabies, once the severe encephalitis symptoms appear, death generally ensues in less than a week, sometimes in three days. Infected farm cats usually go into the woods and die, but if they are hiding about the barn or in mangers, they may bite other animals. If a cat dies in suspicious circumstances, the owner should report the dead cat to the health authorities.

Unimpeachable diagnosis of rabies is possible only by microscopic and biologic means. The cat's brain must be examined in the laboratory; in addition, tissues from the diseased cat are injected into susceptible laboratory animals. The virus recovered from those animals can prove beyond a doubt that the disease is rabies.

PREVENTION AND CONTROL: Suppose you think your cat may be rabid. Contact your veterinarian immediately and take his advice, which may simply be to confine your pet in his hospital to see if it develops the characteristic symptoms as the disease progresses.

Veterinarians are often asked the following questions by pet owners: Why don't veterinarians try to cure animals with rabies? If they can't drink, why aren't these animals given fluid intravenously? Isn't there any serum for rabies? The answer to all these questions is simple. Human beings do not want to handle rabid animals, so practically nothing has been done in the way of treatment.

Prevention is the keynote in rabies control and consists primarily in the vaccination of all animals who might become carriers. Disease control can be made more effective by better supervision of all dogs and cats, and by rigid enforcement of the regulations requiring animal control officers to pick up all strays.

If there is any possibility that infected saliva or other excretion from a rabid cat has entered a cut or abrasion, a person should be given treatments. If taken in time, this treatment causes the human body to develop immunity in the blood, and the immune bodies in turn attack the virus growing on the nerves and destroy it.

To inoculate or not to inoculate cats for rabies is a question often raised. In my state of Connecticut we have not had a case of rabies in cats reported in over thirty-five years. So I will leave the decision up to you and your cat's doctor; telephone your veterinarian's office and ask for the policy in your area. It is true that an ounce of prevention is worth a pound of cure; but I don't take yellow fever shots since we have no yellow fever in my area; but, in the event of an outbreak even one hundred miles away I would make haste to my human doctor.

Virus Pneumonia. From time to time scientists have suspected that humans could transmit an atypical kind of pneumonia to cats and vice versa. There are many cases, well authenticated, of the cats and human members of the same household being sick at the same time, in much the same way. There have been a number of investigations into the nature of the disease and, as a result, it is now possible to identify several distinct forms of virus pneumonia.

Leptospirosis. Of spirochetal origin, the bacterial agent that produces this disease is spread most frequently by rat urine. Whole rat populations are affected at times. It is estimated that from 30 to 50 per cent of all mature rats are carriers. With cats' penchant for killing rats, it is amazing that more felines are not reported with this disease.

SYMPTOMS AND DIAGNOSIS: The disease appears in two forms, the canicola, which closely resembles distemper, and the icterohemorrhagic (jaundice-hemorrhages). The former is often inaccurately diagnosed since it presents particularly difficult diagnostic problems.

Both types produce a number of common symptoms that can be traced to the impairment of certain organs by the spirochetes. These are unsteady elevation of temperature, nausea, lassitude, loss of weight, loose stools, and stiffness. An almost constant symptom in both forms is the congestion of the tiny blood vessels in the whites of the eyes, which may turn a coppery red. The canicola form shows a few additional symptoms. The urine may range in color from orange to chocolate brown and may at times contain blood. The cat is generally quite emaciated when it dies.

The second type (icterohemorrhagic) differs in the symptoms it produces in the manner implied by the name. There is bleeding in the intestines and gums, and sometimes tiny hemorrhages are scattered throughout the body. The vomitus often shows blood; the stools appear bloody.

A further diagnostic symptom is one that a disease of the liver would be expected to exhibit: jaundice. The mucous membranes, skin, and whites of the eyes appear a more and more intense yellow as the disease progresses, until, at death, some tissues may be almost a canary yellow or orange. By the time the yellow has appeared, however, the disease has progressed so far that serious damage may have been done to the kidneys and liver. The difficulty of identifying the disease at an early stage makes it difficult to cure the first cat in an area to contract leptospirosis. By the time the diagnosis has been definitely established, there is usually little hope. Even if the cat should survive, the damage that was done before the treatment was started will often make him an invalid for the remainder of his life.

Laboratory tests on blood serum aids in the diagnosis but unfortunately are not helpful in the early stages of the disease, and when the disease has progressed to that point where the tests are of value it is usually too late to alter its course.

Leptospirosis in a cattery or in a pair of cats is a different matter. If one cat dies, diagnosis by post-mortem and bacterial examination is possible. Then, after the disease has been identified, treatment may be started immediately with those pets that have been infected a shorter time. When the disease is detected at an earlier stage, the cats may—and usually do—recover if proper treatment is given. Urinalyses can be performed on all as a helpful precaution. Every cat not entirely well, particularly those that show indications of a fever, can be treated. If the temperature fluctuates markedly from very high to almost normal, it may add to one's suspicions, for leptospirosis does not cause a uniformly high fever even at the beginning.

TREATMENT: Penicillin and other antibiotics have been found to be useful when given in massive doses, but they should be administered as early as possible. The mortality is high, but some cats do recover with no aftereffects. Laboratory tests with the serum from infected cats, mixed with colored spirochetes, cause clumping of the bacteria and show whether or not a cat has recovered. From my own experience, it would seem that the difficulty in diagnosing this disease and the harmlessness of antibiotics warrant their use whenever suspicion points to the possibility of leptospirosis.

Tuberculosis. When cats have tuberculosis it is more often the bovine, or cow, form. Barn cats that live in close proximity to cattle and often drink unpasteurized milk are most often infected. In Europe it is estimated that 2 per cent of the cats are tubercular. In America the percentage is far less. Attempts to infect cats with the human form of tuberculosis have failed.

The most frequent sites of lesions are lungs, liver, and kidneys. The lungs may become so heavily infected that areas of tissue may die and a tuberculous pneumonia occur.

So far we have no proven case of a cat having infected a human with

TB. They have been incriminated in spreading it to cattle, but there is always the possibility that birds are the true culprits. If a TB test demonstrates that a cat is infected, it is best to destroy it as quickly as possible because of the ever-present possibility of contagion.

14. Noncontagious Diseases

*A*LTHOUGH I have covered the diseases we think of as contagious in the previous chapter, there are many so-called noncontagious diseases that fall in a gray area in that they are transmitted occasionally. Then there is the case of diabetes which may be declared contagious if the current theory that it is a virus disease affecting the pancreas is proven. This theory suggests that there is an inherited familial lack of resistance to the virus, which would explain why it runs in families.

Let's begin by clearing the air about two often misunderstood terms—the suffix "itis" and the common cold.

-itis. The suffix, "itis," indicates inflammation and describes a condition, not a specific disease. If your cat has dermatitis, tonsilitis, hepatitis, encephalitis, or gastritis, it has inflammation of the skin, tonsils, liver, brain, or stomach. None are diseases, rather all are the body's response to some existing problem. When we talk about enteritis and refer to a specific contagious disease, we should call it feline infectious enteritis, or distemper. Enteritis itself may be caused by intestinal parasites or a myriad of other agents.

Colds. It has been said that only human beings and chimpanzees contract colds (which have been described as specific viruses). However, it has also been said there are over 100 human diseases with similar "cold-like" symptoms. Of these 100 maladies, cats certainly contract some, but since there is so much confusion about this subject, I will not refer to the word in this chapter.

DIABETES MELLITUS

The cause of diabetes is unknown at this time and its control is difficult in the cat. In Chapter 2, I discussed the pancreas and mentioned that one of its functions is the production of insulin. The diabetic cat produces little or no insulin to aid in the utilization of glucose either from the diet or produced by the liver. When the glucose builds above tolerable levels some is excreted by the kidneys. Usually the patient drinks more to aid in this process and urinates excessively. The cat loses weight and becomes less active. Cataracts may develop.

Glucose in the urine should suggest a fasting blood-sugar test and when suspicions are confirmed insulin must be given by injection at least once daily. Diet and exercise are all important in maintaining proper glucose levels since a dose of injected insulin combined with a given amount of food results in a given amount of glucose that is burned up by exercise. A delicate balance exists among these elements. Thus, if a cat on insulin eats much less than usual or if there is an increase of exercise, the blood glucose drops to a level inconsistent with life, resulting in coma and death. Unless, of course, the condition is reversed.

You will have to test the urine daily, maintain a rigid diet and uniform exercise to be successful. You cannot make the mistake of administering an extra unit of insulin. In other words you must be a concerned, conscientious owner willing to treat and watch over your pet with great care. The injections may seem repugnant at first, but after a week you'll be an old hand at it.

A queen may do beautifully on insulin with a uniform diet and exercise until she comes in heat, and then problems arise from hormones that interfere with the injected insulin. Such an animal, when stabilized, should have an ovariohysterectomy. Permitted to breed and to have kittens, a diabetic cat may die of stress, and the insulin given while she is pregnant may produce abnormalities in her kittens.

In my opinion, to stabilize a cat on insulin produced for humans, the insulin must be diluted. For a cat one-tenth or less the size of a human being, the dose must be a fraction of the human dose. One drop of full-strength insulin more or less can be critical, and although the syringes are accurate, the human eye may not be. To avoid difficulties, I dilute the insulin with three parts of sterile water, in which case a drop more or less is not as critical.

TETANUS (LOCKJAW)

Cats can become infected with tetanus but, despite the vast number of abscesses that cats have, they seldom do. Tetanus germs cannot grow in air; they do best in mixed infections where the other germs use up the oxygen, at which time the tetanus organisms begin to grow. Whether because the staphylococcus germs that are most commonly found in cat abscesses inhibit their growth or because the abscesses break before the tetanus gets a start, I have never seen a cat develop lockjaw because of external abscesses. I have known, on the other hand, deep, penetrating wounds that caused tetanus.

Symptoms are those typical of tetanus in other animals: the cat slowly stiffens; even the tail stands out straight with its end hanging from the weight. The cat's facial expression changes as its ears are held closer together than usual. There are indications of hunger and thirst but inability to chew and swallow, cessation of defecation and urination, often a pitiful moaning. Finally, dehydration and death.

Treatment with tetanus antitoxin and antibiotics, if started early enough, is often effective.

BACTERIAL PNEUMONIA

Inflammation of the lungs with bacteria of several types causes difficult breathing, high temperature—104°F. and over—prostration, loss of appetite, moderate thirst, and the rasping sound one hears if he holds his ear to the cat's chest. It is hard to mistake the symptoms of bacterial pneumonia.

Pneumonia follows exposures. Cats caught in traps or for any reason forced to remain cold and wet for any length of time are fit subjects. Such exposure in some way reduces the cat's bodily defenses, and pneumonia starts. Cats seldom live through it without drug administration.

The cat with pneumonia should be kept dry and warm. No attempt should be made to reduce its temperature, which is the body's way of helping to discourage the growth of the germs.

Pleurisy may follow pneumonia, with the lungs being adhered to the lining of the chest cavity. Areas of the lungs may break and form pockets and the cat is left with what in a horse would be heaves—emphysema. In that event the cat will no longer have the capacity for a long, fast frolic. It will become short of breath far too quickly, and its breathing may have the wheeze characteristic of this affliction. There is no cure for these aftereffects, but many cats learn to live with them. Antibiotics and even a day or two in an oxygen tent may save an animal with bacterial pneumonia.

SEIZURES OR CONVULSIONS

Epileptic convulsions are fortunately rare in cats, but when they do occur they are a terrifying episode to behold. Apparently the cat in such a seizure has lost contact with the environment and so either does not suffer or cannot remember suffering on recovery.

In such cases, I usually gather the cat up in a blanket, being careful to keep fingers away from the cat's mouth, for although a convulsing cat does not bite aggressively, it will open and close its mouth as it thrashes around. If a finger happens to be in the way of the closing jaws a bite will result. The blanket is to prevent injury to the animal.

If the seizure is too violent try to corral the cat in a closet or small room until the violence subsides before using a blanket, and remember if it does not subside in fifteen or twenty minutes it may last until death.

Observe the actual length of time of a seizure. Such a terrifying episode may seem like ten minutes when it actually lasts only a minute or two.

We can divide seizures into two categories: those produced by brain problems as with epilepsy and those produced by causes outside the brain. Among problems of the brain that cause seizures, there are several diseases that may cross the protective defense of the brain called blood-brain barrier. Tumors are a good example and as they grow the seizures become more frequent and increase in severity.

Both virus and bacterial encephalitis are capable of causing convulsions. In case of either, the spells are milder in the early stages and progress with each subsequent episode until help arrests them or death overtakes the cat. Only a veterinarian can help with this condition and our record is not good in effecting cures.

Anemia can contribute to convulsions as can intoxication. The latter can derive from two sources: bacteria in the stomach and intestines, and unexpelled decomposing roundworms left after a deworming.

Of other conditions outside the brain causing seizures, low blood sugar, heart-lung diseases, liver disease, kidney disease, and too little calcium are the most prevalent. A deficiency of vitamin B_1 (thiamine chloride) can also be numbered among the causes.

Poisoning with antifreeze (etheline chloride), which is a sweetish-tasting material, is probably not common but is observed from time to time. Lead, usually as chips from old paint, many insect sprays and powders must be on the list. Although fortunately not readily available today, strychnine and arsenic will cause protracted convulsions that end in death unless radical treatment is given promptly.

Very sensitive cats, even when in the best of health, have been known to have seizures when unduly excited. When taken for their first car ride, cats may become so terrified they rush wildly about and froth at the mouth. Owners occasionally report that cats attending their first cat shows have had seizures. Whether there are other contributing causes or whether the excitement alone brings on the seizures remains to be demonstrated, but certainly cats that have never had seizures before or since have had violent ones under the stimulus of excitement.

In the terminal stages of rabies the seizures are particularly terrifying.

The most common treatment for seizures is pentobarbital with tranquilizers, but since the dose must fit the problem, leave its determination to your veterinarian.

DIAPHRAGMATIC HERNIA

Trauma, usually from a crushing automobile accident, dog bite, or a fall from a high place, may rupture a cat's diaphragm. The diaphragm is that thin muscle which separates the chest cavity from the abdominal cavity. When the rupture is small, perhaps only a loop of intestine passes into the chest cavity, and few signs of the condition are apparent. More often the rupture is extensive, permitting the stomach and even lobes of the liver as well as loops of intestine to enter the chest cavity. In this situation there is insufficient area for the lungs to expand and labored breathing is obvious. Frequently, even after an injury from an automobile, there is no external sign, except perhaps labored breathing, to warn you of a problem, and X rays may be necessary for the diagnosis in such cases. A swallow of barium before the X rays locates the stomach and intestines and pinpoints the problem.

An injury sufficient to rupture a cat's diaphragm may have seriously injured the liver and lungs, making the cat a poor surgical risk. Sometimes such a problem is so life-threatening that we must take a calculated risk and operate immediately. If the cat's condition permits a few days of antibiotics and time for some healing, the results are a higher surgical success rate.

A ruptured diaphragm usually causes vomiting, as it did in a cat I treated off and on for years for weekly vomiting. He never did seem sick enough to X ray and a blended diet prevented vomiting. When he died of natural causes at fourteen years of age, I requested permission to examine the remains (a procedure called necropsy in lower animals). A small loop of intestine had passed through a ruptured diaphragm—the result of a car accident that took place when the cat was about one year of age.

HEART AILMENTS

The diagnosis of specific heart diseases in cats isn't easy even for experts. The veterinarian is trained to weigh the symptoms carefully. He listens to the heart for leaky valves and for rapidity, which he can also feel in the pulse, easily taken on the inside of the hind legs. He may watch for rapid, shallow breathing, for swelling of the legs and filling of the abdomen with blood plasma. He notices whether the pulse is feeble and thready or full and bounding. With a stethoscope he can tell if the heart is enlarged, and with an X ray and electrocardiogram he can check any findings about which he is in doubt. The layman cannot be expected to develop all these skills, of course, but he can learn to recognize some of the outward symptoms of heart disease so that he can get expert advice before the condition has progressed too far.

The veterinary profession diagnoses an ever-increasing number of heart problems in cats, leading one to wonder if the profession is becoming more adept or cats are having more heart problems. I believe the latter is the case but why I can't say. Once again the effects of environmental pollutants and preservatives need investigation.

One reason heart problems are not easily diagnosed in cats is that their rapid pulse makes faint murmurs difficult to hear. When a murmur develops to that point where it is obvious, the cat may be in an advanced state of cardiac insufficiency. When a heart is not able to pump an adequate volume of blood it tends to enlarge. While this process is progressing the cat may act normally, but eventually if the problem is not corrected weakness and shortness of breath indicate an obvious problem.

Enlargement. It is a simple matter to feel a cat's heart. If you place your hand beneath the cat with the fingers on one side of the chest and the thumb on the other, the pumping heart can be felt clearly, its location determined, and some idea gained as to its size. If you do not know how large the heart should seem, find a normal cat for comparison. (The overwhelming number of healthy cats are normal.) It is not unusual to find the heart enlarged to twice its normal size when the walls have become thinned. The pulse then feels weak and feeble even though the contraction is strong, because the heart muscle doesn't have the power and resiliency it needs. Leaky valves can sometimes be felt as well as heard when the ear is pressed against the chest over the heart.

These facts are about all that the owner can learn by direct examination of his cat's heart. Beyond this he must depend upon observation of general symptoms.

Dropsy. In dropsy the abdomen fills with fluid, sometimes becoming so distended that the cat may seem to be pregnant. Frequently the cat has an abnormal thirst, in which case kidney complications can be suspected and some acidified urine boiled to test for kidney trouble. If it turns cloudy or a white precipitate forms and settles out, the prognosis is unfavorable. In dropsy, the fluid part of the blood is left stranded in the tissues as a result of a heart malfunction and settles in the easiest place— the abdomen. The red cells stay in the vessels. Fluid may also gather under the skin of the legs, lower chest, and lower abdomen.

Caffeine is sometimes administered as a heart stimulant, but since it has been found that caffeine tends to produce stomach ulcers in cats, it must be given sparingly. Digitalis is a good drug for the purpose. Your veterinarian will work with you to establish proper doses of his choice of medications for a given heart problem.

Heart Infections. Cats may develop infections that produce leaky valves. Sometimes fluids accumulate in the space between the heart and its covering (the pericardium). Such infections may eventually produce adhesions of the pericardium to the heart. In other cases infections may inflame the lining of the inside of the heart (the endocardium), with resulting rapid heartbeat and shortness of breath. Quite often this condition is associated with stiffness, indicating a joint inflammation or rheumatism. If either part of the heart is infected, the cat's temperature rises considerably and it pains it to be pressed in the region of the heart. These diseases call for professional treatment and patient care.

Age itself takes its toll of cats, and its effects are often seen on the heart. One has to expect very old cats to become feeble. Their hearts simply are not able to stand the strain of the activities of young cats, and as they grow older they should be treated accordingly.

More and more cats today are being diagnosed with heartworms as this parasite is spreading over so much of the United States. Fortunately, however, it is still a rare problem.

RESPIRATORY AILMENTS

We have already mentioned contagious feline respiratory conditions, which are the most frequent ailments of the respiratory organs. But cats do have other diseases, including, rarely, tuberculosis, that affect the lungs (see also Chapter 13).

Edema of the Lungs. Edema develops when the body is infiltrated with dropsical fluid and the lungs are affected. Shortness of breath is an important symptom of this condition. In addition to the pressure from abdominal distention, the fluid in the lungs puts a burden on the respiratory system. The fluids must be depleted from the body with drugs. Allergies may cause edema.

Emphysema. As an aftermath of diseases of the lungs—and from other unknown causes—sections of the spongelike lung tissue break down, allowing large pockets to form. These pockets often collect mucus. When many such pockets are present, a great deal of the lung tissue is useless and the cat has to breathe faster and deeper to aerate its blood.

There is no cure for this condition, but temporary alleviation of the symptoms is possible. Treatment, however, should never be considered more than temporary relief.

Pleurisy. During pneumonia, when bacteria may have worked through the pleura or coating of the lungs, infection may pass across the chest cavity to the pleura on the rib side. In such cases the two surfaces may adhere to each other in spots when healing is completed. While the inflammation is present, an exceedingly painful pleurisy can result.

Areas of the chest cavity may become filled with fluid, which the veterinarian will have to tap and draw off. Certain areas of fluid may prevent heart and lung sounds from passing clearly. When these areas are tapped with the fingers, a dull thud is heard instead of a hollow, healthy resonance. In "dry" pleurisy a sharp, sandpapery, grating sound is produced with every breath.

Pyothorax. Pyothorax is an infection around the lungs often causing the formation of an overwhelming quantity of pus, which must be relieved. Treatment should be instigated promptly to achieve a cure.

Hydrothorax. Hydrothorax, or fluid in the chest cavity, follows lung infections, growths, or accidents. The cat is unable to obtain sufficient oxygen and shows symptoms of shallow breathing and, frequently, bluing of the tongue and gums. Treatment is a task for the veterinarian, who can draw off the fluid by tapping and prescribe medication to prevent its return.

Chylothorax. Chylothorax is a condition almost invariably caused by injury to the thoracic duct, causing a milklike fluid to form around the lungs. This too must be treated by a veterinarian, who may have to resort to surgery.

Tumors. Tumors in the chest cavity are not common. They are difficult to diagnose but may be suspected when the cat loses weight too rapidly, has shortness of breath, and develops an abnormal distension of ribs. Tumors sometimes occur in the lungs themselves. This kind often sends out buds (metastases) that grow in other parts of the body. Often X ray is utilized to diagnose the presence of tumors in the chest. The conscientious cat owner should have every suspicious growth examined by his veterinarian's pathologist as soon as possible.

EYE AILMENTS

Enlargement of the Nictitating Membrane. This is a condition, not a disease, and is usually a manifestation of other troubles. As you remember from Chapter 2, this membrane—which is sometimes called the third eyelid—seems to rise from behind the lower lid. In a normal eye it often cannot be seen at all, and when it rises up prominently, even though it is apparently not red and inflamed, it can be taken as a signal that the cat is not in perfect health. In extreme cases these third eyelids may rise so high as to completely cover the eye proper. More often, however, they just peek over the lower lid.

A cat with many roundworms nearly always has prominent nictitating membranes. The same is true for a cat with indigestion or constipation and for one with hair in the digestive tract. For once, those who tell you this symptom is a sure sign of worms may be right—but they are not always right. If the membranes are distended with blood, swollen and unlike their normal appearance, and if the rest of the tissue inside the lids and around the eye is also red and inflamed, the cat has conjunctivitis, a condition that may affect only one eye. In such cases, pull down the lid to remove any possible foreign objects behind one of the lids. Lime, fertilizers, powder-type insecticides, and scratches will produce just such symptoms. Has a mischievous youngster with an ammonia pistol squirted some of the liquid in the cat's face? Has a sudden blast of fresh exhaust from a car sprayed the cat or have fumes of carbon dust and gasoline burned it? All these things happen, and they are but a few of the mishaps that, in addition to bacteria, commonly produce conjunctivitis.

When a cat's eyes burn, it seeks dimly lighted places. It may rub its eyes so constantly as to irritate them even more. If the trouble is in only one eye, a scratch or foreign body with or without infection is usually the cause.

TREATMENT: Remove the cause. If only the nictitating membranes are enlarged, have a fecal examination made and deworm the cat if necessary. It may be necessary to treat the animal for hair impaction or autointoxication. Medicines will not always reduce enlarged nictitating membranes.

Since the eyes are so critical to the normal animal it behooves us not to waste time when problems strike but to consult a veterinarian as soon as possible.

On rare occasions cats have one or both of the ducts that lead from the eye to the nose infected and plugged. Tears overflow the lid and moisten and soil the nose. Here again ophthalmic ointments may help to unplug the duct, but it is necessary to use them for several days and many times a day. Sometimes the veterinarian must flush out the tear ducts while the cat is under an anesthetic.

Corneal Diseases. Any injury, however slight, sustained by the cornea usually causes an opacity or bluing. This is the result of the white blood cells invading the injured cornea, trying to protect it from disease, and setting off the process of healing. The white cells, and with them the blueness, disappear as surely as they came, but not until healing is accomplished. If you know that the eye has been injured (watering is usually the first clue), before the whiteness sets in, look closely for thorns, metal chips, or any tiny object penetrating the cornea. Remove it if you can find it. And if you cannot, have your veterinarian look for the problem.

When the cornea of your cat's eye turns white, it cannot see. (Note that whiteness does not indicate a cataract. A cataract is in or on the lens and can be seen only through the pupil.) How long a cat will remain blind in the corneal injured eye depends on how long healing takes. If a deep wound has filled in, the cat will generally carry the scar all through life. Whether it is in a location outside the line of vision determines whether it will interfere with the cat's sight.

Since all these afflictions cause pain, the cat should be kept out of strong light. It may manifest its pain by refusing food, hiding, pawing at the eye, and so on. A "boxing glove" applied to the appropriate paw is often helpful. (See page 161.)

Infections in the cornea may cause abscesses—very serious affairs that need expert attention. The whole eye may become infected and have to be removed. Or it may ulcerate because of bacterial or viral invasion, and day by day you can watch the ulcer growing larger unless its spread is checked by medication or surgery.

A virus infection called herpes virus can produce a disastrous ulcer that, if treated with the wrong medication, can encourage the infection. Fortunately there is an effective antiviral medication for herpes eye ulcers.

Operations to correct ulcers are available and have saved countless eyes. Some are delicate and require a good deal of experience. If your veterinarian finds a problem he thinks someone else is better equipped to handle he will refer you to that specialist.

Even after healing, it is not uncommon to find the healed areas filled with pigmented cells—usually black—that remain during the cat's life. I have seen them in eyes of cats that have had only superficial corneal injuries.

If the veterinarian recommends removing an eye for some reason to save the life of the animal and you think a lot of the animal, don't hesitate in letting him perform the surgery. A one-eyed cat can compensate amazingly well and very often even close neighbors will not realize the operation has been performed.

Glaucoma. This disease, which so far as is known is not inherited in cats, produces slow swelling until the eye bulges. The lens may drop down from the window behind which it normally lies. The internal pressure becomes greater and greater. A similar condition, called hydrophthalmus, is difficult to differentiate from glaucoma, as is an abscess that may have formed behind the eyeball, pushing it forward. In any of these conditions the cornea may appear blue. Treatment usually involves surgery and in hopeless cases the removal of the eyeball.

Protruding Eyes. This condition should not be confused with the naturally prominent eyes that some cats show. In certain cases one or both eyes may be pushed forward abnormally. Such a displacement occurs when the bony arch over the eye is fractured. A tumor in the orbit behind the eyeball can also push it out. Then, too, as a result of accidents, fights, or bites, the eyeball may be knocked or pulled outside of the lids. Because of the inflammation and swelling, which set in quickly, the eye cannot be squeezed back into place. If you find a cat in this condition, smear the eyeball with Vaseline or an ophthalmic ointment and rush it to the doctor, who can slit the eyelid, drop the eye in place, and suture his incision. If the muscles and optic nerve are not injured, the cat may see again.

Cross Eyes. Siamese cats are considered acceptable specimens if they have "casts" in their vision, but ordinary cats have casts or are cross-eyed only as a result of accidents that tear eye muscles. If a protruding eye has been replaced surgically, there may have been a torn muscle, in which case the injured eye may be looking in an entirely different direction from the uninjured eye.

Eyelid Maladies. Lacerations are the most frequent ailments of the lids, and those made by other cats are most common. Any sharp object, hooked under a lid, may tear it so that it must be sutured. Every such wound should have attention. The natural healing process may close the tear, but the lid will usually have a notched, uneven edge. The result will be an ugly, jagged scar that will greatly detract from the cat's appearance.

General inflammation of the lid, caused by infection or injury, is seen occasionally. Appropriate treatment for each will bring about a prompt cure if the cat will leave its eyes alone. If it insists on rubbing them, it may be necessary to apply an Elizabethan collar.

EAR AILMENTS

Canker and Ear Mites. Canker is a term covering many ear infections that manifest themselves by the accumulation of excess waxy secretions. It may be due to irritation caused by bacterial growth. Canker can be recognized by a cheesy odor, a gummy wax in the ear, and frequent scratching. Ear mites, which cause the same symptoms, usually produce a drier, darker, crumbly wax with less or no odor. (See Chapter 13.)

There are remedies for many pet ear problems on sale where pet supplies are sold. Some of them are effective, but since most are quite mild, the manufacturer will never be taken to court for harm done. If you try such a product and succeed, great, but if you see little progress see your veterinarian.

Three per cent hydrogen peroxide has corrected many cases of ear canker, but must be used three times daily. The ear is filled and after each application the ear is gently massaged, in order to float debris out which can then be wiped away with cotton or tissue. But again if good results are not observed in two or three days, telephone your cat's doctor for an appointment.

Deafness. About 50 per cent of blue-eyed white cats are born deaf in both ears. These cats inherit the problem. But deafness due to disease and age is not a common finding in cats (as opposed to dogs). Hardening of the arteries, or sclerosis, rarely causes more than impaired hearing, but when it does there is no treatment.

One of my patients brought in for minor surgery reacted unfavorably to the anesthetic and for all intents died on the table. After injections, heart massage, and oxygen for ten minutes, the heart started pumping and eventually the cat began breathing. This cat was blind and deaf for over a year before partial sight and partial hearing returned. Time was responsible for the partial recovery and not my efforts.

DERMATOLOGY

It seems to me mammalian dermatology is not an exact science and that feline dermatology is practically an untilled field. However, in this section we will discuss briefly what is known at this time.

I am reminded of a battered tom we altered hoping it might have an effect on his sore, riddled, almost nude body. Jerry had lost his hair two years before and the home treatments tried had done nothing for him. Winter was coming again and the owners decided to give him a last chance. After the surgery and many negative tests we decided on a regimen of medicated baths and hormone treatments. After the first bath Jerry declined to make himself available for further medication. Frustrated, the owner telephoned to say the decision had been made to hospitalize him. It was December in Connecticut, and Jerry, an outside cat, had no protection against the cold. A day later the owner telephoned to say the old cat had left the premises and when he returned they would bring him in. Spring arrived and so did Jerry—the owners brought him in —with a full, luxurious coat and solid, if poor, flesh. Jerry has remained a friend of the family for years now and has been an inside cat since his miraculous cure without treatment.

If Jerry had had a parasitic disease caused by mites a cure would have been easy. The diseases caused by parasites are not common but do respond to external treatments as described in Chapter 13.

Other external parasitic problems may be caused by ear mites. (See pages 187–88.) These small creatures look like crabs under the microscope and are barely visible to the human eye. In a severe case the mites, as well as the resultant secondary infection, must be treated. Although oils such as mineral oil will kill the adults, it takes frequent treatments over a thirty-day period to accomplish the feat. It is better to obtain a prescription from a veterinarian to be used twice a week and to follow his advice carefully.

There are three species of large mites that should be mentioned, though they are rare. I call them "motorized dandruff," but properly the condition is called cheyletiellosis. The skin is itchy and as the parasites proliferate there is hair loss, with odor and sores. One method of diagnosis is to investigate any itching lesions on you, the owner.

Treatment consists of an all-out attack, using medicated baths, and since cats are poisoned easily with most of our medicated shampoos you should consult your veterinarian for the proper treatment. I use rotenone (discussed elsewhere) and suggest that bedding be washed regularly or burned if not washable.

I remember a young couple who insisted their pet had lice. I asked how they had made the diagnosis and they smiled and reported that they had contracted pubic lice from the animal and they had to see their physician to correct the problem. When I told them that that type of human louse would not live on their pet a silence filled the air—strange glances passed between them.

A large parasite, the flea, is considered by many to be the cause of dermatitis in cats. I am a doubter since the cause-effect principle has not been scientifically established. Most cats have at least one flea now and then and the proponents of this theory suggest that the cat is allergic to the saliva of even one parasite. They point out that the bite of one flea causes an allergic reaction. In my experience cold weather sees the end of the dermatitis although a few fleas usually persist through the cold months. Therapy using the hormone progesterone usually corrects this problem but if it recurs the medication may be necessary, off and on, for the life of the cat.

Intestinal parasites seem to affect the skin on rare occasions and may be corrected by destroying the parasites. Sometimes repeated stool checks are necessary to make the diagnosis.

Maggots.   Old debilitated cats or cats with open wounds are subject to flies depositing eggs near the wounds or near fecal material clinging to hair. The eggs hatch in a few hours, sometimes producing hundreds of maggots that invade the wounds or cause a deterioration of healthy tissue, which they eat. Damage by these creatures, often extensive, can result in shock and death if they are not removed in time. A severely affected cat must receive prompt treatment. Since the efficient maggot killers are toxic to cats I prefer to remove them with forceps after clipping the hair around such an invasion and treating the affected areas with antibiotic ointments.

During World War I maggots in the wounds of soldiers were observed to be helpful in keeping certain infections from developing. An agent called alantoin was discovered, which did indeed prevent many infections but it was discovered that the maggots destroyed healthy tissue and the accepted thinking that maggots were helpful has long been shelved.

Cuterebra or "Wolf" Infestation.   There is nothing "cute" about this parasite, which attains a length of one inch and a thickness of almost a half inch under the skin of a cat. Most commonly found in young animals, it is spread by a fly that lays its eggs where rodents are found. The eggs hatch and the minute larva attaches itself to a rodent or cat passing by, burrows into the skin, and lives on nourishment from the host. The observant owner notices a swelling under the skin and sees something moving in the small opening the larva has made. Sometimes a small incision must be made to enlarge the opening in order to extract the parasite. When this parasite is extracted it may be best for an owner with a weak stomach to be seated during the process since a large cuterebra is a shock to behold.

Other Skin Problems.   Allergies are, in my opinion, rarely the cause of skin problems in cats but when present are apt to be caused by food. The offending food must be determined by selective feeding until the cause is eliminated. As with most skin disorders, the extent of the condition is in proportion to the degree of susceptibility and the length of time of exposure. The signs of an allergy may be itching without inflammation, hives, open sores, and pustules from an extended period of ingesting the offending food.

A week without the offending food in the diet is usually ample time to see an improvement. Start with one type of food only, such as cooked filet of fish. If no improvement is observed try a week of beef chunks, and if again no improvement is observed you can forget about food allergy as the cause of a skin disease. With improvement add one type of food each week such as boiled rice, crushed cooked peas, and so on, but remember commercial cat foods have many ingredients and any one ingredient may be the culprit.

I am not aware that inhaled particles have been identified as causing an allergic reaction in any cat.

Bacterial skin infections seem to be more common than other causes of skin infections but superficial infections are difficult to identify since to my knowledge no work has been reported on the normal bacteria of cats' skin. I don't class abscesses, such as those caused by puncture wounds, as skin diseases. Abscesses, usually found under the skin, are discussed elsewhere.

Fortunately, fungus infections are not common in our cats but when present require more frequent and prolonged treatment than many bacterial infections. One problem we must constantly consider is the cat's propensity to lick and ingest all medicine. Culturing a fungus for its identity can be difficult since these parasitic vegetables often grow poorly if at all and when they do grow, it may take weeks before the bacteriologist can help with a diagnosis. Once again, you are dealing with a diagnostic problem difficult even for a veterinarian; so don't waste time with home remedies if you find a skin lesion that is growing. The most important skin fungus disease is ringworm.

Dandruff.   This is a term used to designate constant flaking of the skin. All cats, like all human beings, are constantly shedding off the outer layer of the skin and replacing it with new growth. Some cat owners are concerned when they find even a small number of scales. It appears to be a normal occurrence and a good brushing with a coarse brush will very often rid the hair of flakes. If the cat is scratching, however, it is another matter, and an infection is probably the cause. Often cat owners are advised to feed cod-liver oil, wheat-germ oil, and raw eggs, and told not to feed starchy foods. Vitamins affect skin health, to be sure, but special food supplements seldom effect cures. Some of the unsaturated fatty acids, certain building blocks of fat, are necessary for skin health in rats and children, but whether these food ingredients help coat health in cats remains to be proven.

Dandruff seems to be seasonal with some cats, causing them to shed skin scales at certain times of the year and not at others. You may have read that the use of crude caustic soaps will produce dandruff; yet the daintiest soaps may be the worst offenders. Again it is said that the dry atmosphere of a heated house is conducive to dandruff; yet it is seen in outdoor cats that are seldom in heated rooms. It appears to be a normal occurrence, and, as we have seen, it can be helped by hard, vigorous brushing.

In treating cats for any skin disease, remember that they are inclined to lick themselves. By all means apply an Elizabethan collar, as described in Chapter 10, to prevent excessive licking. If your cat does manage to get a little medication on its paws, it will suffer no ill effects from ingesting small amounts, and with a collar securely in place, the medicine will have an opportunity to do its work unmolested.

Lick Granuloma.   Lick granuloma or "rodent ulcer" is a problem with an unknown cause. Here the hormone oral progesterone cures some cases but so do injections of steroids. Years ago surgery was the only suggested treatment but I have cured many cases by applying a combination steroid-fungicide-bacteriacide five or six times daily. An extensive ulcer of the upper lip may take months to cure with this technique. This malady is called lick granuloma because the cat's licking keeps the lesion open and growing.

I had been supervising the treatment of such a lesion the size of my palm on the inside of a cat's rear thigh with little success since the owner could treat it only two or three times daily. The cat broke her opposite leg, which was set with a splint. Somehow with the awkwardness of the splint she stopped licking the granuloma and it healed nicely without medication during the month the splint was in place. There is something that we do not as yet understand about the rough tongue and/or the saliva that causes this minor skin problem to escalate to a major one.

Although cats have much less cancer than people, feline skin cancer must be listed in this context: It should be treated by surgery, drugs, X ray, or injections by a veterinarian.

Locally applied external chemicals such as turpentine, kerosene, acids, and caustics all may cause skin irritations, many of which demand immediate professional attention.

Feline acne is common, although often overlooked. It is always located under the lower jaw on the chin and may go unnoticed until it becomes extensive. Untreated, the skin may become encrusted and even bleed. Antibiotic creams are a simple cure.

Autoimmune skin disease is one in which the cat for some unknown reason rejects areas of skin just as the heart transplant in man may be rejected.

And the list goes on, with rare conditions the consideration of which space does not permit. Space does permit my urging you to consult your veterinarian if your cat has a skin problem *before* it becomes extensive—your cat deserves at least this consideration.

Hormone Therapy. There is no doubt that certain hormone therapies improve many skin irritations in cats but it is my contention that we are in some way stimulating the defense mechanisms to help overcome infections. In some cases the condition may be cured with oral or injectable hormone therapy but often the condition returns. It should be noted that many of the skin problems that respond to such therapy also respond to the stimuli of cold weather, only to reappear the following summer. Therefore, a combination of external and internal treatment may be the best treatment. Time and research will one day give us more insight into many problem skin ailments.

TUMORS AND CANCER

That lump growing under the cat's skin which develops slowly, that rapidly growing tumor on the shoulder, that soft pliant swelling, those lumps in the breast of your pet—what are they? Will they cost it its life? Should they be removed? Will they return if they are removed? The veterinarian hears scores of such questions. Many cat owners have misconceptions about growths.

A tumor is a growth of new, useless tissue growing independently of the surrounding tissue but not replacing it.

In medical terminology the term *malignant* means a virulent growth that tends to go from bad to worse.

A benign growth is only a relative term. Compared to a malignant tumor, it stays within itself and does not recur elsewhere. But what growth could really be benign? A wart? Even so small and seemingly innocuous a growth causes itching and sometimes pain. No tumor is really benign in the common sense of the word.

Cancer is a malignant tumor. The word comes from the Latin, meaning *crab*. This implies that it is a growth which invades other tissue by extending crablike tentacles. But this is an old definition, hardly acceptable in the light of newer knowledge. There is cancer that grows in a lump apparently as benign as any nonmalignant tumor. Then this lump in the lungs, let us say, sends off a bud or cell into the bloodstream that is halted in the skin on the pet's back, where it grows. Careful microscopic examination of the lump after removal discloses that it is tissue characteristic of the lungs, even though it is growing in the skin. This is called metastasis.

Carcinomas arise in the skin, in the intestinal linings, and in all tissues that develop from the same original embryonic sources. Sarcomas are tumors made up of connective tissue—the part of the cat's body that binds it together and supports it.

Under these two classes, carcinomas and sarcomas, fall the various kinds of tumors. If your veterinarian tells you your cat has a malignant melanotic sarcoma, you know it is a tumor of the connective tissue, that it gives off buds or invades the adjacent tissue, or both. Melanotic means black, so it is a darkly pigmented growth. A pigment cell must have gone wild.

What causes these growths? The causes of a few kinds are known. Some believe a virus is the initiating agent of certain forms, if not all. Irritation, such as the constant rubbing of a snag tooth on the lip, certain hormones, contact with irritating chemicals, inhalation of smoke—all are known to cause some types of growths; for others there is no explanation. Perhaps mutations or sudden changes in the characteristics of a cell are induced by irritation and, once started, simply grow out of control.

When a cut or abrasion occurs in an animal, the body heals it by the growth of surrounding cells. Something in the body applies a brake to this healing growth at the right time. If it didn't, every cut might grow out of all proportion. We are not sure what this brake is. The cancer cells have no brake applied by the body and grow by cell division on and on until they overwhelm the host.

Diagnosis of malignant growths is accomplished by removing a section of the growth and preparing it by an elaborate process of slicing and staining until it can be examined with a microscope by a pathologist, who can classify it.

There is always a question of what to do about a growth, and the fact that some growths appear suddenly and seem to stop is no reason to be complacent. Such a growth may remain the same size for years and suddenly grow rapidly. Your veterinarian will advise you as to whether the growth should be treated or left alone. There are gray areas when we may wait and watch, but I usually advise surgical removal if there is much doubt.

In an elderly cat with a growing lesion my suggestion is usually to remove it surgically since I would rather try and fail than not try at all. There is no hope for survival if we do nothing, but if we try there is hope.

We have four main approaches to cancer treatment. The first, and most popular and successful, is surgery, followed by chemotherapy, immunotherapy, and X-ray therapy; the last three are not necessarily in order of preference.

Cancers of the bones of the face, of the tongue, lips, and throat are perhaps the most frequent ones in cats. White cats have a rather high incidence of cancer on the edges of the ears. Growths in and under the skin are observed from time to time but lung cancer even in homes where people smoke is rare. If you find an unusual swelling I suggest it be removed and sent to pathology for a diagnosis. Then you will know what to expect in the future.

Do not confuse cancer with an abscess. The latter appears over a day or two whereas the former, even a wildly growing lesion, will usually take weeks or months to register a dramatic change. Salivary glands may be infected and the resulting swelling may appear more serious than it is.

It is interesting to note that in a survey concerning the incidence of cancer, dogs had twice the incidence of man, and cats had half the incidence of man. So here again we see an indication of the remarkable constitution of this remarkable species.

DEFICIENCY DISEASES

Negative as well as positive factors cause disease. There are the obvious cases of suffocation: a carrying cage or shipping crate may be insufficiently ventilated, and when it is opened, the pet is found dead. Lack of oxygen, obvious as it is, constitutes a deficiency disease. There are many more subtle deficiencies.

Some deficiencies produce what should be called conditions, not diseases. A disease is a morbid process with characteristic symptoms. Thirst is neither a disease nor necessarily the result of disease. The symptoms of dehydration are cured by water consumption. Anemia is a disease in one sense, a condition in another. Millions of humans go about in an anemic condition. In general, deficiency diseases are quite easily cured, simply by furnishing the body with the missing elements.

In my opinion the only nutritional deficiency disease that occurs with any frequency in cats is eclampsia. Mothers producing a lot of milk, yet receiving only muscle meat to eat, develop the shivering, trembling symptoms. These are relieved by an injection of calcium gluconate or similar substances.

Although the layman seldom sees deficiencies in his pets, cats used by scientists in food studies have exhibited the same symptoms as dogs, including those of blacktongue. These studies showed that the cures were the same as for any other species—supplying the deficient essentials.

Studies show that cats require vitamin E (tocopherol). Only minute amounts are needed, but it must be fresh. Any rancidity in oils containing tocopherol renders the vitamin worthless. Wheat-germ oil is often fed to cats and sometimes cod-liver oil or fish oil mixed with it. The combination is so frequently rancid that it does more harm than good. There is usually enough vitamin E in natural foods so that no additional supplement is required. Most of the canned cat foods have additional vitamin E added to them.

An insufficiency causes the disease steatitis, commonly called yellow fat disease. It is most common in overweight cats and causes great pain in the animal. They lie around, appear unresponsive, and show the pain when we try to pick them up. Before this disease was recognized as a vitamin deficiency disease, it was a common problem; today it is almost unheard of.

Anemia. The word "anemia," which refers to a symptom, not a disease, has been mentioned as a sign of many conditions in felines. Some anemias are caused by the mechanical loss of blood, some are caused by a failure of the bone marrow to produce enough red cells, and some are caused by the cat's developing an immunity to its red cells. Still others are caused by a destruction of red cells in excess of the body's ability to produce them.

Viruses, bacteria, toxic substances, parasites, malnourishment can all cause anemia, and once again your veterinarian is trained to unscramble the evidence to make a diagnosis of the cause.

A shortage of oxygen to the tissues is present in anemia. We have considered the obvious form but not the symptoms. *When an animal suffocates, the pink color of the tissue turns blue.* A lack of oxygen in the tissues can be produced by many causes other than lack of air. The blood may simply be unable to carry oxygen about the body. This, in turn, may result from a diminished supply of red cells in the blood. There may be too few, or the chemical composition of their components may be inadequate.

A home test for anemia is to look at the gums and tongue of the suspect—are they bright pink or pale? If pale, your cat may be anemic. Press the gum above an eye tooth firmly and note how rapidly the pink color returns. A slow return may be an indication of this problem. This is called the color and refill test and is helpful information to pass along to your veterinarian.

Why do signs of anemia appear suddenly in a chronic disease condition? I say "suddenly" because one day a cat may appear normal in behavior and the next be stumbling, with rapid breathing and depression. In such a case there have been enough red blood cells to transport oxygen one day and too few the next. There is a critical number of red cells above which life appears normal and below which the cat appears desperately sick. A simple blood test will indicate the percentage of red cells in the blood.

Some ordinary diseases alter the proportion of red and white cells, not by reducing the number of red cells but by increasing the number of white cells. This is not anemia. Diseases that produce toxins or attack the blood-building apparatus of the body produce anemia by reducing the number of red cells.

A lack of iron or copper or both causes anemia. Insufficient iron is responsible for a shortage of hemoglobin, and though there may be a full quota of red cells, they can't pick up and transport oxygen. Copper deficiency also causes anemia. Copper is not part of hemoglobin, but affects its formation.

Nicotinic acid deficiency (a cause of blacktongue), a shortage of vitamin B complex factors, pyridoxine deficiency all cause anemia.

Rickets. Rickets is a result of a lack of one or more of these factors: vitamin D, calcium, or phosphorus.

Mineral Deficiencies. Minerals of great consequence to pets, especially cats, are calcium, phosphorus, and iron, but in passing we must recognize that the absence of others causes dire consequences. Phosphorus and calcium must be in proper proportion for good bone development. Iodine is essential. Its lack causes goiter in animals, and when pregnant females are iodine-starved they may produce abnormal young called cretins. Common salt is also essential. Since 99 per cent of the calcium in the body is found in the skeleton, obviously a calcium deficiency results in poor skeletal development, as we saw in the case of rickets. But calcium does more than develop bone. It is necessary to proper nerve function and acts almost like some vitamins as a catalyst or "marrying agent" among other minerals. Bad teeth may be traced to a fluorine deficiency. Cobalt and boron, though needed in minute quantities, are essential in preventing certain illnesses. Potassium deficiency causes paralysis, and so forth.

Vitamin Deficiencies. The subject of vitamins has been covered in Chapter 3.

A number of deficiency diseases of an odd nature are due to what are known as inactivators. For example, a substance in raw fish destroys vitamin B, causing a deficiency, which in turn produces a paralysis known as Chastek. Cooking destroys the inactivator, which is, of course, why we recommend that fish be cooked for our pets.

In the section on foods and feeding I mentioned the essential amino acids, a deficiency of any one of which may be a disaster. Recently the amino acid arginine has been found to be so essential that in a young animal one meal without this ingredient can result in death from ammonia intoxication. Older animals are not affected.

Hypervitaminosis. Just as a lack of certain nutritional elements in a diet causes problems, so may an excess of certain elements. Excesses of calcium, phosphorus, vitamin A, and vitamin D should all be viewed as problem producers. Time and research may prove that certain combinations of vitamins and minerals, taken in excess, are dangerous. One well-documented problem resulting from an excess of vitamin A has been seen all too frequently in cats fed exclusively on liver. Excess bone formation develops around the vertebral bones of the neck and chest causing a rigid spine in that area. Pressure on nerves may cause partial paralysis of the forelegs. Such a cat, before paralysis develops, is said to walk in "boat fashion."

Friends of mine had a Siamese cat named Boyd who was so old they decided to cater to his desires toward the end of his life and fed him a diet almost exclusively of liver for his last two years. Boyd was found dead in his bed at just under twenty-one years of age. I doubt a younger cat would have lived for two years on such a diet and I would urge you not to try it.

SALMONELLA INFECTION

This ubiquitous organism of which over two hundred serotypes (varieties) have been identified is rarely found in cats unless they have been stressed. Overcrowding, surgery, and injuries may weaken an animal, permitting this bacteria to gain a foothold and produce a serious disease. Vomiting and diarrhea are the signs. A diagnosis can be made only by culturing and identifying the agent in the laboratory. In young animals there may be a high mortality in spite of intensive treatment.

ANAL GLAND PROBLEMS

If your cat twitches or chews on its tail, appears unnecessarily nervous, sometimes jumping up suddenly and running across the room for no good reason, or licks under its tail, investigate to determine if the anal glands are infected. These two small glands are part of the skin and are situated just under the anus, one on each side. Their secretions are passed out of the body through ducts that discharge into the rim of the anus. The normal secretion of the glands is yellowish and oily-looking, but when bacteria cause infection, the glands may become filled with nasty, purulent, blackish, brownish, or bloody material.

To relieve the cat of this infection, use the following method: Place him on a table and have an assistant hold his head and shoulders tightly against the table. With your left hand lift the tail straight up, holding it close to the base. With a piece of cotton held in your right hand, squeeze just below the anus. The contents of the glands will be expelled into the piece of cotton. This should be repeated once a week until no more infected matter can be expressed.

If you are not successful consult your veterinarian and he will be glad to show you how to accomplish this feat.

PARALYSIS

Posterior. Usually posterior paralysis has a sudden onset and the cause and extent must be determined to indicate the treatment and outcome. In some cases, an embolism of the major artery leading to the back legs prevents blood from nourishing the muscles and nerves. Usually the rear legs are cold to the touch in comparison to the forelegs. Medication and surgery or both may be lifesaving. The condition is called saddle thrombus and is associated with heart infections.

Injury to the small of the back is a more common finding. In some injuries, pressure is exerted on the spinal cord, with the extent of the pressure determining the extent of the paralysis. Many injuries of the back recover with tender loving care, but others require X rays and surgery to relieve pressure.

Tumors and infections of the spinal cord may also cause posterior paralysis but these are rare in the feline.

Foreleg. When a cat receives a blow just above the shoulder joint, nerves may be injured, resulting in paralysis of that leg. It is called radial nerve or brachial plexus paralysis and may be permanent or temporary depending on the degree of injury to the nerves. In my experience if the cat has some use of the shoulder joint we can be somewhat optimistic of recovery. If, however, the leg hangs down with a sagging shoulder the prognosis is less favorable. Sometimes recovery requires months and many cats never use the limb again. If the nerves are injured beyond repair, scar tissue develops between the severed ends and the leg will be dragged along the ground, eventually resulting in abrasions and infections. I usually advise amputation in such cases as described in Chapter 17 on elective surgery.

HORNER'S SYNDROME

Tumors, infection, or injury may cause a sudden strange group of symptoms in the cat, including poor co-ordination, one pupil that is larger than the other, and a protruding eyelid. A frightening set of problems that are solved either because of or in spite of our treatments. I say "in spite of" because years ago we did not know this to be a nervous-system problem and many animals recovered without treatment. However, if one of my cats were afflicted I would administer antibiotics for a possible infection while working up the cause. When caused by bacterial infection the response to antibiotics is sometimes dramatic.

15. Health Hazards in Hospitals, Boarding Establishments, and Shows

$\mathcal{C}$AT owners sooner or later face the question: What shall I do with my cat when I have to leave him? There are a number of other questions closely related to this first one. If the pet becomes sick, shall I keep him at home or leave him in a veterinary hospital? Shall I exhibit my pet in a show? Is it safe to allow my cat free access to neighborhood animals?

Actually all of these general questions are part of a still larger one: To what extent shall I isolate my cat?

In order to answer these questions intelligently, there are certain basic facts you should know. Every proprietor of a veterinary hospital or a boarding kennel, every dog warden and humane-society officer, knows these facts. If every pet owner knew them as well, sickness among pets might be greatly reduced. Omitting for the moment any consideration of the emotional side of the question, let us discuss only the purely physical factors, the health hazards that "mingling" entails.

Let's assume that every cat owner and every cat handler is honest, and that every person owning an animal he or she knows is sick will isolate it. Let's assume, too, that no Humane Society warden knowingly puts a sick cat in the pound. And last, but not least, let's assume that no veterinary hospital exists without isolation wards where cats are segregated according to the type of disease they have. It is obvious that none of these assumptions can be completely true. Pet owners are no more and no less ethical than other groups of people. Certainly not all of them are sufficiently concerned about the health of other people's pets to isolate their own when they know them to be sick.

But suppose that all these things were true. Could you even then be certain that your cat could be safely placed with a lot of other healthy animals and never contract a disease? Even if your cat were completely immunized against all diseases for which we now have vaccines, you could not be 100 per cent sure.

The average cat show probably furnishes the best example of the risk involved whenever animals are brought together, in spite of the fact that every cat exhibited is supposed to be a healthy, properly inoculated animal. Although veterinarians may examine all cats at the entrance gate and reject those that are sick, cat shows are still one of the means by which disease is spread.

In the British Isles a cat exhibited in a cat show is quarantined for two weeks prior to the show. Since the incubation period for most contagious cat diseases is five to seven days, a cat contracting a disease would be contagious a week later, although not obviously sick. The two-week interval has been successful in minimizing the spread of contagious diseases.

Here is another example of the way disease is spread. The cattery owner accepts Mrs. Williams' pet in all good faith. The cat is placed in a room with many other cats. All of them appear to be in good health. After three days the cattery owner notices that Mrs. Williams' cat is sneezing. She isolates him in another room. But suppose your cat had been in a cage in the first room. Many cat diseases are spread by droplet infection through the air. A day after you take your cat home he starts to sneeze. You telephone the cattery owner immediately and take your cat to her to cure. She tells you your cat was contented and well on its first visit. But the chances are she remembers Mrs. Williams' cat, and when two days later she finds that most of the cats in that room are sneezing, what is she to do? Whose fault is it? Is the cattery owner under obligation to take your cat back and keep it until it is cured or dies? Legally such an occurrence is considered along with lightning, wind, and fire as "an act of God." Pure slander! But lawyers have to have a pigeonhole for everything, and so cat diseases are blamed on God.

Perhaps your cat contracts feline distemper while being boarded, and when you return she is dead. The owner of the cattery has spent hours, half sick herself because of worry over what has happened, trying to nurse the cats under her care to health. You are hurt, indignant, and angry that your cat has been lost. Perhaps you refuse to pay even the board. Actually, considering the work and worry she has had, you owe the cattery owner far more than if nothing had happened.

Needless to say, no cattery owners ever *want* such things to happen. It hurts them every time it does. It causes worry, anguish, extra work, and loss of money. So what, then, should be one's attitude? Shall every pet owner say, "I left a well animal; now he's sick. You're to blame"? Or shall he look at it from a reasonable point of view, difficult as that may be when one's pet's health is involved?

It is impossible to assemble a large group of animals of any species and be 100 per cent certain that no one is infested with parasites, is incubating some disease, or is an immune carrier. As long as this is true you can't board a pet and be 100 per cent sure the pet will be well, and neither incubating a disease nor showing symptoms of it when you call for it.

The best and safest thing you can do is to leave your pet in a cattery where veterinary attention is given or where the owner knows diseases well enough to be able to recognize the first symptoms and is willing and able to treat them properly. It is, of course, essential that there be an isolation ward in conjunction with the boarding facilities. And above all, every cat should be properly immunized against the diseases for which vaccines are available before being exposed at boarding establishments, shows, and even to apparently healthy cats in your neighborhood.

Far worse health hazards exist in allowing city cats to wander freely. Cats picked up by public agencies are usually destroyed at once, usually in a high altitude chamber, or even less commonly today than some years ago in a carbon-monoxide gas chamber on the truck that transports them. I consider both methods repugnant. If they are held, the chances are at least even that they will be placed in a large cage or room with other cats. One sick or carrier cat among the lot infects all the rest.

If your tomcat knows where a queen in heat lives and if he is healthy, you may be sure he will be camped near her home, and so will all the other toms that know—another potent source for the spread of infection.

Unquestionably cats can contract diseases in veterinary hospitals. The most careful veterinarian, in the best of faith, accepts animals, apparently free from disease, for operations. Two days later those same animals may be sneezing and filling surgical wards with invisible virus-filled droplets. Even though ultraviolet lights and germ-killing vaporizers may have been installed, they are not a 100 per cent guarantee that a few healthy cats will not be infected. I have never known a veterinarian to tell me that no disease was ever contracted in his hospital. But neither can the superintendent of a hospital for humans make that boast. Who doesn't know of at least one case of a patient in a hospital contracting virus pneumonia or some other of the contagious diseases? What of the diseases that sweep through the infant wards, or the women who even today are infected with "childbed fever"? I doubt that the risk of leaving a pet in a scrupulously clean veterinary hospital, complete with isolation wards, is as great as the risk of contracting a disease yourself while in a hospital.

Remember that not everything that happens to your pet in a hospital or cattery happens *because* it is there. Many of these things are the result of normal health hazards; many are the direct result of the age, habits, idiosyncrasies, food, and appetite of your pet.

If you leave an old animal, remember that the older it is, the nearer it is to the end. If your pet should die of a heart attack or a kidney ailment, even though lawyers blame the death on God, be just enough to call it old age, remembering that it had to die sometime. And be grateful it wasn't in your arms. You were spared a heart-stopping anguish.

Many states require that the boarding facility keep the body until the owner returns home no matter how much the animal decomposes. Veterinarians maintain freezers to put them in, but legally the bodies may not be disposed of until permission is granted.

You may have left a very fat pet and return to find it thin. You should be pleased that your pet has lost dangerous excess weight. Or a comfortably fat pet may have grown too fat by the time you call for him. A few days' attention to his diet will correct that.

Remember the characteristics of the breed and of the individual animal. If you know your Siamese will refuse the wholesome food of the institution where you leave him, then supply your own food. If you take him for frequent "vacations" he will have another home and may come to enjoy it.

If you own a lively cat, the first day after you take him home his stools will probably be quite loose. This does not necessarily mean he is sick. Excitement after confinement—not sickness—often causes loose stools. Your pet was probably in a small run or even a compartment; at home he has the whole outdoors to run in and he jumps and frisks. Expect loose stools until he gets back into his old routine.

Most cats seem thirsty after leaving boarding establishments even though they have had pans of water in their cages. This is normal and to be expected.

Your cat may seem ravenous. This is not strange. He's been introduced to a new food and you take him back to the old one. Of course he enjoys it.

The overhead in any establishment caring for cats is surprisingly high. It is based on costs and usually about a 10 per cent profit. Perhaps the simpler places that are family operated can charge less and come out ahead. But here, it is important that the place be clean and not overcrowded. When in doubt about a place to leave your pet, phone your veterinarian and ask him what establishment has the best record of keeping animals healthy.

Which brings us to this observation: If you find a boarding accommodation for your pet that suits you, keep using that establishment and don't shift around. In time your pet will become immune to infections, and your troubles are over. Just as children in a certain school and community become immune and thereafter are glad they did have childhood diseases so they don't have to have them later, so pet owners can be glad their pets were first protected against all the diseases they can be protected against by inoculation and then by having built up natural immunity to the others.

One other factor or risk in boarding pets is escape. If your Persian cat suddenly bites the cattery assistant, jumps out of the cage while that person is recovering from the pain and surprise, and escapes out of a window, that is your responsibility and not the cattery owner's, unless you warned him that the animal was vicious.

The tendency of most human beings to blame the other fellow for their own shortcomings is evidenced to the fullest in their reactions to the loss of a pet in a boarding institution. If you will consider the facts as I have presented them, you will see the problem in a fairer light.

One precaution you can and should take: Consider the age of your pet. Kittens are far more likely to die than are grown cats, because they have less resistance. Intestinal parasites and viral diseases are more harmful to young animals than to older ones. Knowing these facts, you will be wise to keep your kittens isolated, as far as it is in your power to do so, until they are over a year old. Thereafter the ravages of diseases will be less severe.

After you have read this book you will be in a better position to judge where your pet contracted any disease, because knowledge of the incubation period will help you.

One final thought: The risk to health where pets congregate or are congregated is unavoidable. It can, however, be greatly reduced. Nothing does more to minimize the hazards than proper vaccinations. If you neglect to take this simple precaution, you not only are not doing the sporting thing to the pets of others, but you are failing to take the most obvious step to protect the health of your own. Do not hesitate to ask your veterinarian for advice in this area.

16. What You Can and Cannot Catch from Your Cat

*N*EARLY EVERY cat owner wonders, at some time during his or her cat ownership, whether there is any danger that cats can transmit diseases. The answer is yes, they can. I think, though, that the danger to cats from human contact is even greater. I have seen cats infected by their owners with upper respiratory infections, for example, more than the reverse.

By combing the medical literature for reports of authentic instances where cats have infected human beings, you can find an impressive list. The list can also be quite frightening if you forget that in most cases the diseases are extremely rare. It was nearly always quite a surprise to find that he "caught it" from a cat. The following diseases can be contagious: tularemia, rabies, cat scratch fever, virus pneumonia, ornathosis, diphtheria, tuberculosis, brucellosis, typhus, pasteurellosis, ringworm, creeping eruption, favus, amebiasis, salmonellosis, trypanosomiasis, leishmaniasis, dog tapeworm, fish tapeworm, liver fluke, episthorchiasis, schistosomiasis, strongyloidosis, scrub typhus, leptospirosis.

We also find other cases in which cats are suspected of having infected human beings. The suspicion in each case is based on the fact that cat and man were in close contact and both had the same disease: leptospirosis, plague, histoplasmosis, toxoplasmosis.

Are there any diseases in the above list which you, as a cat owner, really know anything about (aside perhaps from rabies)? Have you ever, among all of your acquaintances, known of a single person having contracted a disease from his or her cat? Probably not. Bearing this in mind, let us consider several of the diseases cats have been known to transmit to humans.

On the basis of my own experience with thousands of cats and their owners, the following, from the lengthy list of possibly transmissible diseases, are those to be watched for: rabies, tuberculosis, virus pneumonia, cat scratch fever, ringworm, and visceral larva migrans. In Chapter 13 you will find these diseases—except cat scratch fever and visceral larva migrans—described as they affect cats. Here we consider their danger to human beings.

Rabies. Rabies contracted from rabid cats is unknown in many sections of the world but the disease is a real danger where rabies is prevalent. If you live in an area where rabies is found, and your cat begins to act abnormally, hides and sulks, take the necessary precautions. Put the cat in a room by itself and watch it carefully. Do not handle it. Perhaps it is only coincidence, but in cases in which human beings contracted the disease from cats, every one was bitten by a cat that previously had become asocial and wanted to hide. Possibly it was under the sofa and the cat charged suddenly and bit the person's leg. Possibly it was in the tall grass behind the house and, as the person walked near where the sick cat was hiding, it sprang, bit, and scratched the person's calf or ankle.

Tuberculosis. Tuberculosis definitely can be contracted from cats but usually it is the bovine form, not the human. Cats living in contact with cattle, walking in their mangers, breathing their breath, drinking raw milk from cattle whose udders have tubercular lesions, can transmit the disease to humans. Cats which unaccountably cough or grow thin can be tuberculin tested. If they test positive, they should be destroyed mercifully. In fact, when they are a public danger, they should be eliminated just as the United States Government destroys every cow which proves to be a "reactor."

Virus Pneumonia. Virus pneumonia may be a far greater danger than has been realized to date. Since there is more than one form of the disease, no cat sick with virus pneumonia should be kept where a human being might come into contact with it. However, we need not destroy the cat since, with proper treatment, many of the cases recover fully.

Cat Scratch Fever. Cat scratch fever had a great deal of publicity in the newspapers in 1951 and 1952. Again it makes news because it is so unusual—the commonplace things never do. It is a case of "man bites dog." Cat scratch fever is probably a virus disease.

The symptoms of cat scratch fever in a human being begin with a painless swelling in the lymphatic glands near the scratch a few days after the scratch is received. These glands are located in many places both inside and outside of the body cavity. Those under the skin can be felt in the throat, the neck, under the arms, and in the groin. The infection often spreads to all the lymph glands. The body temperature rises and there is general ill feeling. Sometimes the glands break down and suppurate and the skin may show pustular eruptions. The person recovers spontaneously and, according to one investigator, administration of certain antibiotics hastens recovery.

One of the strange facts about cat scratch fever is that cats themselves cannot be infected with the virus, but seem to be merely the bearers of it. Every cat whose scratch has infected a man or woman was found to be healthy. In one household, three members contracted the disease from one cat. Such an animal should perhaps be declawed rather than destroyed.

Ringworm. The most common disease transmitted from cat to man is ringworm. Many a cat shows no evidence of the disease, yet passes it on to every member of the family. This is especially true in the case of long-haired cats. If ringworm suddenly starts, with its reddish round or oval spots, and your physician is sure of his diagnosis, then examine the cats with meticulous care. Even if you did not contract it from them, you are almost certain to transmit it to them and they will continue to infect you.

Ringworm is easy to cure on man and cats if the proper mixture of drugs is used. In fact, a large number of our clients have, on their own responsibility, used the remedy that was given them for their cats and speedily cured themselves and their children as well as the cats.

Visceral Larva Migrans. From time to time the media and especially the sensationalist press inform the public of the disastrous effects of dog and cat roundworms in humans and there is a grain of truth in their statements. We know the eggs of the common roundworm can live for years in the ground, even in cold climates, and we know that humans can ingest them. They have caused serious problems in children who, after eating the microscopic eggs, have had migrating larvae find their way to an eye and other organs.

There are several points to consider concerning this problem. In the first place the disease is usually confined to children under five years of age, and is most prevalent in children who have the habit of eating dirt.

The solutions are to prevent the child from ingesting dirt, to deworm any cat or dog with these parasites, and to dispose of excrement properly. Although fecal analysis is desirable to identify the infested animal, treatment of this condition is so well tolerated that there is no harm in using one of the many over-the-counter forms of piperazine as a deworming agent. Just follow the directions on the package.

Proceed with caution in treating very young or debilitated kittens. These five-inch-long worms are not always easily passed by kittens. If they are killed by a medication and decompose in the weak kitten the intoxication could be the straw that breaks the camel's back. In small or weak individuals consult your veterinarian before a treatment. He may advise the deworming be done in the hospital where supportive injections and enemas may be indicated.

Bacterial Infections. Perhaps we should mention infections caused by cat bites. These infections do occur but no more frequently than infections caused by any other skin wound from a relatively clean object.

Bacteriologically the cat's mouth is cleaner than ours by far, and after literally dozens of cat bites I have never had more than some local discomfort.

It is probably safer to kiss your cat than your spouse, although I don't espouse cat kissing.

Chaga's Disease. This protozoan disease has been reported rarely in the United States, but may be a cat-carried problem in some areas of the world.

Fleabite Dermatitis. Some people become sensitized to the bite of the cat's fleas. Each bite will produce a large welt with inflammation and itching. I have known many people with such a problem.

Salmonellosis. A large family of bacteria found commonly in nature may affect cats. They may live in the intestine without causing a problem or they may cause diarrhea, sometimes with blood. I have never heard of a cat transmitting it but it is theoretically possible. Culturing is necessary to identify the culprit and your veterinarian will supply helpful medication.

Cutaneous Larva Migrans. An uncommon problem passed from cats to man is the larva of the hookworm. It may be ingested by eating soil contaminated with hookworm eggs; in other cases, the larva, hatched from the eggs, may penetrate the unbroken skin. In either case the parasite works along in the skin causing an extremely itchy condition. After the itching phase some children develop a lung problem.

In over thirty years of practice I have never heard of such a case in my area; the condition is thought to be more common in Mexico and Central America.

Tapeworms. If a flea eats part of a tapeworm segment it may transmit the parasite when the cat ingests the flea. The same problem has been reported in young children. The children, with sticky fingers, pet the cat, a flea may stick to the fingers, and since infants put their hands in their mouths so often, the ingested worm-infested flea may produce tapeworms in the infant.

Scabies. A tiny mite called Otodectes produces an itching skin rash, usually on the cat's head, which may affect people. On man the rash is often on the inner surfaces of the arms or on the body; but as far as I can determine the mites do not reproduce on us. Where these insects bite, intense itching occurs. The problem is easily diagnosed and easily eliminated with medication.

Toxoplasmosis. After all the publicity surrounding this disease and the danger that cats present because of it, especially to pregnant women, one would think that cats were too dangerous to keep as pets. A little serious thought would reveal that the danger is grossly exaggerated. If any cat owner is careful in changing the contents of the cat's pan, especially if the cat appears to be sick, there is little likelihood of contracting the disease, especially since there are only two to three weeks when the sick cat can transmit it. We know that many persons have had the disease without knowing it and have built up resistance to it. We know too that thousands of persons have contracted it from eating rare meat and raw eggs. To date it has not been proven that any human case was contracted from a cat. In man the symptoms are similar to those of a cold with perhaps muscular stiffness.

Leptospirosis. At present this disease is being studied, but it appears to be of small concern to cat owners because its effects on cats are not severe. It is quite probable that cats have the disease and recover without their owners realizing that their pets were ever sick.

Leptospirosis is caused by a spiral-shaped bacterium that may enter the body through the mouth or the genital organs. It is being recognized as a much more common disease of cattle than had been suspected and is transmitted via milk or urine. Cats drinking unpasteurized milk can contract it; barn cats are often exposed to the disease.

Cases severe enough to be recognized generally show jaundice. Although two forms of the disease are recognized—the jaundice-hemorrhage and the canicola—they are difficult to differentiate. They have not as yet been sufficiently studied in cats for us to be able to state which form is more prevalent. In human beings the canicola form of the disease often passes for influenza.

Of all the other diseases on the transmissible list, tularemia is a good illustration of how little we have to worry about. It is considered primarily a rabbit disease, and only three cases of tularemia were diagnosed in cats by the State Health Laboratory of Connecticut. Three cats out of the thousands in that state are indeed a very small percentage.

Actually then, we have little to fear from our cats so far as the transmission of diseases is concerned.

Indeed, if it were a problem, a high incidence would be found among veterinarians, their assistants, and workers in boarding establishments, yet this is not the case.

*O*NE of the advantages of feline practice for the veterinarian lies in the fact that cat lovers do not request many unnecessary surgical procedures. The dog lovers have tails cut, ears cropped and removed, not to help the animal in any way but to please the owner. To breed for beauty is one thing; but unnecessary surgery to create beauty somehow seems uncivilized to me.

But there are a few procedures we recommend to cat owners to make their pets more satisfactory companion animals or to alleviate or shorten a period of discomfort for their cats.

SPAYING

Spaying, properly called ovariohysterectomy, is one such operation. After fasting and a physical examination one of several injectable anesthetics is administered. The surgery may be performed with such agents alone or in combination with gas anesthesia.

The surgical site is clipped, scrubbed, and a sterile drape placed over the animal. In the meantime, the surgeon dons his sterile mask and cap, scrubs, gowns, and puts on sterile gloves.

There are several variations, but in all of them the ovaries as well as most of the uterus are removed. Any blood vessels must be ligated (tied) and the incision sutured internally and externally.

When performed by the average veterinary surgeon fatalities are virtually nonexistent.

A stitch or stitches may have to be removed in a week or ten days, during which time the queen is usually quiet for the first two days and quite normal thereafter.

Many queens are spayed when in heat and even when pregnant with uniformly good results.

For many years opinions about the results of spaying (not spading) a queen were bandied about by "experts" on a purely conjectural basis. Mr. James found his queen became obese; Mrs. Jones found hers did not change. Even veterinarians couldn't agree.

Considerable research now shows that spaying young adults has little effect on the general characteristics of the animal, except for the fact that mating cycles, and the attendant urges, are eliminated.

This is true with one qualification—that the operation be done when the animal is nearly full grown or later. This is very important. Studies show that when animals are spayed at an early age, their glandular development is abnormal. In order to produce a chicken that will be large, awkward, lazy, and fat (a capon, in other words), the operation should not be put off until the bird is full grown. If it were, the result would be merely a sterile rooster. One reason for spaying queens young is to prevent the queens of vicious strains from becoming dangerous as they get older. If they are spayed as kittens, they tend to remain more gentle.

The fact that some spayed queens get fat is not in itself a valid argument against spaying. Unspayed queens, too, get fat. Some of the most grossly overweight cats I know are whole animals. They are simply overfed. If they had been spayed and placed in the hands of the same owner, his or her explanation for the overweight condition would have been that the queen had been spayed.

Actually, some cats are often altered young to advantage. Ornamental queens probably develop more handsomely if they are spayed before their third month. They grow to be larger, quieter, slower, and are more inclined to drape beautifully over the furniture. Usually the most beautiful cats are the ones that have been spayed early.

Spaying a queen has a number of definite advantages:

1. The animal is spared the risk attending birth.

2. The owner is spared raising or having to destroy unwanted kittens.

3. The owner avoids the annoyance of males surrounding his home, spraying on his front or back doors.

4. The spayed female does not wander at certain seasons as the unspayed female does.

5. Food is saved, since a pregnant, or lactating, mother consumes more food than a spayed one.

6. Considering the risks of pregnancy and birth, a female's chances for a longer life are actually greater if she is spayed.

7. The uterus is subject to infection and both the uterus and ovaries are potential cancer sites.

CASTRATION

Another elective surgical procedure is the removal of the testicles from tomcats.

Much the same arguments hold for castration as for spaying. Generally it is done to make males stay home. Those that congregate around the abode of a queen come home punctured with tooth marks from the frequent fracases attending such meetings.

There are many other reasons for castrating. Cats of strains whose members tend to become vicious with age are often rendered gentle and lovable when castrated young. Castration also tends to prevent indiscriminate wetting in the home and prevents obnoxious odors.

Tomcats that are of no use for breeding become stay-at-homes, and much expense in their care is saved. Uncastrated toms so often come home infected that the family has to face veterinary bills to cover treatment. If castrated after maturity, their ratting and mousing ability will not be impaired and in general they will be more satisfactory pets.

It seems to be the opinion of many that animals should not be spayed or castrated because copulation is essential to health. This is not the case. Any animal, whether whole, spayed, or castrated, is just as healthy if it is never bred as those that are used for breeding. Only a small percentage ever copulate in their whole lives. This is true of many species, not of our pet cats alone.

DECLAWING

In recent years the minor surgical procedure called declawing has been refined so that it is now a common veterinary practice. To the veterinarian it is minor, but not to the cat, in spite of the fact that the operation is performed under general anesthesia. Recovery from ten toe amputations is not exactly a pleasure for the cat. I suspect that someday we will have an injection to immobilize the nails, but if so they will have to be clipped regularly. Of course most cats can be trained not to scratch the furniture and shred the draperies by disciplining them with a fly swatter and at the same time providing a scratching post. A scratching post may be a fireplace log with an interesting shape for aesthetics. In addition, pieces of carpet remnant may be fastened to furniture under attack.

Frankly, I do not like to declaw any cat, but sometimes it boils down to killing an animal or declawing it. I must accept the lesser of the two evils.

There is, however, a genetic alternative. Cats can be bred to be "soft-pawed." These animals inherit the tendency to keep their nails retracted and are not inclined to exercise them on draperies, rugs, or upholstered furniture. The giant wild cats do not use their nails except to kill and a percentage of our domestic pets carry the genes too. It is my understanding that, whereas in the United States soft-pawed cats are rare, in Japan, for example, one cannot find a cat that scratches. Such an animal virtually never introduces nails into clothing or flesh when held close, and even when terrified, such a cat will bite in self-defense but never use the claws.

I know of no American breeders interested in producing such cats; but in my opinion such a breeding program is a golden opportunity for those who truly desire to improve this species as companion animals.

As mentioned previously, a declawed cat can climb trees, although not with quite its previous agility.

HEMATOMAS

When a cat scratches an ear excessively, as with an advanced case of ear mites, a blood vessel may rupture, resulting in a blood clot between the layers of skin. This is called a hematoma and should be corrected by surgery. I list it under elective surgery since it is not a life-threatening event, but left untreated it results in a shriveled ear sometimes called a "potato-chip" ear. The accompanying sketch illustrates one of many sur-

A hematoma in the ear, and one of many surgical treatments to facilitate rapid healing without puckering. The drain, which is moved back and forth to prevent the middle strip from healing, is removed when the sides have healed.

gical techniques used to correct this condition, all of which are done under general anesthesia.

RUPTURED ABSCESSES

Perhaps the most common problem in cats is the abscess caused by the bite of another cat. When a joint is infected by a bite the problem needs professional attention. However, many abscesses are small when they rupture and heal uneventfully. When the abscess is large, leaving a huge area of open raw tissue, then elective surgery will correct the problem in a fraction of the time Mother Nature alone takes. The cat is the only animal I know that will heal readily without complications when such an area is sutured closed. In man or a canine, such suturing results in the development of infection under the sutured area, which usually leads to another abscess. Not so with our feline friends.

Such abscesses are usually located on the head or forelegs if the cat is a fighter or around the tail and back above the tail or the rear legs. The latter occurs if the cat is a pacifist and would rather run than fight.

If the abscess opening is larger than a half dollar I like to suture it; this is still an elective procedure since the cat will recover either because of or in spite of anything we do.

REMOVAL OF AN EYE

Enucleation is the medical term for the removal of an eye. There are eye problems with which the cat can live but would be better off with the eyeball removed. Certainly a chronically infected eye is one, and a swollen blind eye another. In both cases there is pain, which we have the capability of relieving by enucleation.

When this suggestion is made to many owners their response is often to elect euthanasia. What a tragedy! This most adaptable of animals adjusts to life with one eye and conducts himself as any other cat. The lids are sutured so that hair covers the area, and there is no grim, open, fleshy cavern. Loss of an eye, it bears repeating, is not a valid reason to destroy a cat.

AMPUTATION

When a leg is useless, subject to infection, and in the cat's way, as with permanent nerve damage, it may be an advantage to amputate it. If a foreleg is involved, the cat has a problem climbing trees, but not so with a hind leg. Of course the only time trees are necessary is to elude a dog, so such an animal should be kept indoors.

Here again, as in the case of eye removal, many owners are reluctant to have a disfigured pet around them. Given a choice, the cat, if he were able to communicate, would no doubt opt for an amputation. Such a cat leaps to the window sill as usual and with one front leg he will leap to the mantelpiece as usual.

I would urge you to accept amputation over misery or death for the cat. Remember, the cat lives for the present only and doesn't consider how unfortunate he is as compared with the way he was in the past.

18. Geriatrics

THE SUBJECT of geriatrics has been woefully neglected in all species, it seems to me, and that includes man. Virtually no research has been done with the feline in mind.

The first question to consider is, "When is a cat in its geriatric years?" Even this has not been defined and the fact that we see old-acting young cats and young-acting old cats adds to the definition problem. Since there is good evidence that age is a genetic factor, I think a cat's life expectancy is determined at birth and, barring disease, accidents, and poor nutrition, it will live out those predetermined years.

On the average I think ten years places most cats in their golden years. One of the first signs of old age may be detected by placing the cat in the dark with a light source behind you. If the eyes appear brighter and perhaps larger as they reflect the light, the cat most likely has lenticular sclerosis, a hardening of minute arteries in the lenses of the eyes. Since the cat does not see as well as in his younger days it must dilate his pupils more widely to admit more light and this is the reason for the brighter night-shining eyes. In the daylight the pupils that were once black are now gray—the more hardening of the arteries, the grayer.

This is an indication of what is happening throughout the body. Sometimes this sclerosis affects the delicate membranes of the inner ear; whereas the cat failed to respond in days gone by due to aloofness alone, impaired hearing now makes the aloofness seem exaggerated.

However, of several advantages the feline has in general, one worth mentioning is the fact that their hearts are remarkably free of the degenerative changes we recognize in canines and man. The pathologists verify this in their studies of old cats' hearts.

However, in older cats one organ does appear to suffer more degenerative changes than the others and that is the kidneys. On post-mortem examination we frequently see gnarly, shrunken kidneys, which can be readily palpated in the living old cat.

I should point out that in spite of such kidneys a normal amount of urine is passed; but the urine does not have the waste materials that must be passed to maintain life. Such a situation is, for a time, compensated for by an increased intake of fluid: in one cup of urine the cat passes the wastes it used to pass in a half cup. In time there is further degeneration and it becomes impossible for those filtering plants to work well enough to sustain life. With most animals the kidney failure causes stress on the heart, which must pump more blood to be filtered by the kidneys; since it is overworked, the heart eventually fails. This does not appear to be the case with cats. In any event it seems to me that the feline's kidneys, not the heart, are their Achilles' heel.

If there is a problem in eliminating the wastes of digestion in the old cat, then nutrition should be considered as one means of, if not prolonging life, at least making the last years more livable.

Since I will talk about a change of diet, and many owners know their cat will eat one food only, let me hasten to add, as was mentioned earlier, that you can teach an old cat new tricks and you can change its diet. You may have to do it gradually but you can do it.

The problem with most commercial cat foods lies in the quality of the protein contained in them. This protein produces excessive nitrogenous waste materials, which stress the kidneys. So, if you give a high-quality protein such as wholesome beef, chicken, or fish you may help your old friend a great deal. Since we believe cats cannot live on such protein alone, add a little ground cooked vegetable—about 10 per cent. A quarter teaspoon of brewers' yeast powder all well mixed together with the meat and vegetables makes a satisfactory diet, which should be rounded out by a daily mineral-vitamin supplement and one-eighth pound of cooked beef liver or chicken liver once a week.

The concerned owner does more than pet, hug, feed, and admire an old cat. He takes a few minutes to feel the pet gently all over for lumps and bumps. He examines the ears every month or so for infection or tumors. He keeps tabs on the cat's teeth and nails and combs and brushes the animal regularly.

And with the advancing years, a cat must be protected when it is outdoors against a threatening dog or cat that may be too fast for old muscles and reflexes. Since its senses are not so acute, the geriatric cat is at a greater disadvantage with vehicles, too.

When it's cold or rainy, exposure is the last thing one should permit. And changes of routine should be avoided.

For the old pet who has had the comfort of home for years, a boarding establishment is not a desirable solution when the masters must be away. It is best to have someone visit your home and feed and water the cat or, if that is impossible, take it with you. Use a carrier and no one will know your cat is in the motel room with you.

It is most important to observe changes in an old cat's functions and attitude before a problem becomes too serious, so don't hesitate to consult your veterinarian. I like to get a laboratory profile on an older cat while it is still healthy—then if at a later time signs of ill health are observed a second profile will show which test values are changing and direct us to the source of the problem more easily.

A profile could be a urinalysis, a fecal analysis, and blood tests, and of course your comments as to your friend's condition. This is particularly important in animals, as they can't tell us where the problem lies.

The whole business of good care for the geriatric cat is basically common sense, but unfortunately common sense is a rare commodity especially when people deal with animals they take for granted.

There is something about an old cat that makes it a little more majestic, a little more noble than a youngster, and, with years of love invested in it, a little more important; so be concerned and the golden years will be brighter and perhaps longer.

According to Guinness Book of World Records the authenticated oldest cat was a female owned by Mrs. Alice Moore of Devon, England. She was put to sleep November 5, 1957, in her thirty-fifth year.

19. When the End Comes

$\mathcal{T}$HE death of a pet is a very serious problem to a great many people. Too many otherwise intelligent pet owners simply can't bring themselves to realize that every life has a limit. When their conscientious veterinarian assures them it is time to say good-bye to their pet, instead of taking his advice they say good-bye to the veterinarian and take their pet to another, who may prolong its miserable life to the advantage of no one, least of all to the patient.

It is interesting and helpful to consider the life expectancy of cats. If you know what to expect in advance, you will not be surprised at death, nor will you ask the impossible of your veterinarian.

In the table below, the average age at death means *from natural causes* in cats that have survived infanthood.

Table VIII

BREED	AVERAGE AGE AT DEATH	OLDEST KNOWN BY THE AUTHOR
Domestic	12	22
Longhair	12	16
Siamese	12	23
Manx	12	19

Unless our cat dies suddenly from unknown causes, there comes a time when we must ask ourselves, "What's best to do? Shall we let him die as a result of old age, general breakdown, a growth, kidney disease, or other causes?" Or shall we bravely say, "He has led a good life, he's no longer enjoying what little is left of it, he's blind and deaf, he's in some pain; we'll have him put painlessly to sleep"?

It takes courage to make such a decision. To do so always makes us wish that our pet could live as long as we do. When the time comes for the owner to decide what to do with his aging pet, there are some general facts which he should know and questions he should consider, which may make the decision easier for him.

There is no pain to euthanasia if properly administered. A veterinarian can inject a few cc's of an anesthetic into a cat's vein and soon the cat droops his eyes, nods his head, sighs as he feels release from pain, goes to sleep. He just never wakens.

An animal does not miss tomorrow. Suppose that you couldn't think ahead. If you had no imagination, you couldn't project yourself into the future. Mentally and physically you would live only in this moment—not even two seconds in the future. We can anticipate a fine dinner party and see images of it in our mind's eye. We can look forward in winter to next spring's flowers and thus make our winter more bearable. But an animal lives in the present alone, without any thought of the future. If he dies, his existence merely terminates. He is being deprived of nothing, for he has no conception of the future.

The death of a pet is not his loss so much as ours. The home will be empty without his presence. True, for the past year he probably hasn't been the friend we knew and loved; he's been ailing and not himself. But propinquity has endeared him to us and we see him as he used to be; we remember all the fine qualities he once had. When we hesitate to bring his life to an end, we are unconsciously thinking of ourselves. We may even allow him to suffer pain and discomfort because *we* don't want to lose him; we don't want our serene existence upset by no longer having our pet.

He's going to die someday. We must face this fact, even though we shrink from it. Isn't it better to stop his suffering by terminating his existence by our own volition than to allow him to linger in pain or extreme old age?

What might he say if he could think? He would probably say something like this: "I don't want to leave you any more than you want to be without me, but please give me comfort and freedom from misery. I can't see, so I bump into furniture. I can't hear you. I no longer enjoy the meals you prepare for me. I'm a burden to you, and certainly no good to myself. If I go outside, I might be crushed by an automobile. What good am I, anyway? Couldn't you be unselfish and grant me a blessed release?" And he might well add: "And if I gave you so much fun and companionship, get yourself another pet to fill my place, just as quickly as you can. Start giving him the attention you gave me when I was young. It will give you lots to think about and help to keep you young."

Is he in pain? The determination of the presence of pain is simple in a cat with a recent fracture. When he moves or is moved he will utter sounds of pain. However, when pain arrives gradually, as with arthritis, this animal, which is noted for his stoicism, will not cry or demonstrate discomfort other than by feeble attempts to move about. He no longer considers it worthwhile to attempt the leap to his favorite overstuffed chair and even moving to food and water is an effort. Many old animals suffer in silence unnecessarily.

Ask your veterinarian. Opinions are what you pay a veterinarian for, and although some will insist the decision of ending an old life is yours, others attempt to analyze the situation and help with your decision. I try to make a decision as if the patient were one of my own cats.

This brings to mind the other side of the coin—the owner who decides a condition is hopeless when with a little effort in the form of treatment the condition can be corrected. This type of owner is usually sincere and perhaps has watched a previous pet linger too long before death. I think the opinion of a trusted veterinarian should have a great deal of weight in the final decision.

It is a common occurrence for an old cat to leave the home and wander aimlessly until, exhausted, it finds a sheltered spot and curls up to die. Such an animal will not respond to calling and is usually so secreted that it is never found. This is not the way an old friend should be treated and such a situation should weigh heavily on the owner's conscience.

Make the decision and have the strongest member of the family carry it out. Do not permit any form of "dark age" euthanasia.

METHODS OF EUTHANASIA

The methods employed in euthanasia in the past—and, unfortunately, even today in some places—are largely responsible for the fact that so many people simply refused to consider ending a pet's life. These methods were shocking, inhumane, and often clumsy. Usually the animal was shot, gassed, or electrocuted. The drugs that were occasionally used were unsatisfactory: the injection of strychnine was certainly inferior even to shooting; ether and chloroform brought a kinder death, but even with these there was violent struggling.

Today there are a number of drugs available that are both quick and painless. When you decide that it is best to terminate your pet's existence you have every right to insist that drugs of this type be administered. The best of these, in my opinion, are the barbiturates; and of them I prefer sodium pentobarbital. When injected into a vein, its effects are almost instantaneous. A sudden sleep overpowers the animal and in a matter of seconds it is completely unconscious. The heartbeat and breathing cease; the end comes quietly and quickly. I have administered this drug to many pets in the presence of their owners, and without exception they have been tremendously impressed by the humane and painless death it has brought. The drug can be given by mouth in capsule form but it takes longer for the cat to die.

The lethal dose of sodium pentobarbital is usually considered to be one and a half times the amount required for anesthesia. In nearly every case such an injection is adequate, but I have known cases in which it produced only a prolonged deep sleep and a second injection was necessary.

To eliminate even the possibility of such occurrences, I administer three grains for each five pounds of the animal's weight. A dose of this size is completely and immediately effective.

In spite of the fact that sodium pentobarbital is inexpensive and easily available to qualified persons, it has not been adopted as widely as it deserves to be for euthanasia. If your local humane society or dog warden is still using the methods of a decade or so ago, you will be doing a service to both the pets and pet owners in your community by discussing with the proper authorities the possibilities of using pentobarbital.

This may mean a change of regulations but since regulations are made by people they can be changed by people. At this time most states are in the process of changing or have already changed these unfortunate laws to the benefit of our pet animals. If your state is dragging its feet, put your shoulder to the effort for the good of the pet population.

When the decision for euthanasia has been made, the question remains of whether to watch the procedure or to leave the old cat in the hands of the veterinarian.

Some insist on watching and comforting the animal to the end. Some think the old pet will think it is deserted and consider leaving not a responsible act. Others want to watch because they want to be sure it is done and done humanely.

Personally I have never remained with one of my own pets while it was euthanized. I have left the animal in good hands and have left the premises to cry in private or to comfort loved ones who will miss the old-timer as much as I.

If you trust your veterinarian he will not break that trust—it will be just as humane as if you were there. The act of euthanasia is on the one hand the most repugnant duty a veterinarian has to perform; but on the other, the most humane.

CARE OF THE REMAINS

Should you have your cat buried? If so, where? The back yard? This is illegal in many cities. In a cemetery for pets? A grave and perpetual care cost about one hundred dollars in some communities. Should the animal be embalmed? Why? What happens after death, anyway? Slow oxidation is the answer. Oxidation is a chemical name for burning. Wood in a fire oxidizes with a visible flame. A decaying stump oxidizes slowly, with no such fanfare. An animal's body oxidizes slowly too. So it is actually a matter of deciding between quick or slow oxidation. Burial or cremation is the choice and I unhesitatingly recommend the latter. What advantage is there in slow oxidation? Isn't it better to know it is over in a few minutes rather than slowly taking place in the ground over a period of years? Chemically, there's little difference; aesthetically, choose cremation.

Years ago we permitted clients to bury their pets on a wooded hillside near our office. It was touching to see people come on every holiday to plant ivy or place a few flowers on the graves, and when some were away on a holiday, florists would deliver flowers for us to place on the graves. It was touching and who am I to judge another. We stopped burials fifteen years ago and this is the first year no adornments or visitors have arrived.

POST-MORTEM EXAMINATIONS

Sometimes the question arises: "Shall I permit a post-mortem examination?" A study made in a large hospital for humans to determine the percentage of persons who refused to allow free post-mortems on their loved ones showed that 26 per cent refused permission. Even though the interviewing doctor could say, "The examination may be of help to you personally; such things run in families, you know," 26 per cent still refused. A similar study at the Whitney Veterinary Clinic revealed the astounding fact that 24.3 per cent refused to allow free examinations on their pet dogs after death. Many of the findings could have been of great help to other dogs, if not always to their owners. Had we kept track of the cat owners, doubtless the results would have been similar.

Occasionally cats die of diseases that are transmissible to their owners. If the veterinarian is willing to risk his health performing a necropsy, one would think the owner should acquiesce. The same applies when such an examination could help the veterinarian to help other cats, or when it would add to our knowledge of cancer, or parasites, or growth, or blood, or heredity.

When your doctor finds your pet's malady of sufficient interest to give his time to studying its body, you need an excellent reason to justify your refusing him permission. If you love pets, you love to see them well. You can hardly do less than to help the doctor help other pets—and perhaps, incidentally, yourself.

1. Q. How can oil or Vaseline be given a cat that fights and refuses to swallow it?
   A. Applied to face and legs, it will be licked off.

2. Q. How early may a cat be spayed?
   A. Any time after birth, but it is better to wait until she is five months old.

3. Q. How early must she be spayed to avoid her first heat?
   A. Before she is five months old.

4. Q. How early can a tom be castrated?
   A. At two or three months of age.

5. Q. Can a queen be spayed safely after she has had a litter?
   A. Yes, at any time. However, more involved surgery is required.

6. Q. Can a tom be castrated safely after he is a year old?
   A. Yes.

7. Q. Do cats have asthma?
   A. Yes. Something very much like the human variety.

8. Q. Are cats strictly carnivorous?
   A. Zoologically speaking, yes, but they eat vegetable foods and thrive on them in addition to meat.

9. Q. Is beef the natural food of cats?

A. Studies of cats gone wild indicate that rodents are the natural food of cats.

10. Q. Is a brush best for grooming a cat?
    A. A comb with strong teeth spaced twelve to the inch serves best.

11. Q. Are cats' nutritional requirements the same as for other pets?
    A. Very similar, with exceptions. Unlike a guinea pig, a cat makes its own vitamin C; unlike a rat, it needs only a little vitamin E.

12. Q. Is catnip the best tonic for a cat?
    A. Its odor serves as a mental tonic. If eaten, it is a weak nerve stimulant.

13. Q. Does a cat come in season only once a year?
    A. She may have one season after another in rapid succession if not bred. Another series may occur in four or five months.

14. Q. Can a queen become pregnant while she is nursing a litter?
    A. Yes. She often does.

15. Q. Must a cat touch another with distemper to become infected?
    A. The virus lives for months on an infected premises.

16. Q. Can you teach a cat tricks?
    A. Yes, as easily as a dog.

17. Q. How can a cat be made to stop clawing furniture, wallpaper, etc.?
    A. Keep its claws trimmed. Train it. As a last resort, your veterinarian can operate.

18. Q. Can cats have tuberculosis?
    A. Yes. Two per cent of European cats were found to have the cattle form.

19. Q. Do cats have convulsions from eating meat?
    A. Only indirectly, if they become constipated. Toxins such as those from food-poisoning organisms and worms, or certain poisons, may cause seizures.

20. Q. Are blue-eyed white cats always deaf?
    A. No, but many are.

21. Q. Are tortoiseshell and tortoiseshell-and-white cats ever of the male sex?
    A. This color is inherited as a sex-linked characteristic. About one in 5,000 are males.

22. Q. Does diarrhea come only from improper feeding?
    A. It comes more often as the result of disease—distemper, coccidiosis, etc.

23. Q. Are phenol disinfectants safe around cats?
    A. No. Never use them or phenol derivatives as disinfectants.

24. Q. Are cat distemper and dog distemper one and the same disease?
    A. They are caused by totally different viruses. Dog distemper does not affect cats and vice versa.

25. Q. What makes a cat's breath bad?
    A. Bad teeth, infected mouth and lips, kidney disease, poisoning, to name a few causes.

26. Q. Is ear canker the same as ear-mite infestation?
    A. No. Mites are small insects that produce a dry, crumbly wax; canker is a bacterial and/or fungus infection that generally produces a sticky wax.

27. Q. When a lactating female develops violent trembling and becomes prostrate, is it a sign of poisoning?
    A. It is probably eclampsia, caused by inadequate amounts of calcium in her diet.

28. Q. How can one make a cat eat what's good for her instead of only beef kidneys?
    A. Make her hungry enough by starvation.

29. Q. Can cats reason?
    A. They condition easily but do not reason.

30. Q. Can an orphan kitten be raised on cow's milk?
    A. Yes. It is similar to cat's milk in composition.

31. Q. How does one pick up a vicious cat to avoid being scratched?
    A. Gather the cat up in a heavy blanket.

32. Q. Should cats be inoculated?
    A. By all means.

33. Q. Does mineral oil, when given every day in the food, help constipation?
    A. It is much better to feed laxative diets. Mineral oil tends to absorb the fat-soluble vitamins so that they become wasted on the cat.

34. Q. Does altering a tom predispose him to urinary problems?
    A. There is no evidence that altering has any relation to urinary problems.

35. Q. How do mange and eczema differ?
    A. Mange is caused by a mite; "eczema" is due to an infection, either bacterial or fungal.

36. Q. Does it pay to grind cat food?
    A. Yes. You can incorporate all the things that are good for your cat in one mixture.

37. Q. Do well-cared-for cats live longer than those that fend for themselves?
    A. No one knows. Overfat cats may not live so long as leaner ones, but the age of feral cats is not accurately known.

38. Q. What are the chief advantages in castrating a male cat?
    A. He stays home, has few fights, urinates sitting down, and his urine loses its acrid unpleasant odor.

39. Q. How long should a cat take to deliver a litter of kittens?
    A. A few hours. However, normal deliveries lasting twenty-four hours are not uncommon.

40. Q. Can cats have rabies?
    A. They can and occasionally do.

41. Q. What does a ringworm look like? Can people catch the disease?
    A. It is not a worm but a fungus infection that produces bald patches of ring or oval shape, with quite clearly defined margins. Yes, we can catch it from cats and also spread it to them.

42. Q. How many common intestinal parasites are found in cats?
    A. Several species of tapeworm, several species of coccidia, roundworm, hookworm, and rarely whipworm.

43. Q. How much water does a cat drink a day?
    A. There is no standard amount. If she has much milk, she'll want very little water. If she has salty fish she will drink a lot.

44.   Q.   Do cats change their teeth as they get older?
      A.   Only to lose their baby teeth.

45.   Q.   Can cats be washed safely?
      A.   Yes, if they are dried and not exposed to cold until dry.

46.   Q.   At what age should kittens be weaned?
      A.   Start at six weeks and be finished at eight or nine.

47.   Q.   Can cats digest vegetables?
      A.   Very well, if the starch granules have been cracked by cook-
           ing.

48.   Q.   Is thirty pounds a good weight for a cat?
      A.   Certainly not. A human being proportionately heavy would be
           a circus curiosity. It is a very bad weight.

49.   Q.   Can cats be raised in outdoor cages safely?
      A.   Most can, but cats in outdoor runs may sit out in the rain and
           develop pneumonia.

50.   Q.   How many litters of kittens can a female have?
      A.   Many have had twenty litters in a lifetime.

Acknowledgments

White Persian, Blue Acres Doll Baby of Les Cygnes, owned by Mr. and Mrs. Paul Swan, Les Cygnes Cattery, Independence, Missouri.

Short-haired black. International News Photo.

Russian Blue, imported from England by Mrs. Blanche Warren, Casa Gatos Cattery, Idyllwild, California.

Peke-faced red tabby, Pineland's Pepper Pat, owned by Mr. and Mrs. Robert B. Treat, Jr., and Robert Treat 3rd, Callavorn Cattery, Porter Hill, Middlebury, Connecticut.

Siamese. International News Photo.

Abyssinian, Double Champion Chirn Sa-hai Ani, owned by Mrs. Richard O'Donovan, Chirn Sa-hai Cattery, Tarrytown, New York.

Smoke Persian kittens, owned by Mrs. H. N. Bellows, Bellows Falls, Vermont.

Manx, Grand Champion Guthred of Manx of Glen Orry, bred and owned by Misses Ruth and Ellen Carlson, Glen Orry Cattery, West Chicago, Illinois.

Blue Persian, Grand Champion Purri-Isle's Bobadil, owned by Mr. and Mrs. L. I. Olsen, Purri-Isle Cattery, West Palm Beach, Florida.

Tortoise calico cat, owned by Mrs. Mollie Brennan, New Haven, Connecticut.

Black Persian, Double Grand Champion Hermscrest Natajha, owned by Mrs. Frances M. Herms, Hermscrest Cattery, Tarrytown, New York.

Burmese, owned by Mrs. Blanche Warren, Casa Gatos Cattery, Idyllwild, California.

Persian, Grand and Double Champion Leilani's Petitepointe, owned by Mrs. Walker Johnston, Azulita Cattery, San Diego, California.

Index